Look Back In Anger

The Miners' Strike in Nottinghamshire — 30 Years On

Look Back In Anger

The Miners' Strike in Nottinghamshire — 30 Years On

Harry Paterson

Five Leaves Publications
www.fiveleaves.co.uk

Look Back in Anger
The Miners' Strike in Nottinghamshire
— 30 years on
by Harry Paterson

Published in 2014
by Five Leaves Publications,
PO Box 8786, Nottingham NG1 9AW

ISBN: 978-1907869952

Designed and typeset by Five Leaves
and Four Sheets Design and Print

Printed in Great Britain by Imprint Digital

Contents

Acknowledgments

The first thing I learned when starting to write this book, is that it wouldn't be written alone. My name might be the only one on the cover but it really is a team effort. *Look Back in Anger* probably wouldn't have appeared at all without the input of others. The reader will, hopefully, indulge me for a moment while I pay tribute to some individuals without whom there would be no book.

Firstly, my deepest gratitude is extended to my father, James Stewart Paterson. Confronted by a rebel child, determined not to learn to read simply because 'The Auld Yin' insisted he would, he eventually raised a son with a deep and abiding love of books and for language. Throughout my career he has been not only my staunchest supporter and critic but also my unofficial editor. A supremely intelligent man, with a traditional classical education behind him (a rarity, in those days, for a working class lad from a poverty-blighted family in Alloa), The Auld Yin is, rarely wrong on matters of grammar, syntax, spelling and punctuation. His observations, comments and critiques have been invaluable at every stage of my career and so it has proved here too. Thanks, Dad.

Mick Wall is one of the world's most respected and successful authors, journalists and broadcasters in the field of contemporary music, Mick's friendship, mentoring and practical advice sustained me in the darker moments when confidence was low and doubt set in. Mick also gave me my first real break in my day job; that of music journalist and from there everything else flowed. After thirty-five years at the literary coalface no one knows better than Mick, and I got his accumulated wisdom, knowledge and experience *gratis*. Sincerely and fraternally, brother.

Few have a deeper knowledge of just about every aspect of the miners' titanic struggle than former NUM official, author, social historian and activist, Dave Douglass. Widely known throughout the labour and trade union movement, Dave was right in the thick of events during the year we'll never forget. His strength was in his ability to deliver insight and analysis regarding the decision-making process of the NUM leadership, the areas where that differed from the views of the wider membership, those aspects of the dispute most commonly misrepresented in the dozens of accounts since and perspective from outside Nottinghamshire.

As an author with several titles to his name and some forty-odd years in the industry and the NUM behind him, you'd expect the man to have picked up a thing or two and so he has. I've leaned on Dave's own published work for some parts of the book that are not directly concerned with Nottinghamshire. Where there might be errors, they are mine. Where there are none, thank Dave.

Dave's opposite number, you might say, David Amos, deserves a mention, too. Doctor Amos, as he subsequently became on leaving the pit, is a rarity, as I soon discovered; a former strike-breaker prepared to defend his position and go on the record. In addition, he provided access to and copies of important documents from his private archive, all of which have, I believe, lent richness and depth to the text.

Ross Bradshaw, my editor at Five Leaves, is probably the bluntest and most witheringly honest man I've encountered in my career thus far (with the possible exception of *Classic Rock* magazine's Senior Features Editor, Dave Everely; hi, Dave). From savaging my first efforts with a finely-honed blend of genuine wit and excoriating scorn, Ross has, nevertheless, been a true believer. He believed in the book, he believed in me and, thanks to him, what you now hold in your hands is infinitely better than it ever would have been had I been left to my own devices. 'Lenin does Mills and Boon' indeed, Ross. Thanks for everything, pal. Let's do it again sometime.

SheWhoIsNeverWrong, my wife, Sue Paterson; miner's daughter and child-veteran of the Great Strike herself. As well as not killing me during a year in which I left a trail of papers, documents and books all over the house so that, at any time, I could lay my hands on whatever I might need, she has cheerfully shouldered the burden of running every aspect of our lives and those of our kids. Sue also provided the excellent photo of Bestwood headstocks which formed the basis of the cover artwork by Pippa Hennessy of Five Leaves.

It's often been suggested by Sue that I'm not the easiest of people with whom to live. Those who know me will, I'm sure, share my astonishment on learning this. Despite that, Sue has ensured, often at great personal inconvenience, that I've always had the time to do what I needed to do to meet the deadline. Managing all this with a debilitating illness as well is an act of humbling selflessness.

My most heartfelt thanks must be extended to Henry Richardson, Ray Chadburn, Keith Stanley, Bob Collier, Kevin Parkin, Michael Hogg, Brian Walker, Eric Eaton and Jimmy MacDowall as well as to the many other former miners who gave generously of their time but wished to remain anonymous. These men, more than any others, have made the book, for better or worse, what it is.

Thanks must go to Notts NUM Ex- and Retired Miners' Association, the NUM both in Nottinghamshire and nationally, former members and officials of the Communist Party, Labour Party, Socialist Labour Party, National Coal Board and TUC.

Let the record also show my gratitude to the following; James Reeve for the loan of various research materials; journalist, author, recovering Trot and, stylistically, one of my biggest influences, my good friend David Osler; the incomparable Seumas Milne, something of a journalistic hero of mine; my boss at *Bass Guitar Magazine*, Joel McIver, for his interest and encouragement; Paul Mason; artist and cartoonist, John 'Brick' Clarke; former NOD official, Brian Evangelista; Jim Aspinall; Louise McDaid; Ken Capstick; Mel Hepworth; Nobby Lawton; Sam Metcalf; widow of Gordon and sister-in-law of Dennis, Helen Skinner and all the contributors to the excellent Facebook page, 30th Anniversary of the Miners' Strike.

I suppose I ought to mention the members of The Order of The Jack; a noble fraternity which meets bimonthly to consume Jack Daniels and fine Indian cuisine. Neil Cross, Phil Meynell and Gavin Fowkes, members of that illustrious Order, have actually been of no help whatsoever. Indeed their continual and merciless ribbing might even be described as a hindrance. They did, however, provide light relief and a distraction when the going got tough so, er, thanks, brothers.

Finally, thanks to all those who follow my work in the various publications for which I write and who emailed to express interest, support and encouragement and to all my friends on Facebook who did so much to promote the book and spread the word. I was touched by your kindness and remain so.

Look Back in Anger: the Miners' Strike in Nottinghamshire – 30 Years On is dedicated to the memory of Maurice 'Mog' Wake and Iris Wake. 'Loyal to The Last,' may they both rest in peace.

Introduction

In 1983 there were around 174 operational deep-mine pits in the UK, employing a total workforce of over 230,000 people. At the time of writing, Spring 2013, following a fire at Daw Mill in Warwickshire (which will see the pit close and its 650-strong workforce lose their jobs) there are now just three; Kellingley and Hatfield in Yorkshire and Thoresby in Nottinghamshire, employing barely 2000 miners.

From the vantage point of thirty years later, it must be difficult for younger people to fully grasp the significance of the 1984/1985 miners' strike. Equally, it must be difficult to understand the impact that this, the most bitterly-charged industrial dispute in British history, had on everything that followed.

During the year-long battle which, in certain parts of the country, assumed a genuinely insurrectionary character, over 20,000 people were arrested and/or hospitalised, two hundred served time in custody and/or were convicted and jailed, 966 were victimised and sacked for fighting to preserve their jobs and their industry, three died foraging for coal, two were killed on picket lines and another was killed trying to ferry a strike-breaker across a picket line and into work.[1]

In the Nottinghamshire coalfield, of vital strategic importance to both the National Union of Mineworkers (NUM) and Thatcher's Government, the battle raged perhaps more fiercely than anywhere else in the country. Fewer than 2000 men finished the year on strike from a total workforce of nearly 32,000. The story of that dispute is without parallel in British industrial history and those on strike endured suffering, hardship and loss on a scale incomprehensible to many today. For what, though? As the strikers themselves saw things, for nothing less than survival; the survival of their industry, the survival of their trade union and the survival of the jobs and prospects of the generations which were to come.

Nottinghamshire saw men in their fifties, nearing retirement, with absolutely nothing to gain but everything to lose, fighting for the jobs and futures of men young enough to be their sons; in some cases, men who *were* their sons. Men who crossed picket lines and betrayed the very people who defended them only, as the irony of the years that came later showed, to be betrayed themselves; by John Major and the Conservative government and by the breakaway Union of Democratic Miners (UDM) who so effectively aided the opponents of the NUM and the trade union movement.

Of course, the working miners emphatically rejected any charges of 'scabbing,' 'class treachery' or collusion with the Government. In their view, publicly at least, they were fighting, equally passionately, for trade union democracy and the right to work.

Despite the dozens of volumes written about this most seismic of industrial disputes, which to this day divides families and communities, very little has been written about the dispute in the crucial Nottinghamshire coalfield. Apart from a handful of first-hand accounts, memoirs and diaries from strikers and one from a working miner, there has not yet been a book that places Nottinghamshire in its correct historical context. This work attempts to rectify that. It seeks to set events in the county in their proper place; to recount the year-long battle in the local coalfields, using many new interviews with key protagonists, and to gauge its importance within the strike as it unfolded nationally.

The pre- and post-strike years are also examined. The legacy of the General Strike, the history of the NUM, the formation of the UDM, the miners' last stand against Heseltine's pit closure programme in 1992-1993 and the corruption scandals involving key UDM leaders are all included, with the intention of providing a comprehensive and detailed overview of the strike, and its impact with Nottinghamshire taking centre stage.

During the research for this book, many little-known, underappreciated, underreported and previously unknown facts were unearthed. The reader will discover that much of the received wisdom regarding the miners' strike is challenged and disputed: the question of a national ballot, Roy Lynk's real motives and role in the formation of the UDM and the controversial dismissal of Henry Richardson from his post as Nottinghamshire Area General Secretary and much else.

Finally, while attempting to provide an objective historical study of the strike, this book, nevertheless, seeks to serve as a tribute to Nottinghamshire's striking miners and their families. As one Welsh miner put it, "We were solid. Rock solid. For months, we had not a pit anywhere with even a single scab. Compared to the Notts boys on strike, we had it easy. We couldn't do anything else. Doing what they did was like being behind enemy lines and those men were heroes." Their stand deserves recognition and respect. For that reason alone a written account of their struggle would have been worthwhile. There is, however, another.

A thirty-year old industrial dispute might appear to have little relevance to people and their lives today, yet nothing could be further from the truth. Today's employee-employer relations are the partial legacy of that tumultuous year. So too is the seeming acceptance that mass unemployment is now an acceptable norm; the widespread resignation that working for a living now involves minimum-wage labour on zero-hour contracts with minimal employment protection in service industries. After all, there are virtually no mines left in which to work, or steelworks, docks and shipbuilding — little manufacturing of any real kind left in the UK. While one shouldn't underestimate the wider historical processes at work: world recession, the collapse of the Soviet Union and the triumph of neoliberalism, for the younger generation, the Britain in which they live today is partially the result of the miners' strike and the processes that the end of that dispute set in motion. That all this was powered by class-hatred and a conscious intent to destroy British trade unionism only compounds a historic tragedy.

The miners' strike was a very British war. Germany, for example, places state-owned industries at the centre of its mixed economy and views trade unions as an essential component. While no self-respecting socialist would view the German model as a viable, or even desirable, long-term solution to the contradictions of capitalism, it does show an alternative to the class-based scorched-earth policy pursued by Thatcher's Government; even within the parameters of the free market, there was *still* an alternative.

Economics, though, were only ever a secondary factor where the miners were concerned. At the heart of the dispute was an agenda driven by ruthless class considerations; the elimination of effective trade unionism, the eradication of anything pertaining to socialism or any alternative to a system the continuing survival of which depended on the impoverishment of the working class and the institutions which sustained it. The miners' strike was about all of these things and more.

Accordingly, the dispute is rich in lessons and it throws up questions which remain unanswered: what kind of world do we have? What kind of world do we want? What is the purpose of an economy? Is it to serve the needs of the many or the needs of a few? Is it there to serve the needs of anyone at all or is it some kind of fixed, inevitable process to which we are all naturally subservient?

As global austerity sees entire economies plunged into chaos, the miners' strike and the issues over which it was fought are, today, more relevant than ever. Through the medium of its history I hope the reader will ask some of those questions and maybe, just maybe, formulate some answers.

Part 1:
The Story
of the Blues

Chapter 1:
Back to the Future

"Those who cannot remember the past
are condemned to repeat it."
GEORGE SANTAYANA

Mining communities were close-knit environments breeding a distinctive tribal culture. Along with the job of mining itself, often passing down the generations from grandfather to son and from son to grandson, so too was handed down the collective history and folk-tales: of tragedies and triumphs, betrayals and loyalties, victories and defeats, socially, industrially and politically.

Traditionally occupying purpose-built villages and estates, often situated cheek-by-jowl to the pits in which the men toiled, miners shared values and common goals. These communities were often highly self-contained. The miners and their families organised their own social activities and institutions. football and cricket teams, allotments and social clubs. A sense of social cohesion, qualitatively different to that of any other group of workers, was often the result.

The work itself, brutal, dangerous and, in the days of private ownership, claiming lives and limbs in an ever-escalating tally, induced a sense of camaraderie and bonded man to man and miner to miner. A 'them and us' attitude, common amongst any workforce where danger and sudden death were constant

17

threats, ironically, not unlike police and soldiers, knitted strong threads which became the very fabric of mining culture.

Loyalty to one another and to the Union was taken for granted and often formed the bedrock of these communities. Illustrative of this is the account by former NUM official, activist and author, Dave Douglass, of a miner who worked during the General Strike.[2]

Only a young lad at the time, he was ostracised from the Hatfield community for the rest of his life. Many years later, by that time an old man, the local Miners' Welfare voted on whether or not to allow him membership. The vote went against him and his social exile continued until his death. Similarly, members of the Miners' Union Jack Memorial Club in Goldthorpe, in 1956, held a vote on whether to lift the ban that had been imposed on miners who had returned to work before the official end of the 1926 dispute. With a span of nearly thirty years and the deaths of some of the miners having since occurred, the members still voted by ninety votes to thirty-six to uphold the exclusions. As broadcaster, journalist and author Michael Crick dryly observed, "Miners have long memories."[3]

While this may seem harsh, cruel, even, to those from outside the mining tradition, it is part and parcel of the culture. It is an unbreakable tenet of trade unionism that picket lines are inviolate, sacrosanct. No one took this, the first commandment of trade unionism, as seriously as miners did. Picket lines are class lines and to cross one is to unequivocally cross the other. The faith, trust and confidence in one's fellow miners to watch out for each other when facing the dangers of the coal face extends equally to union activity above ground and away from the pit. The miners learned early and learned hard that if unity really is strength then disunity, divisions and siding with employers and the government is to stab your own in the back in the most inexcusable fashion. Strike-breakers, yellow-dogs, blacklegs, scabs, call them what you will, occupy a position of contempt in mining history and never was this more vividly shown than in the Nottinghamshire coalfields of 1984 and 1985.

For older miners, Nottinghamshire's behaviour was simply the logical extension of an area that gave birth to the strike-breaking company union of 1926 and saw the emergence of a class collaborationist philosophy dubbed 'Spencerism'. Typical of those holding this view is former NUM Vice President, Keith Stanley. Speaking at the David Jones Memorial Lecture in 2010, Stanley, for his entire working life a Nottinghamshire miner, had this to say. "We are renowned as 'Scab County' and it's obvious why that name has come about. The [Nottinghamshire] miners, in 1926, broke the strike and the Spencer breakaway union was formed. And then again history repeated itself in 1984 when the Nottinghamshire miners refused to come out on strike, the majority of them, and again, a breakaway union was formed: the UDM."

Add to all that poverty-level standards of subsistence, the norm until the latter part of the twentieth century, and, unsurprisingly, miners have historically been among the most class-conscious and politically advanced workers anywhere to be found.

Any real understanding of the strike of '84/'85 depends on an appreciation of these factors. Almost every major event in British mining history, from the General Strike of 1926 onwards, exerted *some* influence on the way the NUM's battle against pit closures and the destruction of effective trade unionism unfolded. Where Nottinghamshire is concerned, that understanding is even more critical.

If ever there was a more painfully appropriate slogan for Nottinghamshire miners than Santayana's celebrated line from *The Life of Reasons*, it's yet to be written. Indeed, history provided Nottingham with a stark warning from its own mining past and in an eerie replay of events surrounding the General Strike, the period following the '84/'85 strike featured reruns of some of the same incidents that had been visited upon the labour and trade union movement at the end of the earlier dispute.

In NUM folklore, the General Strike of 1926 sowed the seeds of Nottinghamshire's class treachery and collaboration with Thatcher, providing an ignoble precedent for the County's strike-breakers during the events of '84/'85 and afterwards. This was all aided and abetted by the TUC reprising its shameful role of 1926 in its refusal to uphold the mutually-agreed 1982 'Wembley Principles.' This is the received wisdom and while nothing about the 'Miners' Great Strike for Jobs' is ever that simple, it's a view that has a great deal of validity.

For the strike-breakers themselves, this was nothing but mere historical coincidence, if they even considered it at all. Whatever the private motives of the 25,000-plus Nottinghamshire men who defied their leadership and the majority of their fellow union members nationally by continuing, or returning, to work, their public stance was that of resisting an undemocratic and dictatorial leadership. Subsequent events, not least the corruption which embroiled Nottinghamshire's new Spencerists, the UDM, showed this to be, at best, a tragically mistaken course of action. Any pretensions of an honourable crusade in the name of democracy were left discredited by Arthur Scargill's Cassandra-like predictions coming to fruition, the unmasking of key working miners' activists as state assets and the jailing of UDM leader and proven thief, Neil Greatrex.

In any event, whatever one's subjective view, there is a powerful argument for tracing the psychological start of the strike as far back as 1926. Certainly, the NUM's conduct during the later dispute was shaped, in part, by the events of sixty years earlier. Arthur Scargill was always quick to remind his supporters and critics alike of the implications of that period and frequently urged them to draw, as he saw things, the correct conclusions. Today, as we survey the virtual disappearance of the entire mining industry, who could say he was wrong?

In the year before the General Strike, in 1925, a round of wage cuts was attempted by colliery owners. Due to the combined efforts of the railway and transport workers, in solidarity with the NUM's forerunner, the Miners' Federation of Great Britain (MFGB), which linked up with the National Minority Movement — a Communist Party-created trade union caucus — the colliery owners were beaten back. On the day strike action was originally scheduled to commence, Friday 31st July, 1925, the government announced it would subsidise the mining industry for a period of nine months while a specially convened commission conducted an inquiry. Mistakenly, this was hailed as a victory and quickly became known as 'Red Friday'.[4]

The Miner's Federation of Great Britain rejected the findings and vowed to fight. The slogan summing up their stance, and around which opposition was built, was coined by MFGB leader

A.J. Cook. "Not a penny off the pay, not a minute on the day," he defiantly asserted and battle was joined.

From May 1st, around 900,000 miners were locked out, with the TUC then declaring a General Strike from May 3rd "in defence of miners' wages and hours".[5]

The climate was charged, with the Government in fear of revolution breaking out. The Russian Revolution, not yet ten years old, cast a long shadow and the Communist Party of Great Britain, barely six years old itself, exerted influence out of all proportion to its numbers. Cook himself, despite his formal membership of the Independent Labour Party, was a supporter of the Communist Party (CP) and worked closely with its members throughout his tenure as General Secretary. His future successor, Arthur Horner, at the time of the strike, an Executive Member of the South Wales MFGB, was also a CP member and was a key strategist during the dispute. The short-lived Councils of Action, which sprang up all over the country, often evolving from existing Trades Councils, also numbered a high percentage of CP members and sympathisers and, in many cases, were founded and organised by them.

This was also a time of real union power and influence. Forty-five percent of the UK workforce belonged to a trade union,[6] and of those the mighty MFGB numbered close to a million-strong.

For the Labour Party leadership and for the TUC General Council as well, these were not facts that induced a sense of joy. More concerned, as oppositions are wont to be, with proving itself a safe pair of hands with the nation's purse-strings than with actually winning the dispute, the leaderships of the organisations found their fears of insurrection pushing them into undermining the strike and betraying its participants. Something which the miners never forgot and which was to live on in the collective consciousness of the generations of NUM members that were to follow.

Ernest Bevin, General Secretary of the Transport and General Workers Union (TGWU) during the last-ditch negotiations prior to the formal declaration of the strike, was emphatically opposed to such a course of action, urging his fellow-negotiators that, "No mention should be made of a possible general strike, for fear that it would place a weapon in the hands of our opponents." When the talks broke down and the strike was underway he was at pains to protest, at every available opportunity, that it was most certainly *not* a political dispute but an entirely industrial one.

As far as the Government was concerned, this was a show-down that had to be met. Insurrection, revolution and revolt, all of which it felt were but a step away, had to be crushed and the working class brought to heel.

Winston Churchill, not yet airbrushed by revisionist history as the valiant defender of British freedom and implacable foe of Nazism, was responsible for a key part of the Government's propaganda offensive. And who better? His CV included ordering troops into Tonypandy in 1910 when, as Home Secretary, he broke the resistance of striking miners in the Rhondda, the creation of the brutal and sectarian Black and Tans in Ireland and, predating Hitler by some years — a man upon whom he would lavish fulsome praise and admiration[7] — advocated the enforced sterilisation of the poor and their incarceration in purpose-built labour camps.

Under Churchill's editorship the Government's official strike bulletin, *The British Gazette*, was, frankly, unhinged in its attacks on the TUC, entirely consistent with the establishment's fervent belief that the General Strike was merely a precursor to outright Bolshevik insurrection. Churchill immediately grasped what the General Strike meant for Britain's ruling class: "Either the country will break the general strike, or the general strike will break the country." The hysteria continued. The Communist Party General Secretary, Harry Pollitt, was jailed for 'seditious intent and incitement to mutiny,' Churchill cranked-up the attacks in the *Gazette* and the BBC was conscripted as a partisan arm of the Conservative Party, point-blank refusing to broadcast any alternative view, from either the TUC or the Labour Party, that might counter the avalanche of disinformation and outright untruths raining down from the Government. "I do not agree that the TUC have as much right as the Government to publish their side of the case and to exhort their followers to continue action. It is a very much more difficult task to feed the nation than it is to wreck it," he remarked with a notable absence of that fabled British sense of fair play.

The TUC General Council felt trapped. On the one hand, outright abandonment of the miners was, *at that stage*, simply unthinkable. On the other, the establishment's terror of revolution was shared equally by them. It was this fear of unleashing forces beyond their control, the terror of a militant, organised working class pushing the strike all the way through to armed uprising, that informed their decision to limit the action. Instead of calling on all 6,500,000 union members to come out, the call for action was restricted to just workers in the key industries of rail and docks. Barely 1,500,000 union members were actually on strike for the full period of the dispute. Then, as now, there were few people more conservative than many trade union officials.

In the years following the Russian Revolution such fears were justified. Syndicalism might have peaked but its legacy lived on; the idea of the trade unions as a vehicle that would not just improve workers' conditions but effect a wholesale transformation of society was widespread. No less an experienced revolutionary than Leon Trotsky was to remark, "The general strike is one of the most acute forms of class war. It is one step from the general strike to armed insurrection. If carried through to the end, the general strike brings the revolutionary class up against the task of organising a new state power. A real victory for the general strike can only be found in the conquest of power by the proletariat." With such a leadership as that constituted by the TUC General Council, such an outcome was, to put it mildly, unlikely. The Communist Party leadership, too, despite the principled activities of its rank-and-file, played directly to this narrative with their self-defeating slogan, 'All power to the TUC General Council.'

During this time Cook toured the country tirelessly, working for victory and drawing crowds of tens of thousands to listen to his impassioned pleas for resistance. In contrast to his reluctant TUC comrades, victory was not to be feared and only the utmost commitment to the cause would be countenanced. In ill-health and of no financial means beyond his union salary, he refused to draw anything other than the 'lock-out pay' given to his members, many of whom were, literally, starving.

Meanwhile, in Nottingham, the situation was considerably bleaker than most other areas of the country. As of April 1926, there were 6,143 recorded as officially unemployed while an additional 1,447 were noted as being 'on short time' or 'stood off.'[8]

leadership to be so treated.

Of all the various trade and craft unions represented on the Trades Council, the MFGB had but a single delegate, a miner named Tom Willoughby. However, the town was notably left-wing and support and sympathy for the miners' cause was high. On May Day, the day before the strike commenced, a huge public meeting assembled on the Forest Field where the town Alderman, H. Bowles, assured the attendees that all present would stand firm with the miners. Other speakers included Nottingham West M.P. George Bowman, who treated his audience to a fiery denunciation of capitalism, while the President of the Trades Council warned that unless the government backed down it would feel the wrath of the entire labour and trade union movement raining down upon its collective head.[10]

Nationally, the mood was little different with most trade unionists more than willing to take on the Government in defence of the miners. With the general level of class consciousness at an all-time high, again largely the result of the impact of the Russian Revolution, the feeling was one of confidence and determination. A genuine belief that victory could be won was popular.

The General Strike was to last just nine days and end in abject defeat. After less than a fortnight, during which middle class volunteers supplemented the army in running and maintaining essential services, the TUC gave in. After seeking assurances that the Government would honour the recommendations of the Samuel Commission, it was all over. Nothing was gained from the sacrifices of millions of working class people. Even more contemptible, in the MFGB's view, was that a plea by the TUC that no strikers be victimised or sacked and that those already sacked be reinstated, was loftily dismissed by the Government on the grounds that it could not instruct private employers as to whom they should, and should not, employ. The TUC acquiesced only to see more people come out on strike than during the official action itself as, not just the mine owners, but employers everywhere interpreted the Government's stance as a green light to victimise the perceived radical elements among their own workforce. But by May 13th, the conflict, without any kind of settlement, was over; or so most thought. For Britain's miners, the real battle had only just begun.

Abandoned, isolated and alone, the miners battled on for a further six months, some even holding out for nine. The hardship and poverty they and their families endured was offset only partially by the reservoir of solidarity, goodwill and support from working class communities all over the country. Soup kitchens and other relief efforts sprang up, the Co-op organised donations and food parcels but it wasn't enough. Starved back to work, by the end of November the majority of miners were back at the coalface. In the wake of the defeat, blacklisting, victimisation and purges of activists swiftly followed with many miners never working again, hastened to early deaths in conditions of malnutrition, poverty and abject squalor.

Just prior to the official collapse of the strike, on October 5th, in Nottingham, a meeting took place which would echo down the generations and change the course of trade unionism forever in the mining industry. The owners of Digby and New London pits facilitated a meeting at their Eastwood base. Among those present was the then Labour MP for Broxtowe, George Spencer. Originally a miner himself, Spencer served first as a County Councillor, representing Stapleford, before his election as an MP. First elected to Parliament in 1918, he was also an official of the Nottinghamshire Miners' Association, affiliated to the MFGB. Spencer was involved in a series of unsanctioned talks with colliery owners in an attempt to bring an end to the strike and win back jobs for sacked men, inn return for no-strike deals and other concessions to the collicry bosses. At his urging the men voted to abandon the strike and return to work.

He was immediately expelled from the MFGB for strike-breaking, or 'scabbing' in common parlance, and thus set in train the series of events that would see his name become a byword for class treachery, collusion and disloyalty in NUM folklore. His later expulsion from the Labour Party would see Spencer serving out his remaining parliamentary term in ignominy, speaking from the Liberal benches. An associate and confidant of J. Havelock Wilson, the right-wing head of the seamen's union, Spencer's union-busting activities were financed, in part, by Havelock and by donations from grateful colliery bosses. Havelock, too, was later expelled by the TUC for his part in the strike-breaking as he encouraged his seamen to continue working during the nine-day stoppage.

At the same special conference that endorsed Spencer's expulsion, on the 7th October, the MFGB also approved the expulsion of the Digby pit delegate, Cyril Pugh, for his part in organising the return to work. A Communist Party member from Kimberley, Pugh, realising the magnitude of his mistake, attempted to then persuade his members to go *back* on strike. With his credibility in shreds, there was little support for his changed stance. After a period of penance, he was readmitted to the Nottingham Miners Association (NMA) in 1928, eventually rising to the position of Executive Committee delegate. He was also elected to Kimberley Parish Council.

As for Spencer, with his political career now in tatters, he turned his attention fully to the miners. In conjunction with the colliery owners, he set up a company union in direct opposition to the official MFGB affiliate, the NMA. The new organisation, the Nottinghamshire and District Miners' Industrial Union (NMIU), was again funded by both the colliery owners and Havelock Wilson, along with donations from local right-wing businessmen. Based mainly in the Dukeries coalfield, in north Nottinghamshire, Spencer and the pit owners set about building up the new union's membership in their efforts to destroy the NMA.

The new union proclaimed itself 'moderate' and 'non-political.' In reality, it was ferociously political; unashamedly right-wing and uncompromisingly opposed to all that genuine trade unionism represented. At that time, as well as the mines in the hands of private owners, the cottages and homes of miners were owned by the colliery bosses. With the collapse of the strike and the widespread victimisation that followed, strikers were in a highly vulnerable position. With huge pres-

26

sure exerted on the defeated workers to join the company union and the threat of evictions and destitution adding impetus to Spencer's campaign, many chose to capitulate and leave the NMA for Spencer's NMIU.

The colliery bosses, in the ascendency, derecognised the NMA and all other MFGB sections and sacked and victimised its members. The battle between the two unions for the hearts and minds of miners was protracted, bitter and violent and raged all over the Nottinghamshire coalfield. Eventually, matters came to a head at Harworth Colliery. Situated in the very north of the Notts coalfield, Harworth was, geographically, nearer to Doncaster in the South Yorkshire Area. The consensus and culture at the pit, however, were very much in the spirit of the new 'moderates.' Despite this, it still boasted a recalcitrant militant element and NMA loyalists there struck again, this time demanding their union be recognised by pit management. The struggle raged for six months with the strikers and NMA loyalists beaten, arrested, evicted and imprisoned.

The owners of Harworth colliery, Barber Walker and Co, owned the majority of pits in Nottinghamshire along with the miners' homes. In the typically incestuous manner of the ruling class at the time, its chairman, Major Thomas Barber, was also chairman of the County Council, responsible for, conveniently enough, policing in the Nottinghamshire towns and villages. Not for the last time, the state was pressed into service on behalf of the interests of private business. The police, in conjunction with the pit owners, waged a campaign against the NMA striking loyalists with miners routinely beaten, arrested, sacked and then evicted from their company-owned homes.

When the strike was finally over, culminating in 'The Harworth Riot' with police running amok, breaking down doors and beating miners and their families in their homes, the strike leaders were prosecuted. Harworth NMA President, Michael Kane, was tried and convicted of riot and sentenced to two years hard labour. A further seventeen were also charged and convicted with eleven, including a miner's wife, given sentences of between four and fifteen months hard labour with the other five fined and bound over to keep the peace.

From the militants' point of view, one significant outcome from the events in Nottingham was the start of the erosion of

'Mondism' as any kind of useful guide to improving workers' pay and conditions. Named after the industrialist Alfred Mond, Mondism had been a growing strain of thought in the trade union movement that the way forward for workers was to abandon class struggle and, instead, cooperate with business owners to improve productivity. This, in turn, would lead to rising earnings and improved living standards for the workforce; a crude forerunner of the 'trickle-down' theory. With cowed working miners now earning even less than before the General Strike, its uselessness as any kind of practical guide became apparent. Indeed, following the NMA's strike for recognition, there was a growing realisation that miners' pay and conditions in Nottinghamshire were even lower than those of miners in the MFGB-recognised areas.

The Labour Party, however, instead of giving its support to the NMA and MFGB to press home its propaganda advantage, and to capitalise on the widespread indignation at the treatment of the strikers among Nottinghamshire residents, urged both sides to settle their differences. Eventually talks led to George Spencer being readmitted to the MFGB and to securing the Presidency of its Nottinghamshire arm and finally, in 1937, his breakaway company union merged fully with the NMA.

For many of today's NUM activists, this was the point at which Nottinghamshire contracted its historic 'Scabitis'. This resurfaced in 1984-85 when Nottinghamshire miners again embraced the bosses' and government's cause, defied the strike and worked as normal.

Chapter 2:
Brother, Can You
Spare a Dime?

*"Poverty is the parent of
revolution and crime"*
ARISTOTLE

If the twenties had been hard for the miners, the thirties were
to prove brutal. The Wall Street Crash of 1929 sent shockwaves
around the globe; leaving virtually no economy untouched by
its impact. The world plunged into The Great Depression.
Wages plummeted still further while inflation, unemployment
and destitution soared. Moreover, the effects of the economic
slump weren't confined to purely fiscal matters. Authoritarian
regimes and dictatorships sprang up and, following the rise of
fascism in Spain and Italy; weaker nations were invaded,
annexed or conquored.

At home the decade saw the Jarrow Marchers and the formation of Ramsay MacDonald's National Government. In the
General Election of 1929, Labour had emerged as the single
largest party but one without an overall majority. Completely
thrown by the demands of the new period, Labour was soon in
turmoil regarding its desire to prove itself a natural party of
government but simultaneously beset by demands to slash
public spending in order to preserve the Gold Standard. In 1931

MacDonald took the steps that would see him damned in the eyes of Labour Party and trade union activists for generations to come. With just two Labour MPs he formed a National Government in coalition with the Tories. Like Spencer before him, MacDonald was expelled from the Party and was replaced by Arthur Henderson as leader.

The public spending cuts, of which a portion meant a ten percent cut in pay for sailors, led directly to the Invergordon Mutiny. For two days on the 15th and 16th of September, 1931, around a thousand sailors openly mutinied in protest. The City panicked and a run on the pound ensued. Forced to abandon the Gold Standard and the spending cuts as a result, in the subsequent General Election, on October 27th, MacDonald's machinations reaped their reward. The Labour Party was almost wiped out in a swing to the Conservatives which saw Labour retain a rump of only fifty seats.

For the miners, it was difficult to imagine a worse set of circumstances as they struggled to recover from the effects of the General Strike. From around 1929 to 1933, the UK's trade was nearly halved while in heavy industry the fall was around thirty-four percent. By June 1932 there were 3,500,000 unemployed with nearly a further 2,000,000 barely existing on part-time hours. The areas hit hardest by the slump were the traditional mining areas of South Wales, Yorkshire and the North East of England, along with Scotland and Northern Ireland. In some of these areas unemployment reached seventy percent.

Welfare was a purely contributory affair and for millions of workers who had never earned enough to make regular contributions, only charity offered even a partial relief to their circumstances. Disease, malnutrition and premature deaths rose in the mining areas worst affected.[11]

All these factors impacted on the MFGB whose membership at the turn of the decade was around fifty percent of that at its mid-1920s height. Its members were earning around six shillings a day which was barely half that earned by dock workers. It's worth bearing in mind that while the trope 'greedy' miners 'holding the country to ransom' entered, virtually unchallenged, into our popular culture, miners were, historically, at or near the bottom of industrial wage-earners; the move towards the top only changing as late as the latter half of the twentieth century.

Along with wages declining, standards of health and safety were also on the slide as mine owners pushed for greater profits in the challenging times the thirties represented. One of the worst results of the disregard for human life displayed by colliery managers was seen at Gresford Colliery on September 22nd, 1934. The pit exploded, killing 265 miners, many of whom were teenage apprentices. In the subsequent inquiries, many breaches of the law and intimidation of MFGB safety reps were uncovered but instead of lengthy jail sentences, the owners and managers received only token fines.

As the decade went on a gradual improvement in the economy started to return some stability to the UK. The pound was devalued, following the UK's exit from the Gold Standard, leading to a cut in interest rates from around 5.9% to about 1.1%. This had the effect of strengthening British exports against those of countries which had retained the Gold Standard. The small recovery that resulted fed a drop in unemployment from the middle of the decade onwards. This largely bypassed the deprived mining areas of Nottingham, Yorkshire, Scotland, Wales and the North East. The historically prosperous South East received most of the benefit. Government-backed regeneration projects including new roads and financial assistance to the ship building and steel industries, designed to stimulate those areas most affected, were simply inadequate in addressing the high levels of unemployment, poverty and associated social ills.

Meanwhile, war was brewing across the Channel and many miners were doomed to die in the fight against the Nazis. But first there was Spain.

In 1936 the Spanish Republic faced Franco's Fascist uprising and notable miners' leaders flocked to the banners of the International Brigade to aid the fight against fascism. The Spanish Civil War also saw Hitler lending arms and tanks to the Spanish fascists as the Nazi leader used the war as a dry-run for some of Germany's later campaigns in World War Two.

The MFGB gave unconditional support to the International Brigade. Hundreds of its members enlisted, taking up arms against the enemy of the international working class. Will Paynter, the South Wales leader, and Thomas Degnan of Yorkshire were joined by hundreds of politically-conscious miners and other trade unionists from all parts of the UK; over 200 miners from South Wales alone.

At home, meanwhile, the MFGB fought against the embargo of arms to the Spanish Republicans imposed by the Government which had signed a non-intervention treaty. To circumvent the embargo, the MFGB introduced a member's levy to raise funds for the International Brigade so the Republicans could purchase their own arms. The militant Areas donated quickly, with South Wales reaching its target in less than two weeks. Recently-readmitted Nottinghamshire, on the other hand, added to the contempt in which it was held by other MFGB sections, following its conduct during the General Strike, by refusing to contribute to the levy. The Area insisted that if the leadership wanted to send cash to the Spanish fighters, then it should come from the Union's political fund and not their members' pockets. Not the most admirable of positions to take, especially considering some of its own members had joined the International Brigade including twenty-three year-old Frank Ellis. The Hucknall miner joined up in 1937 and was captured by fascists near Burgos, eventually released and repatriated in 1938.

As World War Two ground on, anti-Communist hysteria and discrimination throughout industry, and the mines in particular, receded slightly as Britain's ally, the USSR, won grudging admiration for the sheer scale of both its sacrifice and commitment to defeating Nazism. Possibly something of that feeling influenced the Government's decision to, at first, tread lightly where striking workers were involved. The Government was forced to consider the needs of its non-combatant workforce to a greater degree than at any time previously. The mutinies, strikes and protests of the First World War could not be countenanced while facing the far greater threat of Nazism. It's often overlooked that Churchill's War Cabinet was not Conservative but an administrative coalition with two of its five members being Labour MPs, with several others, outside the immediate War Cabinet, also holding various ministerial portfolios. The most strategically-important of these posts was that of Minister of Labour and National Service, held by Ernest Bevin. As the leader of the biggest trade union in the UK at the time, the Transport and General Workers' Union, he was an obvious choice to be tasked with keeping the peace with the country's workforce.

The powers the Government had arrogated to itself were as draconian as any that preceded them. They were, initially, wielded with a light touch. The Emergency Powers Act and Defence Regulations theoretically gave the government complete control over all aspects of labour and industrial relations. Similarly, Order 1305 of Defence Regulation 58AA banned, without exception, strikes and lock-outs of any kind and the 1941 Essential Work (General Provisions) Order, gave sweeping powers to the Minister responsible to move workers whenever and to wherever he might decide.

These had little impact on workers with 900 strikes taking place within the first few months of the War.[12]

Short-lived they might have been but under the new powers they were most certainly illegal and yet very few convictions followed and those that did were mostly of the 'slap-on-the-wrist' variety. Under conditions of war, the power of the industrial workforce was greater than usual and, while this was to change later, ministerial fools were, at first, reluctant to rush in where angels feared to tread. Cooperation not conflict, unity not dispute, were the maxims of the times.

Strikes actually *increased* steadily until 1944, many in defence of workplace conditions and matters of safety. Mining was particularly affected with stoppages, in part, triggered by the introduction of the 'Bevin Boys.' These were untrained and inexperienced workers conscripted from other industries. The Government had created a coal shortage by conscripting some 36,000 miners into the armed forces, leaving the remaining workforce seriously undermanned and in no position to meet the demand for coal. As Aneurin Bevan would caustically observe, "This Island is made mainly of coal and surrounded by fish. Only an organizing genius could produce a shortage of both at the same time." The crisis was highly dangerous for the Government, most power and industry could not function without coal; the entire war effort was threatened with collapse, hence the industrial conscription of the Bevin Boys.

Miners were involved in many local and area stoppages and disputes throughout the war and from 1938 to 1945 accounted for 44.38 percent of all strike action in the UK. Two were of particular significance and the first of these, in January 1942 at Betteshanger Colliery, in the Kent coalfield, finally saw the Government crack down on the strikers. The miners there came

33

out in a dispute over the levels of allowances for working difficult seams. Under the provisions of Order 1305 over a thousand
miners were subsequently fined between £1.00 and £3.00 each
with three MFGB officials sentenced to jail. The miners
remained undaunted and the strike continued and spread,
bringing out other pits in solidarity. On January 28th the
Government conceded defeat, with the Home Secretary dropping the prison sentences with only nine miners having paid
their fines.

The second dispute, in 1944, erupted when the government
announced that the national average industrial wage had risen
to over £6 per day. Face-workers in Britain's pits were earning
barely £5 per day, with surface-men earning even less. In
protest miners flooded out of the collieries in the historically
militant coalfields of South Wales, Yorkshire, Scotland and
Kent to be joined by their comrades in Lancashire and Durham.
Nearly 250,000 miners were involved in the protest. With the
action taking place on the eve of the Normandy landings, the
strikers were savaged by the Conservative-supporting press. In
response one South Wales miner, with over thirty years at the
coalface behind him, retorted, "... The argument that a strike
would let our soldiers down was countered by men who had
brothers and sons in the forces who, so they claimed, had urged
them to fight and maintain their customs or privileges. They
argued that they must retain something for those absent ones
to come back to, while the suggestion that we should wait for
further negotiations was swamped by the reply that we had
already waited a long while..."[13]

Or, as a more succinct adage, common among miners at the
time, had it 'Fighting fascism abroad, doesn't mean we have to
accept it at home.' Again, the government was forced to retreat
and restore differentials; the miners leaped from 81st place in
the industrial pay league to 14th.[14]

On May 8th 1945 Churchill announced the end of the war.
The Nazis had been defeated and war-ravaged Europe could
begin the process of rebuilding. The British electorate was
desperate for change and eager to finally build the "Land Fit for
Heroes" promised them by Lloyd George at the end of the First
World War. Then, no such vision had materialised and the
inter-war years were the toughest in living memory for millions
of working class people. In 1945 there was a determination that

this time things really would be different; nothing less than a brave new world was the aspiration of millions of UK citizens.

Churchill wanted to hang on to office until at least victory in Japan could be formally announced but, under pressure from Labour, decided to call a General Election. Possibly swallowing some of his own mythology, he believed the electorate would return to office 'The People's Hero' on a tide of gratitude for his inspirational leadership during the War. In a career littered with many under-reported errors of judgment, this was to be his biggest yet. No doubt the collective memory of millions of workers regarding his role during the General Strike played a part, too.

Labour campaigned on a self-proclaimed 'socialist' programme, promising the full introduction of the recommendations contained in the 1942 Beveridge Report; a cradle-to-grave welfare system, introduction of National Insurance, creation of a free-at-the-point-of-use National Health Service and the nationalisation of the commanding heights of the economy. A famous electoral leaflet from the campaign read, "Labour is a socialist party and proud of it." Conservative and establishment thinking was that 'the country wouldn't stand for it' and the mood was one of complacency. On July 5th the nation delivered its verdict. Labour won one of the biggest parliamentary majorities it would ever see. Gaining a convincing 49.7 percent of the vote and a total of 393 seats, the party increased their number of seats by 239 to finish with an overall majority of 146.

The Conservatives lost 204 seats to fall to 211; a 36.2 percent share of the vote. The 'natural party of government' was unprepared for such a shift in public mood. Labour won 11,967,746 votes, the Tories 9,972,010 with the Liberals relegated to the third-party status they would maintain to the present day, with 2,252,430; just 9% of all votes cast.[15]

Churchill was ejected from office to be replaced by Clement Attlee. Ironically, for the leader of such a radical party (at the time), Attlee was seen as a rather woolly figure on the soft-left of the party, eventually moving firmly to its right. Snidely observed by Churchill to be nothing more than "A sheep in sheep's clothing" nevertheless even his own wife, Violet, observed, "Clem was never really a socialist, were you, darling? Well, not a rabid one." With such an unassailable majority and overwhelming mandate behind him, one imagines Attlee paid little heed to his detractors. In any event, he had rather more pressing matters with which to concern himself; nothing less than the rebuilding and the transformation of an entire Island.

The miners waited patiently as, over the next two years, the new Labour Government nationalised, piece-by-piece, large swathes of the manufacturing base and the economy; The Bank of England, inland transport, iron and steel. The new postwar consensus was exactly that; an understanding among the more far-sighted custodians of British capital that if revolution abroad was to be staved off at home and the increasing menace of communism kept at bay, an accommodation with the working class had to be made. However, the new welfare state was not going to be funded by the British ruling class so someone else had to pay. The tab was picked up by those at the sharp end of British imperialism. The postwars gains at home were paid for by those in the Colonies as a huge transfer of wealth from abroad to the UK was overseen. For all Labour's claims to socialism at home, overseas the Attlee government was as reactionary as that which it had succeeded, overseeing the founding of NATO and enthusiastically prosecuting anti-communist and pro-colonial anti-insurgency campaigns all over the Middle East, Africa and Asia.

Eventually, on January 1st, 1947, the miners' new dawn arrived; 'Vesting Day'. The day the coal mines were finally taken out of private hands and into the hands of 'the people.' The newly established National Coal Board erected commemorative plaques at pit-heads which read, "This colliery is now managed by the National Coal Board on behalf of the people."

Mining villages saw marching brass bands, union banners flying proudly in the breeze and a mood of celebration sweeping the pit communities. At last, the hated private owners were displaced. No more would miners work in foul, dangerous and investment-starved mines for a pittance. Sealing the deal was the appointment of two of 'our own' to the new National Coal Board; the union's own Ebby Edwards and the TUC's Walter Citrine.

In preparation for the new era, plans had been made as early as 1942 for the evolution of the union into a single, national, centralised body. A specially appointed sub-committee of the MFGB had drawn up a blueprint to merge the various regions and sections into a single structure of which all miners in the

UK would be members. Ironically, in November 1944, the founding conference of the newly established National Union of Mineworkers took place in Nottingham.

In reality, not a great deal had changed. Far from being a national union, the new organisation retained most of the old federal structure of the MFGB. In contrast to most other trade unions, the NUM was a vast, sprawling beast with many sections, divisions and bodies. Most of its component parts were individual independently-registered trade unions in their own right, all exercising a high degree of autonomy, despite the new national rebranding. This was both a source of strength and a serious weakness.

Nottingham's own Nottinghamshire Miners' Association had existed since 1881. It wasn't until 1888 that the MFGB was established in South Wales. The MFGB was never, as implied by its name, a single, unified and centralised trade union; in reality it acted as a kind of coordinator and administrative apparatus for its many affiliates and sections, most of which were fiercely protective of their autonomy and independence. Local customs, agreements and practices were jealousy guarded. In 1898 the South Wales Miners' Federation emerged, joining the MFGB the following year. In 1907, the Northumberland Miners' Federation was founded and in 1908, the Durham Miners' Federation. And so, area by area, region by region, the MFGB grew to its nearly one million-strong height, in the mid-twenties, by the joining of various regional mining bodies and associations.

One thing the creation of the NUM did do was to give many miners the feeling of now belonging to *two* unions; firstly, as members of their own local body and then to the newly established national union. From that moment on there were often disagreements and differences as to which authority held supremacy. For Nottingham's striking miners in 1984, they grew wearily accustomed to strike-breakers citing their own region's perceived local autonomy and decision-making process as justification for their betrayal of the strike. In response, the strikers coined a phrase that one would often hear throughout the year, whenever arguments regarding the legality of the dispute were exchanged; 'National trumps Local.'

The feelings of exultation and bright hopes for the future soon began to wilt as the reality of a nationalised industry, still operating within the confines of a market economy, made itself felt. Despite the appointments of Edwards and Citrine, many of the pit managers were the still the former private owners or managers. After being generously compensated they were employed by the NCB on substantial salaries. This added to a sense of resentment and a feeling that all was not as it had been promised. Of particular offence to the miners was that compensation was paid to former owners who had already closed their collieries.

Added to that was a complex set of checks, balances and production targets that didn't apply to other nationalised industries. These had the effect of artificially making the industry appear unprofitable.[16]

To further complicate matters the Government asked the miners for a voluntary sixth shift so that production targets could be met. Given that the much-cherished and long-fought for 'five-day week' was something of a miner's Holy Grail, It was only a matter of time before the unrest brought further industrial action. It finally arrived with a strike at Grimethorpe, spreading swiftly to other pits. For many disillusioned miners there was a determination to resist treatment by the chiefs of the nationalised industry which was perceived as little different to that of the old private owners. Certainly, there was still great danger in working 'down't pit' with conditions, at some, barely improved from the bad old days of private ownership. One of the worst postwar disasters took place at Creswell Colliery in the north of the Nottinghamshire coalfield on September 26th 1950. A fire started about a mile from the shaft and eighty miners perished. In terms of worst first days on the job, pity the poor apprentices tasked with digging a mass grave for their incinerated comrades.

Looking back at the record of Labour governments in the postwar period, Arthur Scargill was to remark, in an interview with *New Left Review* in June 1975, that "The one thing that annoys me is that we've got one set of standards when we've got a Tory government and a completely different set of standards when we've got a Labour government." A sentiment which, had it been articulated in the 40s and 50s, would no doubt have received a sympathetic hearing from miners everywhere. The future NUM President would go on to assert that "... a Labour government should never, ever find itself in a position of conflict with the trade unions... if it does then it has nothing in common with socialism and nothing in common with working class principle... I'm not prepared to pay for the crisis of capitalism at the expense of the people I represent."

The next twenty years, up to 1970, saw pits closing at a steady rate. Significantly, more were shut under Harold Wilson's Labour administrations than under Thatcher during her entire three-term tenure in Downing Street. 290 pits were shut during the Labour years compared to 'just' 160 under Thatcher. Wilson's love of nuclear power and his stark assertion that "We are redefining and we are restating our socialism in terms of the scientific revolution.... the Britain that is going to be forged in the white heat of this revolution will be no place for restrictive practices or outdated methods on either side of industry" couldn't have been clearer; coal was outdated and, if he had his way, the industry was on the way out. Life in the nationalised mines was becoming increasingly hard for the NUM rank-and-file to stomach.

From Vesting Day, the number of pits dropped from 980 to 850 by 1955. Fifteen years after that, the number had dropped to 292. Job losses were enormous. From around 700,000 the workforce sank to 287,000 which the 1972 Wilberforce Enquiry would come to describe as "a rundown which is without parallel in British industry in terms of the social and economic costs for the mining community."

There were several reasons why the expected opposition had, thus far, failed to materialise. Firstly, the postwar settlement had led to a consensus that even Conservative governments recognised, albeit with varying degrees of enthusiasm. The Macmillan years oversaw the closures of pits in full consultation with the NUM. Possibly of more significance, however, was that despite the miners' reputation for militancy and the union's strong syndicalist and socialist heritage, its leadership was unmistakeably to the right of its members. For now, the lid was on but, of course, could not be kept there indefinitely.

The period also saw the emergence of a new, fighting left and the rise to office of members of the famous (or infamous, depending on one's politics) Yorkshire Caucus. Among them, a young Arthur Scargill who was destined to revolutionise the NUM. Under the men-toring of the Communist Party's local Industrial Organiser, Frank Watters, and its National

Industrial Organiser, Bert Ramelson, Scargill was more than ready to challenge the entrenched right-wing in the Union's leadership; intent only on a quiet life and cosy relations with both the Board and Governments, of whatever shade, at the expense of the members' jobs.

The 'October Revolution', as it was to become known in Scargill mythology, started at the Yorkshire Area Council on October 11th 1969 when Scargill, then the Woolley pit delegate, proposed the union strike over the hours that men above ground had to work. The Left won the vote by eighty-five votes to three. At least that's the official account. Among miners who took part in the action, though, there is an insistence that this was an entirely unofficial rank-and-file action that bypassed the leadership completely.

Since, by then, the local and regional wage-rates had vanished to be replaced by a national rate, the National Power Loading Agreement, the usual divide and conquer tactics (used as often by the NUM's right-wing leadership as the Government) of playing one area off against another was a non-starter. Now the members united around the new common goal. Formal opposition from the NEC was irrelevant: the strike was organised and driven from below by the rank-and-file.

Although a protest against the government's handling of the industry, it was equally a protest at a passive NUM leadership which had meekly presided over falling wages and an enormous number of closures and redundancies. The miners' position at the time was that 'if the industry shuts tomorrow, we still require paying for working in it today.' The Left picked up the gauntlet and slammed it into the twin faces of the NCB and their own leadership.

The strike spread from Yorkshire. At its zenith, the action involved over 130,000 miners from around 140 pits, spearheaded, as usual, by the Scottish, South Welsh and Kent Areas; soon to be joined by Derbyshire, Nottingham and Midlands miners. It was devastatingly effective and there was no production in some pits for the entire two-week duration of the strike. Although flying pickets were not a new device it was the first time that they'd been deployed to such an extent and with such success.

The confidence of the NUM Left soared and there was a conviction that the time of participating in the demise of their own earnings and conditions was over. While not securing the formal objective of reduced hours enshrined in an official national agreement, a fudge was agreed to save the collective face of the NEC: verbal approval of regional negotiations to secure the eight-hour day for surface-workers was approved. No one was under any doubt; the strike had been a success and had secured its objective. The Yorkshire militants had proved that there was a mood to fight and, given the degree of rank-and-file militancy and initiative, the membership could be roused to take on both the Board and the Government.

The following year at the NUM's Annual Conference, Scargill, responding mockingly from the podium to Yorkshire President Sid Schofield's denigration of the Left as "adventurers", starkly declared "...let the Coal Board be warned: the miners last October showed that they have been passive long enough and I suggest to this conference that if we have people in 'splinter groups' who are going on 'adventurous' paths... then I am proud to associate myself with them."

The stage was now set for the miners' finest hour: the toppling of a Conservative Government.

In 1971 Conference made a change to the NUM rule book which was to have far-reaching consequences. Instead of a two-thirds majority required to sanction strike action, fifty-five percent would now be sufficient.

By the time 1972 arrived, miners' pay was among the worst in industry. From the leap from 81st place to 14th in the industrial pay league in 1944, the long, slow slide in pay, terms and conditions had matched the decline of the industry as a whole and, following the moral victories of 1969 and 1970, there was a slim majority in support of strike action. Following an overtime ban the NUM launched its first fully national and official strike since 1926 on January 9th 1972. It was, by any criteria, an unqualified success. Following the Battle of Saltley Gate, a personal triumph for Arthur Scargill and one which was to enter the annals of NUM history, the miners won virtually all of their demands and a twenty-seven percent increase in pay.

The Left's ascendency continued as Scargill, buoyed up by his very public role at Saltley Gate, was elected in 1973 to his first full-time official's post: Area Compensation Agent. Another decisive victory for the Left, Scargill polled more votes than his two right-wing opponents combined: 28,050 votes compared to

Jack Smart's 9,824 and Tom Roebuck's 8,336. Less than a year in the job before his next move up the ladder, even Scargill's most vociferous critics conceded he was an outstanding advocate for his men in his new role. Ruthlessly pursuing the NCB in the wake of the Lofthouse Colliery disaster, in which seven miners had died, Scargill's case was a meticulous and clinical offensive from which the NCB could not escape liability. This early success in his new position only served to elevate both his profile and the esteem in which rank-and-file NUM members held him.

Scargill was a shoo-in as the Left's chosen candidate, following the death of Yorkshire President Sam Bullough. Although perceived as something of a loose cannon by the Communist Party and by no means always in agreement with them, Scargill nevertheless secured their support along with that of the rest of the Left. Following the enhanced publicity he'd received following his role in the Lofthouse Enquiry, he romped home by an even bigger margin than that of his election to Area Compensation Agent. The then Area Vice President, Jack Leigh, might have expected to win but in the event polled only 7,126 votes and was even beaten into third place by South Yorkshire's Jack Layden with 7,981 and by Scargill with 28,362 votes. As President of the NUM's biggest, and one of its most militant Areas, Scargill was now in a key position from which, along with other recent Left candidates who had won elections to the NEC, to influence national policy and push the national leadership ever further left.

The subsequent events seemed to be almost inevitable. The Left formulated a wages claim, backed by Conference, which was rejected by the NCB. The usual overtime ban was followed by a ballot for strike action in February 1974. The members made known their views on the NCB's position and returned an eighty-one percent majority in favour of striking (Scargill must have been particularly proud when his own Yorkshire Area came back with over ninety percent in favour of action).

The miners' cause was further boosted when the Pay Board released figures showing that, contrary to the Coal Board's claims, miners were earning significantly less than those in other heavy industries. Against the backdrop of the three-day week and the success of NUM action, Conservative Prime Minister Edward Heath called a General Election for February

28th. Heath and the Tories campaigned around the question "Who Governs Britain?" The unions or the Government? It was a close-run affair but the answer was: not the Government. A hung parliament resulted and although polling more individual votes than Labour, the Tories won fewer seats and were unable to form a coalition with the Liberals or the Unionists (who had rejected the Tory whip). Heath resigned and Wilson was back in Number Ten, albeit in a considerably weaker position. With no room for manoeuvre, he granted virtually all of the NUM's demands.

The NUM had been lucky. Heath had made an appalling and unnecessary tactical blunder calling the election when he did and the Conservatives lost by only the very narrowest of margins. Still, a trade union had toppled a Tory Government and the feeling was very much one of "what's not to like?" It would be a few years before the 1974 victory would be seen to be a poor second to that of 1972 but, as an old footballing adage has it: you can only beat what's in front of you, and that the NUM certainly did.

For the critics of Nottinghamshire, citing Spencerism as an incurable disease in the body politic of the Nottinghamshire miners, 1972 and 1974 threw up questions that have yet to be answered. In both disputes, Nottingham was as solid as any other Area. Whatever the part some felt Spencerism had played in the 1984 dispute, curiously, it bypassed the disputes of the 70s.

In any event, things would never be the same again: economies around the world were starting to free-fall, energy crises loomed and the end of the postwar boom had arrived. More significantly for the NUM, however, was that just around the corner, the most determined enemy the miners would face was commencing her own climb to power.

Chapter 3:
Anarchy in the UK

"When morality comes up against profit,
it is seldom that profit loses."
SHIRLEY CHISHOLM

Nottinghamshire is probably more famous for Robin Hood than anything else. In the same way, one imagines, that Merseysiders must tire of incessant questions from tourists regarding The Beatles, so Nottinghamshire's residents are resigned to their City and County being defined by the mythical outlaw; either him or Brian Clough, a fellow non-conformist of similarly legendary status. Of course there is and always has been a great deal more to the area than a mere folk-tale and, in the postwar years, it was Nottingham's light and heavy industry, not tourism, which drove the county's economic engine.

World-famous for its acclaimed 'Nottingham Lace', the City was a hub of the textiles industry and the 'Lace Market', during the years of Empire, was responsible for a large part of the UK's textiles exports. The legacy is still visible in the carefully preserved architecture around Stoney Street.

Bicycle manufacturer Raleigh, tobacco manufacturer John Player (now Imperial Tobacco) and Boots the Chemist were all important concerns in the postwar period and accounted for substantial numbers of the county's workforce. All these, though, were eclipsed by the National Coal Board which, in 1983, just before the strike started, had twenty-seven pits in the Nottinghamshire coalfield (along with four workshops). Second only to Yorkshire, with fifty-six pits at that time, mining in Nottinghamshire directly accounted for the jobs of 32,493 miners, mechanics, electricians and drivers, plus support, office staff and managers. David Amos, a former working miner who went on to receive his doctorate writing about the strike and the UDM, of which he had been an official, says his studies revealed that an additional 6.1 jobs for every one mining job, relied on the pits in Nottinghamshire: power-station workers, drivers, freight, haulage, catering, printers, health and safety equipment manufacturing companies and many more.

For the Nottinghamshire miners, the period from 1974 up to the strike was, in contrast to the economic decline sweeping the rest of the UK, one of relative prosperity, affluence and good future prospects. The Plan For Coal, agreed by the Labour Government in the aftermath of the 1974 strike, promised long-term investment and new technology to bring the UK's mining industry fully into the 20th century and make it the best in the world. New mines were sunk and opened and young men, with no previous familial or trade union connections with mining, flocked to the Nottinghamshire pits where substantial wages could be earned. For a while all was well and Nottingham's miners were, with the possible exception of the Kent men, with the lucrative across-Channel markets on their coalfield's doorstep, the highest-paid in the country. This was thanks to NUM President Joe Gormley.

Born in 1917 in Lancashire, Gormley started down the pit at fourteen and, rising through the NUM ranks, emerged as national President in 1971. He would hold office until his retirement, eleven years later. The very antithesis of his successor, Arthur Scargill, he was typical of the old-school labour aristocracy who saw their roles not as challengers to capitalism but as its accommodators. The Gormley-style trade union leaders were very much a part of the system and while ostensibly representing their members, would not do so at what they perceived to be the expense of the system as a whole. Pragmatism, realism and compromise were the watchwords of the right-wing code by which they lived and worked: code among the Left for treachery, sell-out and betrayal.

45

Gormley very much enjoyed the cosy 'beer and sandwiches' relationships he cultivated with the various occupants of Downing Street and the Coal Board chiefs. Often agreeing secret deals and pacts with officials of both the government and the Board, he would then manoeuvre them through the NUM's executive structure, sometimes without even the members of his own Executive being fully aware of his machinations. In one sense, there was nothing at all remarkable about any of this. At the time, it was accepted custom and practice for many of the so-called union barons to behave in such a manner. Oddly, such practices were never condemned by those critics on the Left who routinely portrayed its leaders as conspiratorial, undemocratic 'tightly-knit bodies of men.' By contrast, the Scargill style of union leadership was transparent. No one, at any time, was ever under any illusions as to where he was coming from and what his intentions might be. The Left, in all parts of the labour and trade union movement, has generally been more than happy to be open with, and accountable to, the wider membership, confident, as its representatives usually are, in the power and appeal of their arguments to the rank and file. This was even more so within the NUM, a union filled with highly opinionated and strong-willed men.

The source of Scargill's power was that he both reflected and informed the views of his members and they him. As he was to remark during his maiden speech as national President, "Members have every right to demand total commitment from me as President and to insist that I prosecute resolutions passed at Conference. Loyalty, however, works both ways. I also have every right to demand total support from the members of this union." Homing in on the very essence of what would constitute his future relationship with the membership, he continued, "Leadership is only as strong as the backing it receives from the rank and file." It is well worth the reader bearing this in mind as he or she comes to consider the slander and vitriol which was to rain down on the NUM President's head and the equally insulting portrayal of the strikers as hapless dupes and conned mugs who were unable to distinguish night from day. The point is worth hammering home: Scargill, personally incorruptible[17] and immovably-wedded to his syndicalist-Marxist vision of the miners as the *ne plus ultra* of the socialist transformation of society, was, nevertheless, only ever the embodiment and reflection of the membership's wishes and desires. His greatest crime, in the eyes of the establishment, was to never betray that objective or deviate from his commitment to his membership. If he hadn't existed, the members would simply have invented him and had he 'mellowed' and grown more 'realistic' that membership would certainly have rejected him.

Gormley's power base, on the other hand, derived from his relationships, contacts and arrangements with the government and the bosses of the NCB. At the specific request of Conservative Prime Minister, Edward Heath, he even went so far as to plead with the NUM rank-and-file for the postponement of the 1974 strike until after the General Election; something rejected by his considerably more intransigent members. To no one's surprise, least of all Scargill's, Gormley was exposed by the BBC in 2002 as a state asset and Special Branch spy, informing on his own members and colleagues.[18]

Nevertheless, he was an entertaining, witty and personable presence and enjoyed the affection of many of his members. Widely viewed as the 'wily old fox' responsible for the two highest wage increases the miners had ever seen, he had been fortunate in holding office during a time of industrial militancy when employers were prone to bowing to union power. During his final period in office, Gormley was to make two decisions that would impact on both the NUM and the forthcoming strike. The first of these was to wreck the painstakingly-cultivated national unity of the miners around pay and conditions. In 1966, the National Power Loading Agreement (NPLA) brought all miners together in a single, unified pay-bargaining process, with the workforce in all parts of the country earning a national rate. This went a long way toward overcoming the sectionalism, divisions and local fiefdoms of the NUM's highly-federated structure.

In 1977, however, an Area Incentive Scheme was back on the agenda. The NCB, with the enthusiastic support of the Labour Party, had first raised the idea in the early 70s, ostensibly as a means of increasing productivity. It was fiercely championed by Gormley and the Right who claimed it would restore the differentials between face-workers and surface-workers, which had evaporated as a result of the earlier NPLA, and lead to higher earnings for all miners, generally.

47

The Labour leadership supported such a move as, they claimed, it would enable miners to increase their earnings but not at the expense of the Government's fragile Social Contract, which sought agreement that trade union wage demands would only be of a finite and pre-agreed amount. Of course, it would be the very height of naivety not to assume that the impact the scheme would have on the ability of the NUM to operate effectively as a national unified body, capable of challenging and defeating governments, wasn't also very attractive to the Labour Party leadership. Going a step further, it wouldn't be particularly outrageous to suggest it might well have been the *main* reason for Labour's support.

The Left were opposed to such a move, knowing that it would destroy the miners' national unity and set Area against Area, all the easier for the Regional NCB Directors to play off one against another: a return to the hated practices and conditions of the old, pre-nationalised, private industry.

At first, it appeared to be a no-brainer. Conference, theoretically the supreme decision-making body of the NUM, had previously rejected the proposal. To the astonishment of the Left, Gormley simply ignored the democratically-arrived-at Conference decision and forced a ballot anyway. The Kent Area (supported by Scargill-led Yorkshire), comprised, as both Areas were, of the sort of men not given to responding well to autocratic and high-handed leadership, went to the High Court seeking to overturn their President. The basis of the Kent Area's action was simple and presumed incontrovertible: Gormley was in breach of Rule. 23 by forcing a ballot on a matter already voted on, and rejected, by Conference. To add further weight, the Kent Area's barrister pointed out that Rule. 8 stated unambiguously that the NEC was "... *expressly forbidden from overturning Conference decisions.*" These were the facts and, the Left reasonably assumed, represented a water-tight case. Despite the logic of the Kent Area's position, the High Court ruled in Gormley's favour. The judgment dismissed the NUM's rule book and the wishes of its members, and asserted that a secret ballot was the highest form of democracy superior to any decision by Conference. The decision was upheld on appeal, giving the NEC *carte blanche* to do whatever it felt it could get away with. Of course, governments, employers and right-wing union leaders are much enamoured of secret ballots: far better, for them, atomised, isolated individuals voting in secrecy with only exposure to establishment propaganda to influence decisions. Living, breathing democracy of the robust working class kind, where union members freely exchange views and contrasting opinions and consensus is hammered out on shop floors and in canteens and working-men's clubs, is anathema. Routinely portrayed as press-gangs of left-wing intimidation and bullying, such views reflect the weakness of the Right's position and display contempt for substantive democracy.

Meanwhile, back at the coal face, as it were, Gormley had his ballot and the the proposed incentive scheme was rejected. Surely, now, the matter would end? To the disbelief of the Left, no: there the matter did *not* end. Gormley went to the High Court to receive a ruling *this* time, that a ballot was *not* binding on the NEC after all. Far from it being the 'highest form of democracy' and superior to Conference, *now*, it transpired, a ballot was only an 'advisory guide'. The message was clear: if a Conference decision favoured the Left, it was subordinate to a secret ballot. If a ballot went against the Right, it was merely a 'guide' and an 'advisory' mechanism which could be jettisoned with impunity. Gormley simply ignored the result of the ballot *he* insisted be held in the first place and forced the incentive scheme through on a regional basis.

The Kent miners returned yet again to the High Court (supported still by the richer Yorkshire Area who were footing the bill) to protest that every rule in the book was being broken and that every decision-making body and democratic process was simply being ignored by Gormley. To pile farce upon injustice, Mr Justice Watkins loftily reaffirmed that "The result of a ballot nationally conducted is not binding upon the National Executive Committee".[19]

The legal wrangling was viewed with ambivalence among the wider membership. Most were appalled by their President's contempt for their Union's rules and, by extension, its members. On the other hand, it simply wasn't done for trade unionists to settle differences in court. Furthermore, highly contentious and controversial precedents had now been set.

The unity of the NUM was dealt a damaging blow. The new incentive agreement paid miners a bonus based on output per man and, by the time the 1984 strike finally arrived,

Nottingham miners were, with the possible exception of the Kent men, not just the highest-paid miners in the country but among the highest-paid in industry anywhere. Les Dennis, future picket manager of Nottingham's Linby Colliery, would come to remark at the amazement of Yorkshire pickets arriving at Nottinghamshire collieries in 1984 and encountering miners living in detached and semi-detached private houses with two cars on the drive.

Once the scheme was operational, the South Wales, Kent and Yorkshire Areas dragged the NEC, Gormley and the South Derbyshire Area (among the first implementers of the new scheme, along with Nottingham) back into the High Court in a last-ditch attempt to win an injunction and kill the deal once and for all. To no avail, of course, with the High Court upholding its earlier rulings: the die was cast.

The times were indeed a-changing. The end of the long, prosperous postwar up-swing had arrived and the 70s were tumultuous times. With economic slowdown, not least as a result of the 1973 international oil crisis, relations between the trade unions and the Labour Government were stretched to breaking point. The Government, desperately trying to hold together its shaky Social Contract, in an attempt to restore some economic stability, was savaged by union leaders submitting 'unrealistic' pay claims as their members, thanks to rocketing inflation, saw their wages, in real terms, free-falling and their living standards plummeting.

Culturally, too, music and fashion reflected some of the hopelessness and feelings of disorientation which had set in. Long gone was the Summer of Love, prog rock and Woodstock; to be replaced by Punk, which had spewed forth from the cradle of the 70s in a snarling fury of nihilism, defiance and anarchy. It suited the decade perfectly. Cynical, fervently anti-establishment and concerned only with rejecting all that had gone before, Punk was an apt metaphor for the times and perfectly captured the *zeitgeist* as the 70s drew to a close.

With the advent of the 'Winter of Discontent' complete social breakdown appeared a genuine possibility. Generals and Civil Servants muttered darkly in London's clubland of coups and emergencies. On the streets anti-fascists and trade unionists fought pitched battles with the National Front. Anarchy in the UK indeed.

The Conservatives were returned to government on May 3rd 1979, headed by Margaret Thatcher. Thatcher was cut from very different cloth to that of her predecessors. From the outset it was clear a set-piece showdown with the miners was unavoidable and it wasn't long before the opening salvoes were fired.

1981 commenced with the Yorkshire Area balloting its members, at that time in excess of 60,000 men, asking if they would support strike action in the event of pit closures for reasons other than of proven exhaustion. The miners' leaders knew what was coming and so the mood of the membership was being gauged. With the ballot returning an eighty-six percent majority in favour, there was little doubt as to what that mood was. Just one month later, in February, a round of closures was announced with a predicted loss of around 30,000 jobs and, crucially, not on grounds of exhaustion but 'economics'. As the NUM leadership met with the Board, rumours swirled around the coalfields and attitudes hardened. As usual, with the NUM, the rank and file's thirst for action outstripped that of the Gormley-led NEC. Within days, a strike wave was rolling across the country. Ignoring the leadership's pleas for patience and an official go-ahead, the strike was growing, Area by Area. As it would unfold in 1984, there was no national ballot but, by contrast, no howls of outrage from the media and the Conservative Government regarding the absence of one either. Each Area took its own decision and the fight was on.

Unlike 1984, there were two differences: firstly, the assurances of support the NUM received from the TUC were markedly more robust, and although it never had to deliver on that support, it was obvious to Thatcher and the Cabinet that this wouldn't be a fight involving only the NUM.

Of greater significance was the lack of preparation on the part of the Government. The 'Ridley Plan', of which more later, had not yet been implemented and Thatcher and her ministers were caught unprepared by the strength and speed of the miners' reaction. Cooler Conservative heads prevailed and the Government caved in, calling off the closures and promising further investment. While jubilation ensued in miners' welfares up and down the country over the following few days, the NUM's own set of cooler heads realised this had not been a defeat for Thatcher at all, merely a tactical retreat. The

Government had merely been testing the water. As observed previously, Mick McGahey pointed out that this had merely been a body swerve, *not* a u-turn: this was the NUM's very own 'Red Friday'. There was no doubt in either his, or Scargill's, mind that this had been something of an opening salvo: a shot across the bows, but behind it lay real intent. As Dave Douglass comments, "It wasn't such a phoney war that if there hadn't have been widespread wildcat action, the pit closure programme would have started there and then with twenty-one pits closed in quick succession. I don't think so much as 'testing the water' as quickly getting out of their depth." Be that as it may, the *real* war was yet to come.

In 1982 the final piece necessary for war slotted into place with Gormley's retirement and Scargill's ascension to the national Presidency. The second of Gormley's parting gifts to the NUM, this was an uncharacteristic piece of back-firing blundering producing an outcome that was quite other than the outgoing President had intended. Intent on stopping the Left's darling, the Communist Party member Mick McGahey, succeeding him, Gormley had delayed his retirement until, under NUM rules, the Scottish President was too old to stand for election. This left the field clear for Arthur Scargill, around whom the NUM Left once again united. Unlike the Right who would hesitate, fumble and, ultimately, drop the ball through their inability to agree a single candidate — fielding three who only succeeded in stealing each others' votes — the Left realised this was their opportunity to take complete control of the leadership and no other Left candidate stood.

In typical Scargill fashion, his election campaign was thorough, professional and media-friendly. Equally typical was the forthrightness of his campaigning rhetoric. No one who cast their vote in Scargill's favour could have possibly been in any doubt for what, exactly, they were voting: unyielding, uncompromising opposition to pit closures and an implacable determination to fight the forces of capital wherever and whenever they threatened miners' interests. And, quite often, at times and in places where they *didn't*. Scargill was nothing if not a consistent proletarian warrior, frequently lending his and the NUM's support to other workers' struggles; the nurses' strike and Grunwick being particularly apposite examples.

An exasperated Gormley left his colleagues on the Right to it as they dithered and dallied. When the results came in Scargill received 138,803 votes, 70.3 percent of all votes cast, far in excess of all three of his rivals' votes combined (also, by definition, a mandate far greater than any that Margaret Thatcher ever received for her policies). Bernard Donaghy polled 6,443 (3.3 percent), Trevor Bell (originally Gormley's hand-picked successor) received 34,075 (17.3 percent) and Nottingham President, Ray Chadburn 17,979 (9.1 percent). Chadburn, at that time, was seen very much as a right-winger. He was later to find himself caught between both working miners and strikers as he attempted to manoeuvre a way out of the Nottinghamshire minefield.

Scargill was at pains to ensure there could be no misunderstanding regarding any message he might wish to impart and on 6th July 1982, *The Times* reported the newly-elected President informing that year's NUM Conference that, "Under no circumstances shall I countenance a pit closure programme. We shall never again relive the experiences of the '60s and it would be suicidal of the Government or Board to think otherwise." Presumably to his chagrin, however, the membership rejected calls for strike action on three separate occasions from 1982 up to the dispute commencing in 1984.

Following the second of these, in October 1982, Scargill claimed to have been fed a 'hit-list' of some seventy pits the NCB intended to close. At first, strenuously denied by the Board, they sheepishly came clean but insisted Scargill had 'misinterpreted' the data when, a week later, he ordered the documents' publication in the pages of *The Miner*, the NUM's official journal.

The following year, in March 1983, the NCB ordered the closure of Tymawr Lewis Merthyr pit in South Wales. The miners immediately voted for strike action and sent pickets to other coalfields appealing for support. In contrast to 1984, this time the matter *did* go to a national ballot as the NUM NEC saw this as a national issue. The membership, nationally, yet again rejected strike action. There were regional differences with Yorkshire voting in favour and, somewhat bizarrely, considering they'd refused to strike over the closure of one of their own pits the previous year, Scotland as well.

Dave Douglass says, "That strike, like the 1981 one, was starting to roll, pits in Doncaster like Hatfield Main had already taken decisions to strike when the Lewis men appeared at the gates and called out the Doncaster coalfield. It had every chance of success, like the '81 action but, for some inexplicable reason, the Welsh EC decided to call off the pickets and go to the NEC to authorize a national ballot. It was a disastrous decision: we lost the ballot in the cold light of day, whereas in the heat of a rolling strike action the coalfields would have gone down like dominoes. Worse still, misinformation spread among the Welsh miners that the Yorkshire miners had voted *not* to support them, when in fact there was a majority in Yorkshire *for* strike action.

"This tale caused the South Wales area to say 'fuck 'em', when voting on whether to join the Cortonwood Yorkshire action: they voted *against* strike action. They, of course, were picketed out by their own militants and stayed loyal to the end, but this call for a national ballot with the hope that it would be lost like this one, set a seed in someone's mind. On the other side was the view among the NCB and Government that we would have a ballot and we would lose it."

So the strike didn't happen and the Welsh pickets were left with a lasting residue of bitterness and resentment as miners outside Wales worked as normal while the Welsh pit closed.

On 1st October that year, the NEC released a statement indicating the miners were preparing for war:

> *The National Executive Committee have considered the report of the Union's Negotiating Committee and discussed in detail the Board's response to the NUM wage claim. It is clear that the Board's offer of 5.2% — i.e approximately £3 nett in take-home pay — falls far short of the increase required to restore the purchasing power and basic wage existing in 1974. The dramatic erosion in basic grade rates has seen the miners' slump to 45th place in the Wages Table. The Board has rejected our claim for shorter hours, increased unsocial shift-payment, wages paid on a salaried basis and consolidation of bonus payments. The demand for substantial increase emanated from our Branches/Lodges, resulting in the Resolution passed at the 1983 Conference. In view of this, and of the very serious threat to eliminate "uneconomical pits", contained in the Board's reply to the Union's claim, it is felt that this reply should be sent back to our Branches/Lodges, in order to obtain their views in readiness for a Special Delegate Conference on the 21st October 1983.*

Following the Special Delegates' Conference, the NUM gave notice that from 31st October of that year an overtime ban would be introduced. Although formally in protest at the Board's pay-offer, it was now clear to all that the confrontation over closures was fast approaching and, in preparation for it, the miners knew that reducing coal stocks was of vital tactical importance. Ironically, it was precisely *because* of the success of this tactic that the strike started when it did, in the mild spring of '84, with Scargill castigated as some sort of tactical incompetent for 'calling' the action at such a time. On both counts, such received wisdom is simply incorrect, as the facts will show.

The New Year arrived and with it the catalyst for the longest and most bitterly-fought industrial dispute in British history. 'The Miners' Great Strike for Jobs' as it would come to be known and subsequently immortalised on thousands of commemorative plates and banners, started at Cortonwood on 1st March 1984. George Hayes, the National Coal Board's South Yorkshire Regional Director, gave notice that Cortonwood was to close in five weeks' time.[20]

Considering that just a few weeks previously around 850 miners had been transferred there from the doomed Elsecar pit, on the promise of at least five years' further employment, the announcement sent shock-waves around the Yorkshire coalfield.

Under the NUM's Rule 41, the Yorkshire Area was granted approval by the NEC to strike in protest, following a motion tabled by Cortonwood at the Yorkshire Area Council meeting of 5th March. Here the first of the myths surrounding the strike must be addressed; firstly, Scargill did *not* 'call' any strike at all. As National President, he wasn't a member of either Cortonwood Branch or the Yorkshire Area Council and was not eligible to speak or vote in either forum. The decision was solely that of Cortonwood and the Yorkshire Area, in accordance with the NUM's rule book. The previous Yorkshire Area ballot of '81, returning a majority of 86 percent in favour of strike in the event of closures, added further moral weight to the democratic process. Of course, as usual in the NUM, such procedural mechanics were supplemented with mass meetings of, in some cases, up to 2000 attendees at a time, all over the coalfield, as miners packed out venues to hear the pros, cons and plans for the fight which was now well and truly on.

In Nottinghamshire things were very different. Confusion, doubt and uncertainty were the prevailing moods. With an

Area Executive split between Left and Right from the very onset of the strike, mixed messages and conflicting instructions were the miners' lot.

For miners at Linby colliery, for example, the first they really knew of what was occurring elsewhere was when Yorkshire pickets (at that time entirely unofficial and unsanctioned by any of Yorkshire's official bodies) descended on Nottinghamshire in their thousands. The tone and manner of the visitors, and the nature of their reception, appear to depend on who you speak to. For the Nottinghamshire miners who would reject the strike, the Yorkshire contingent were 'arrogant', 'aggressive' and 'violent' and were not going to tell Notts men what they could and could not do. From the Nottinghamshire loyalists a very different picture emerges: one of good-humoured and friendly men, careful not to offend but determined to be heard as they appealed to their southern comrades for solidarity. It was obvious that the type of Yorkshireman a Nottinghamshire miner might encounter depended entirely on the position of the Nottinghamshire miner. A striker could be assured of friendship, solidarity and bonhomie. A working miner, by contrast, could only guarantee hostility, aggression and, as the working miners saw things, 'intimidation.'

Brian Evangelista, Deputy Manager of Moorgreen during the strike, found most pickets to be polite and well-behaved. "At Moorgreen I've got to say that of the ones I dealt with, I found them generally very well-behaved. For example, one day they came into the canteen at Moorgreen, a busload of Welsh miners. It was quite funny, I won't tell you the Manager's name at the time, but he said, 'you need to go and sort them out, Brian,' I was Deputy Manager at the time. I said 'what do you mean, go and sort them out?' 'Well, they're in the canteen.' 'Yeah, so what?' 'Well they shouldn't be there so you need to go and sort them out.' So I go up the stairs, into the canteen and say, 'Look lads, you're on strike. You can't use the facilities' and they just go, 'OK, boss, we're on our way' and away they went. Next thing you know, the rumours are going around the coalfield that Brian Evangelista threw a busload of Welsh miners out of the canteen at Moorgreen!"

He smiled as he recalled that the incident did little to damage his reputation among NCB management, before continuing, "You had a lot of managers very sympathetic to the miners. *Very* sympathetic. The problem was that at a very senior level you had various people vying to be the next Chairman. They wanted to be the biggest macho-man in the coalfields, Ken Moses being one of them. He was quickly into the armoured buses, the wire meshes and the rest of it. Many of his managers violently disagreed with his tactics but he was the boss and, ultimately, they did what they were told."

Scots pickets were stunned by what they discovered on arrival in the County. Michael Hogg, then a nineteen year-old striker from Bilston Glen colliery, was "amazed" by Nottinghamshire. Today, Hogg is a Regional Organiser for the Rail, Maritime and Transport union (RMT). Hogg had seven brothers all on strike, along with his father and a brother-in-law, and for a committed class militant from a rock-solid pit village, Nottinghamshire was a culture shock. "I visited Nottingham on at least a dozen occasions during the strike, mainly around Ollerton, and was amazed with what I saw. It was the complete reverse of the situation up in Scotland, at least at the start. I picketed Ollerton, Thoresby, Bevercotes, on numerous occasions, as well as the power stations. Our base was the Ollerton Miners' Welfare, until the working miners took control."

Hogg also enjoyed a dubious honour. "I was the first Scottish miner sacked during the strike. I was arrested on the 17th March 1984 and charged with a breach of the peace for aiming a punch at a working miner. I was found guilty in June 1984, fined £500 and the next day dismissed and sacked by the Coal Board, for 'gross industrial misconduct.' I never ever got my job back, despite the review of the cases, as I was an activist within the NUM."

Two of the Scottish striker's brothers were also dismissed and neither won back their jobs either.

Hogg has fond memories of the strike and Nottinghamshire where he made firm friendships which endure to this day. "Jimmy Lees, brilliant guy, Arthur Jackson, Malcolm 'Puda' and 'Froggy' before he passed away. If I could go back and do it all again, I wouldn't change one single thing. Not a single thing. The best year of my life. Definitely."

Maurice Wake was in the canteen at Linby when he first became aware that there were pickets outside his pit, being harassed by both Linby working miners and the police.

Curiosity piqued, he went out to speak to the pickets who explained their presence in an impassioned manner. Convinced of the rightness of their cause, Wake returned to collect his belongings and didn't go back until the official end of the dispute. This instinctive action ensured his place in Nottinghamshire NUM history and his name inscribed on the Linby 'Loyal To The Last' banner over a year later. Speaking in 1993, as the miners' last stand got under way, he explained, "I could never carry on working while other men needed my support. We stick together and whatever the rights or wrongs, of this issue or that issue or the ballot or anything else, you just don't cross a picket line, especially not one put there by members of your own union. I couldn't carry on working when other men were treated like that. It were that simple to me."

Fellow Linby miner Les Dennis recounts a similar experience. "Me and me mate were on nights at the time and there were a bunch of lads across the gate. We pulled over and they explained what they were doing so that were that, for me: we turned round and went home. You don't cross a picket line! The next night, same again but me mate, who was driving, said, 'Don't worry. I can get around them.' That weren't on to me and I told him so. The third night there weren't anyone there so in we went and that was how it was for the first few days, not crossing the picket when it were on but working when it wasn't, waiting for official word from our own officials as to what we were doing."

The Area leadership was confused and uncertain as to how things should proceed. For Area General Secretary, Henry Richardson, one thing was certain: the strike was just, constitutional and legal. After all, Cortonwood and the Yorkshire Area had played by the book and picketing was a perfectly acceptable and time-honoured trade union tradition. For Richardson, a left-winger of the old school, there were important class issues, too: Thatcher wanted to crush his industry so she might better crush his union. There was no doubt as to the side on which he should be. How, though, to deal tactically with the here and now of Yorkshire pickets flooding the Nottinghamshire coalfield and demanding support and solidarity when his own Area had had, as yet, no ballot nor even any kind of in-depth debate? Also, even at that early stage, Richardson knew that support for action from Nottinghamshire was a very long way from being guaranteed.

Further complicating matters was the stance of the other Area officials. Ray Chadburn, the Area President, and one-time national Presidential challenger to Arthur Scargill, in Henry Richardson's words, "...were seen as a right-winger but at least he were for the strike." On the other hand, right-wingers and future UDM leaders, Roy Lynk, the Area Finance Officer and David Prendergast, Pensions Officer, were against their Area taking part in any dispute which hadn't been voted on by the Area membership. This was an action they firmly believed was a Yorkshire Area dispute and no concern of theirs. These initial divisions between the two factions would widen to a chasm with dramatic consequences for all concerned.

Part 2:
Fields of Fire

Chapter 4:
Mac the Knife

"Laws are silent in times of war"
MARCUS TULLIUS CICERO

Margaret Thatcher couldn't have given a clearer warning of her intentions for Britain's miners when, in March 1983, she appointed Ian MacGregor to head up the NCB. The Scottish-born American industrialist had earned his class-war spurs breaking strikes all over America and Canada in the postwar period. Then, at British Leyland, he imported his American-style macho management. As a non-executive director he was central to the dismissal of Communist Party shop steward Derek 'Red Robbo' Robinson.

Following this with a period at British Steel, where he oversaw a reduction in the workforce from 166,000 to 71,000, Thatcher felt he was just the man to deal with the NUM. She wasn't wrong. Mac the Knife, or 'The American Butcher' as he was dubbed by Scargill, approached his new role with vigour.

Following the Cortonwood announcement, MacGregor confirmed the end of the phoney war, one week later, by officially informing the NUM NEC of the closure of twenty pits with the loss of some 20,000 jobs (significantly, not a single Nottinghamshire pit was on the list). Five of them, Bullcliffe Wood in Yorkshire, Herrington in Durham, Snowdon in Kent and Polmaise in Scotland, along with Cortonwood, were scheduled for "accelerated closure," i.e. within the following few weeks.

Now is the time to explode another of the myths regarding the strike. As Dave Douglass reports in his book, *Ghost Dancers,* MacGregor actually met with Thatcher as early as six months *before* the strike where the two discussed ways of kick-starting the dispute and drawing the NUM into battle.[21]

The overtime ban, introduced the previous autumn, had been effective in running down coal stocks. The Government and NCB were well aware that had that continued over the summer, a short strike in the autumn would have been sufficient to 'put the lights out.' Thus was Thatcher advised. The March closure announcements, then, were made with this specific point in mind: the miners *had* to be drawn into battle and broken before the stocks ran down.

This presented the NUM with a dilemma: refuse to rise to the bait and wait until the autumn to strike, when stocks were low and demand was high, or to act now? The weakness of the first option was in justifying it to the membership. If waiting for the autumn was the preferred option, how to justify passively watching 20,000 miners losing their jobs in March? If not to fight in March, why fight later in the autumn? If not now, why then? The rank and file made the decision for the NEC anyway because once the Yorkshire pits were out, Scotland, Kent and Durham quickly followed, all under Rule 41, which gave regions the authority to strike following NEC approval, which was quickly given.

So, to be clear: neither Scargill nor the NEC blundered by 'calling' the strike in March 1984. The Government had deliberately backed the miners into a corner and the choice was stark: fight now with a chance of winning and saving their industry or surrender and guarantee its destruction.

To labour the point a little further, there was no constitutional or legal requirement for a national ballot anyway because, just as in 1981, there *wasn't*, technically, a national strike at all: Area by Area had voted and decided, in accordance with Rule 41, to come out themselves to oppose MacGregor's and Thatcher's closure programme. The controversial Rule 41 read:

41. — In the event of a dispute arising in any Area or applying to the workers in any Branch likely or possible to lead to a stoppage of work or any other industrial action short of a strike, the questions involved must be immediately reported by the appropriate official of the Area in question to the National Executive Committee which shall deal with the matter forthwith, and in no case shall a cessation of work or other form of industrial action, short of a strike, take place by the workers without the previous sanction of the National Executive Committee, or of a Committee (whether consisting of members of the National Executive Committee or other persons) to whom the National Executive Committee may have delegated the power of giving such sanction, either generally or in a particular case and no funds of the Union shall be applied in strike pay or other trades dispute benefit for the benefit of workers without the previous sanction of the National Executive Committee.

Thus, albeit in a strictly formal sense, the 1984/1985 national strike was actually no such thing; it was a series of *Area*, or *regional*, strikes and, as such, entirely constitutional. Of course, there were sound *tactical* reasons for holding a national ballot at a later stage but, equally, there were passionate arguments against, as the reader will see. One thing is clear, however: there was nothing illegal, undemocratic or unconstitutional regarding the manner in which the resistance unfolded.

The NCB and the Government were taken aback at the bypassing of a national ballot. Given the three previous national ballots, all opposing strike action, there was a strand of thinking that surmised a fourth national ballot would take place, which the NUM leadership would lose, and the closures would then sail through unopposed in the face of a union unwilling to fight.

In any event the NUM membership had voted with their feet. Yorkshire, Scotland, the historically moderate Durham Area and the pugnaciously militant Kent Area had been joined by South Wales, most of the North East and parts of Lancashire. The majority of the UK's 174 pits were soon either at a standstill or suffering a huge drop in production. Even Nottinghamshire, where not a single one of the Area's twenty-seven pits was ever stopped completely by strikers, saw a substantial fall in output in the first few weeks as even many of those opposed to a strike stayed away. This was considered preferable to running the gauntlet of Yorkshire pickets, now supplemented by those from Kent and South Wales.

In the meantime, the pro-strike faction of the Nottinghamshire Area leadership, particularly Henry Richardson, was desperately trying to stem the flood of pickets into the Notts coalfields. Richardson saw mass picketing in Nottinghamshire, at that stage, as counterproductive and likely only to harden attitudes amongst the working miners and the undecided contingent. Many Nottinghamshire miners claimed they were at first pro-strike, only to swing into opposition as a result of intimidation and bullying at the hands of aggressive flying pickets from Yorkshire and elsewhere.

David Amos, from Annesley colliery, who worked throughout the strike, explains, "The general feeling, I'd say, right from the off, from the first night the pickets came, was anti [strike]. Well, the weekend before, the NUM had met and agreed Notts were going to have a ballot and I think it was the fact that the ballot was going to be later that week with the announcement of the result the week after that. The main thing I picked up was, you know, 'We're not having people coming down here. We'll make us own minds up what we're doing. We've got our own minds: we know what the situation is.' And so right from the off, generally, among a lot of miners, there was a lot of animosity that pickets had come down."

There is every reason to suppose such claims were little more than a justification for a course of action many had already decided to pursue anyway. Richardson, though, was keen to avoid handing excuses to the working miners and to head off the collapse of the strike in Nottinghamshire before it had started.

Typically, there were meetings and debates held all over the coalfield in the County just as there had been elsewhere. Keith Stanley, at that time a coalface charge-man and rank-and-file union member at Newstead (later to rise to the NUM Vice Presidency), recalls the heated scenes at his local Miners' Welfare on the first Saturday night after the closure announcements.

"We had a Branch meeting on the Saturday night and this was really my first recollection of [Roy] Lynk not doing his job properly. I'd only ever seen him on pit visits and things like that in the past, as he was the Agent for Newstead. But Brian Walker [pro-strike Branch Secretary] stood up that Saturday night, in the Welfare, and you could hear a pin drop while he was talking. It was a good meeting, in terms of numbers: there were probably two hundred men there, probably more. It were packed in the Concert Room. Anyway, Brian stood up and, I thought, spoke very, very well about what had happened to Cortonwood, what would be facing other pits and that we weren't safe in Nottingham, even though it were a productive coalfield."

Stanley was shocked and disappointed at his Branch Secretary's reception. "Then there were people having a go at him. After he'd done they started shouting questions at him and one or two were pretty abusive and more and more people were standing up, shouting, 'Why should we strike? Our pit's not under threat!' There were all kinds of arguments coming from the floor and Lynk just sat there and never said a word and I thought, 'Well, he's Area Agent, Area Official: he *must* understand what's happening to the industry.' So I expected him getting up and speaking, in line with National's position. You know: of supporting people in struggle. But he didn't. I think he'd listened to the people in the hall and realised that the majority were opposed to being out on strike and he spoke only to that section."

Worse was still to come. "I was really, really disappointed. Especially as one of the questions had been: 'Well, it's trade union law that you don't cross picket lines. We've got a picket line on and what are you saying? As a union official are you telling people that they should cross picket lines?' And Lynk says, 'I'm not saying anything of the sort: I'm saying *why* is there a picket line on?' That was the way he answered: he wouldn't come right out and say it [that men should cross picket lines] but that was the way men were being led to think. Well, we were in turmoil after that meeting: people having a peck at each other, the pro- and anti-strike people all having a right go at one another."

Similar scenes were enacted all over the County with the situation at Clipstone's Branch meeting even more volatile. There, the anti-strike contingent jeered and threatened the pro-strike minority, firmly of the view that as their pit was safe from closure so the attitude to Yorkshire should be 'sod 'em: leave 'em to it. Nowt to do with us.'

Brian Walker recalls the difficulty faced by strikers in the first few weeks. "The problems during the strike were enormous for us here. For one thing we didn't have anywhere to be organised. We couldn't use Berry Hill [the official Nottinghamshire NUM offices] so we had to have something independent. North Notts had got Ollerton, they'd got facilities there, but we didn't in South Notts."

The strike centre at Ollerton soon became a slick and well-run affair. As well as organising and catering meals and clothes for children, the premises soon became offices to a host of sympathetic lawyers and benefits experts. One Danny Phillips, a southern-based solicitor, soon became a familiar sight around the coalfield, matching biker boots with his solicitor's trade-mark pin-striped suit as he whipped around the coalfield on his motorbike. Whatever Nottinghamshire had, it was to the young brief's liking, as he stayed on after the strike and started his own practice in the county.

Walker continues, "So I approached Ian Juniper, who should be sainted, by the way. Ian was the Chair of Notts Trades Council and I approached him and asked, could he find us somewhere to operate from? By various means we ended up at the AEUW building, their area offices in Nottingham, and that became synonymous with our resistance.

"At that time the Kent Area were on their way to Notts. They were coming to join us and strengthen our position in Notts but they were turned back at the Dartford tunnel. The next day I get a call from Jack Collins asking what else he could do to help us. Well, we'd got no money coming in from Area so I told him that without some we were sunk." The Kent leader duly dispatched his *aide-de-camp,* Joe Holmes, with £8000 for the Nottinghamshire cause; £4000 for the North Notts Strike Centre and £4000 for Walker's newly-established South Notts Strike Centre.

The emissary from Kent earned the ire of Mrs. Walker when he eventually arrived. Tempted by the exciting array of bever-ages on offer at the Oxclose Hotel, Holmes decided to refresh himself following the long train journey from Kent. Hours after his agreed arrival time he finally fetched up at the Walker resi-dence, introducing himself to Walker's wife with the cheery greeting, "Hello, I'm Joe, from Kent." Mrs. Walker responded acidly, "Joe from the pub, more like."

The funds delivered by Holmes were immediately put to good use and soon the South Notts Strike Centre was busy turning Kent's £4000 into a considerably larger amount. With a degree of entrepreneurial flair that would surely have gladdened Margaret Thatcher's free-market heart, Walker was soon

68

turning a roaring trade in badges, ties and assorted memorabilia.

Things moved quickly over the rest of March and into April, with Nottinghamshire very much at the forefront of events, nationally. On March 14th, following a meeting at the offices of the North Nottinghamshire Mining Board, NCB officials gathered, as they would do daily throughout the strike, to discuss strategy. These early discussions resulted in MacGregor obtaining a High Court injunction to prevent Yorkshire pickets from visiting pits outside their own area. This was merely the opening salvo in a legal war against the NUM that would increase steadily until the Union was bogged down in a morass of writs, injunctions and claims. Of even greater significance, perhaps, was the hard truth that injunctions always need someone to enforce them: a key step in the formation of a *de facto* national police force and the lock-down of Nottinghamshire into what was effectively a police state had just been taken.

Both MacGregor and Thatcher realised that the key to the dispute was Nottinghamshire. If the Board's most profitable and productive coalfield could be kept working, then victory would be that much easier to secure. To that end, under the auspices of its Chief Constable, Charles McLachlan, Nottinghamshire became a county under siege with its striking miners effectively resistance fighters behind enemy lines. Apart from the enormous numbers of police officers at Nottinghamshire's pits, intent on thwarting pickets and ensuring passage into work for the strike-breakers, the force controversially sealed off the region, preventing anyone entering or leaving without having first been subjected to heavy and intrusive questioning. Road blocks were mounted at key junctions around the county and entrances and exits to and from the M1, with pickets' movements subject to the whim of the officers on the ground. Cars, coaches and other vehicles were denied access and ordered to turn around and go home. The measures provoked outrage from civil liberties groups, other trade unions and even those not naturally sympathetic to the strikers' cause.

Of even greater controversy, possibly, were the actions of the police away from the picket lines. 'Civilians' were stopped too and, like the miners, harangued with all manner of questions regarding not just their current movements and intentions, but also concerning their views and opinions: for whom did you vote? Are you a communist? Do you support Arthur Scargill or Mrs Thatcher? Many residents were denied access to their own villages and streets. Children were plied with sweets and winning smiles as officers sought to glean even the most innocuous tit-bits of intelligence: is your dad a striker? What's his name? What pit is he at? Where do you live?

John Lowe, a striker from Clipstone colliery, painted a vivid picture. "We had seen an invasion of our village by the police on an unbelievable scale. From dawn to dusk, two-man foot patrols were everywhere while Transit vans full of uniformed officers cruised throughout the day. The extensive use of roadblocks throughout Nottinghamshire not only saw them encircle the county to keep out the Yorkshire and Derbyshire strikers, but also restrict our movements within it — between pit and pit, and pit and home. We were sewn up tight!"[22]

Anyone then present in Nottinghamshire could have been forgiven for mistaking the coalfield for parts of Northern Ireland under the control of the RUC and the British Army. Indeed, to great controversy, the police were to deploy many of the counter-insurgency techniques developed in Northern Ireland in their efforts to break the strike on behalf of the Government. For many miners, whose fathers and grandfathers had fought in the International Brigade and in the armed forces during the Second World War, such scenes were incomprehensible. Comparisons with Nazi Germany were drawn and inevitable accusations of political bias were levelled at McLachlan's Nottinghamshire force. At this stage the soon-to-be universally despised 'Met' had barely made an appearance, and if the miners thought this was bad they hadn't seen anything yet.

All this was simply part of Margaret Thatcher's plan. Or, to be strictly accurate, part of Nicholas Ridley's plan: for it was he had who authored the infamous 'Ridley Plan' — a secret blue-print drawn up in the aftermath of the 1974 strike and later leaked to *The Economist*. It sought to ensure that never again would a Conservative government be hijacked by a trade union, specifically the NUM. Among its recommendations were:

— *Coal stocks to be increased and hoarded at power stations.*

— *The installation of dual coal- and oil-firing generators.*

— *The importation of coal from non-unionised foreign ports.*

— *The recruitment of non-trade union lorry drivers.*

— *The withdrawal of social security benefits to strikers.*

— *The training, equipping and funding of a large mobile force of police officers to deploy riot and public disorder tactics with the express intention of neutering the hitherto highly effective operations of pickets.*

All these and more would be carried out with clinical precision, not just in Nottingham, but nationwide as the Government, soon to abandon even the pretence of impartiality, determinedly set about crushing the NUM.

The NUM's NEC meeting of 8th March declared the strikes in Scotland and Yorkshire official and voted on holding a national ballot. Twenty-one of the NEC's members voted against with three in favour: Trevor Bell of the Colliery Officials and Staff Association (COSA), Roy Ottey, the Power Group Secretary, and North Wales Secretary, Ted MacKay. The Nottinghamshire Area Executive Committee then met on Saturday 10th March. Events were moving rapidly and it was agreed that an Area ballot should take place as quickly as possible. March 15th and 16th were the agreed dates. Later that same morning the various Branch Committees met and endorsed the decisions taken by the Executive Committee. Henry Richardson and Ray Chadburn had pleaded with the NEC to keep Yorkshire pickets out of the Nottinghamshire coalfield in the days leading up to the ballot: purely a tactical stance, mainly on the part of Richardson who was struggling to hold together his fast-polarising membership. These events took second place, for a while, as the emerging civil war claimed its first casualty.

David Jones was a twenty-four-year-old miner from Ackton Hall colliery, near Wakefield. Although a NUM loyalist and striker, Thursday 15th March 1984 was the first time the young miner had been picketing. On that morning, he and his brother, Trefor, also a striking miner, had gathered with other pickets at Frickley colliery. Their planned destination was Gedling pit in Nottingham. Travelling on separate coaches, the brothers were stopped by police near Clumber Park and denied further access. Hastily revising their plans, Jones and his companions decided to abandon Gedling and walk to Ollerton colliery while Trefor's coach found an alternative route into

Gedling. On such small decisions do matters of life and death hang: had David not changed his mind at the last minute, he would probably have lived through the events of that evening, something that was to haunt his parents and induce lasting bitterness. The decision of the police to illegally stop Jones's coach and refuse it further access to the Nottinghamshire coalfield only added to the storm of controversy regarding the policing of the dispute in Nottinghamshire.

The official version of events at Ollerton colliery is contested, to one degree or another, by those who were present. Although none who were there, or were subsequently caught up in its aftermath, are likely to forget the events, the precise cause of Jones's death remains a matter of dispute. Henry Richardson is one of those unlikely to forget that evening.

"I got a phone call about one o'clock in the morning from Jimmy Hood [then Ollerton NUM Branch Secretary, now Labour MP for Lanark and Hamilton East]. He said, 'Henry, we've got problems. We've had a picket killed. I need you out here now.' I couldn't drive at that time so I had to get a taxi and off I went. We met at Jimmy's house and the Ollerton Branch Committee were there. It was terrible. I said to Jimmy, 'Look, whatever happens, we can't sit here. We need to get to the pit and see what's going off.'"

Richardson recalls, "There's a pub near the pit and the road running down to the pit and as we approached, we could see a couple of bonfires burning and all these faces in this eerie light, lit up by floodlights. There were *thousands* and the Bobbies were just stood there, not doing anything. The atmosphere was *terrible*. There were people picking up tables and chairs from the pub and throwing them onto the fires to keep them going. There were people there, and these were some of them, who had absolutely nothing to do with this industry at all: that were just one of the problems. At this stage, we didn't know how the lad had been killed or what the hell had happened."

It appears that following Jones's death, at the time attributed to a rock thrown by a person unknown, the Ollerton Committee officials pleaded with working miners not to go into work as it was felt such a course would only serve to inflame an already volatile situation. As indeed it did. Richardson recounts an enraged mob of thousands bellowing 'Kill! Kill! Kill!' and says the crowd were set on burning the pit to the ground. It was

72

at this point that some miners feel the strike in Nottingham was already lost. As Dave Douglass, then the Hatfield Delegate and a key organiser of Yorkshire pickets, remarks, "If you're prepared to step over the body of a dead miner, not yet cold, for the sake of a few quid, you have to think no amount of bloody ballots will bring people like that out on strike."

The manager in charge of the shift ordered the strike-breakers to stop work and return to the surface, lest a riot ensue.

Richardson and Hood made the decision to inform Arthur Scargill and returned to Hood's house to make the call. The NUM President, accompanied by other members of the NEC, eventually arrived and, according to Richardson, immediately grasped the potential of the situation to spiral out of control. Hoisted onto the shoulders of loyalists, Scargill was deposited onto the roof of a car whereupon he produced a loud hailer — "God knows where he got that from," chuckles Richardson — and called for calm. Richardson is admiring of his President's handling of the situation. "He had everyone calmed down straight away. They were hooked."

At Scargill's instigation, a respectful two-minute silence was requested and observed with the demand that all police present remove their helmets: an instruction with which the police sensitively (and sensibly) complied. Following this Scargill spent a few minutes lowering temperatures and cooling passions, whereupon he insisted the strikers move on as nothing of any good could be accomplished at that time. To Richardson's relief, the previously murderous crowd then quietly and peacefully melted away. "He was bloody brilliant. God only knows what would have happened if he hadn't been there. The lads would've got into the pit and probably killed the scabs."

For the Jones family, the events of that evening were to bring unimaginable pain. Later, in November, a taxi driver attempting to carry Welsh miner David Williams across the picket line would be killed. A concrete block was dropped onto his cab killing him instantly while Williams escaped relatively unscathed. The Jones family were to remark bitterly at the contrast between the reaction to that death and that of their son. An almost lynch-mob mentality, a mass hysteria, gripped the media and the politicians alike as the most blood-curdling calls for retribution were aired. This stood in stark contrast to the muted reactions to Jones's death. The respective investigations and outcomes couldn't have been more different. While the two Welsh miners responsible for the death of Wilkie were handed down life sentences for murder,[23] no one was even questioned as a potential suspect over Jones's death. No one was ever charged and the Jones family have never received a satisfactory explanation for the death of their son.

Scargill did his best to offer some comfort to the family and an oft-repeated tale sprang from his visits. On one occasion, crouching to offer condolences to Mrs Jones, the family later joked that she had accomplished something Thatcher never could: She had put Arthur Scargill on his knees.

Afterwards, the family's attitude to the strike only hardened, with Jones's father joining the Workers' Revolutionary Party. In one sense, this was unsurprising. After all, as the Jones' family saw things, having a son die in defence of his job, his industry and his class, was never going to lead to a softening of their position and a willingness to see the class enemy's point of view.

The Nottinghamshire Area then called an Emergency Executive meeting and, in view of the volatile feelings running through the County, as a mark of respect for the Jones family, agreed the entire Area membership would be called out until the ballot result came in (Bentinck pit, under the Presidency of Neil Greatrex, defied the instruction and worked as normal). An official statement to that effect was issued:

> The National Coal Board's announcement on March 6th of their intention to close over 20 pits with subsequent losses of jobs in excess of 20,000 caused deep resentment throughout the British coalfield. In the past year, we have witnessed the loss of 21,000 jobs and closure of 23 pits, in this latest round of savage butchery against one of Britain's major basic industries.
>
> The National Union of Mineworkers following the fullest consultation with its membership decided in October 1983 to impose a national overtime ban from November 1st 1983. This action has proved extremely effective resulting in the loss of approximately 10 million tonnes of coal production, with a cost to the National Coal Board of over £300 million. Coal stocks have decreased on the CEGB [Central Electricity Generating Board] from 35 million tonnes to 22 million tonnes and currently stand at 22 million tonnes inside the industry instead of the 33 million tonnes that would have existed but for the ban.
>
> The National Executive Committee on the 8th March agreed

that Areas should be allowed to extend this action allowed Areas
to take strike action in accordance with National Rule 41.
Already, 80% of the British coalfield is at a standstill and we
have seen widespread picketing throughout the past three days.
Two events have occurred in the past 24 hours which have exac-
erbated an already inflamed situation.

The National Coal Board have obtained a High Court injunc-
tion in the name of Nottinghamshire Area NCB Directors, which
restrains the NUM Yorkshire Area from picketing other than at
their own individual unit. The use of Tory government anti-
Trade Union legislation is against the NUM and TUC policy
and as a consequence, brings the Coal Board into direct conflict
with the Union as a whole. The Notts NUM had already issued
advice that members should not cross picket lines where they
existed and the Board's use of Tory legislation seeks to divide the
NUM in its application of National and Area action.

The tragic death of a picket in the early hours of this morning
has brought home to everyone how important it is that the
miners have total unity at this time. In view of these events and
because of the Board's decision to utilise Tory legislation against
a constituent part of our Union, the Notts Area NUM instructs
all its membership not to cross picket lines at any pit or unit in
the county. It is noted that a picket line now exists at every pit in
the Nottinghamshire Area and the Union feels certain that all
our members will respect this basic trade union principle.

The NUM Notts Area, Yorkshire Area and National Officials
re-affirm that the individual ballot vote scheduled to take place
in Nottinghamshire from 6.00pm tonight to 6.00pm Friday will
proceed as planned and members at all the pits that are in
dispute can attend for the purpose of casting their votes.

Speculation as to how much influence Jones's death may have
had on how the Nottingham miners voted can only ever be just
that. For the strikers, it certainly stiffened their resolve. After
all, if surrender came now then their comrade's death would
become an even greater tragedy and terrible waste. For the
strike-breakers, some felt Jones's death was the responsibility
of the Yorkshire pickets and even of Jones himself. "If those
yobs had stayed in Pudding Land and minded their own business, it wouldn't have ever happened," asserts one Nottingham
strike-breaker who worked at Bevercotes. Unsurprisingly, he
wishes to remain anonymous. It would be a rash man who
would have made such a callous statement in the days following the young miner's death.

Keith Stanley had hoped that the events at Ollerton would
finally ram home to the Nottinghamshire miners just what was at

stake. He had hoped that they would close ranks against the NCB and Government following the death of one of their own. The laboured, although carefully-worded, statement from the Area officials was intended to do just that. They and Stanley couldn't have been more wrong and, once the results were in, Stanley recalls that, "I don't think I've ever felt so low in my life."

The question on the ballot paper was stark and left no one in any doubt as to what, precisely, was at stake: "Do you support strike action to prevent pit closures and a massive rundown of jobs?"

A total of 27,551 miners voted and of those, 20,188 voted to defy their National Executive Committee, their colleagues elsewhere in the country and continue working. That left just 7,285 who had voted to strike. In percentage terms, 73.5 percent of Nottinghamshire miners voted to work (this compared with the Area, as a whole, voting against strike action by fifty-four percent ten years earlier, in the 1974 strike. Although then, of course, the Area did strike as, nationally, the vote was overwhelmingly in favour of action).

Blidworth had the biggest percentage of those voting for strike action, with forty-six percent, but not a single NUM Branch anywhere in Nottinghamshire achieved even fifty percent. The lowest pro-strike vote came from Bestwood Industrial, with only four percent in favour.

It got worse for the loyalists as an even higher number returned to work, with around 5,000 of those who had voted for the strike either immediately siding with the strike-breaking majority or drifting back over time. Whatever the intentions of the working miners, they had sided with Thatcher and MacGregor. The Government and NCB campaign against the NUM had been gifted victory in the first battle of the war.

On Sunday March 18th the Nottinghamshire Area held a special conference. With the working miners now in the driving seat, Richardson, Chadburn and the minority pro-strike Branch officials were routed. It was decided that an immediate return to work would be ordered. Other agreed actions were to instruct the NEC to ban pickets from Nottinghamshire and to reconvene with the intention of sanctioning a national ballot of the entire NUM membership. The County had set itself against the prevailing mood and the coalfield plunged into civil war.

Branch	Yes	% for	No	% against	Spoiled papers	Blank papers	Total votes
1. Annesley	161	20	642	80	0	0	803
2. Babbington	159	23	562	77	6	0	727
3. Bentinck	229	16	1,065	82	6	0	1,300
4. Bestwood Industrial	11	4	255	96	0	0	266
5. Bestwood Workshops	56	16	310	84	1	0	367
6. Bevercotes	384	34	751	66	2	0	1,137
7. Bilsthorpe	238	25	760	75	8	0	1,006
8. Blidworth	399	46	461	54	2	0	862
9. Bolsover*	341	43	479	58	1	0	821
10. Calverton	233	21	1,088	79	2	0	1,373
11. Clipstone	344	28	907	72	0	1	1,252
12. Cotgrave	401	29	1,017	71	1	0	1,419
13. Creswell	395	45	488	55	2	0	885
14. Gedling	261	21	1,001	79	2	0	1,264
15. Harworth	312	30	753	70	0	0	1,065
16. Hucknall	208	23	711	77	4	0	923
17. Linby	276	34	562	66	2	1	841
18. Mansfield	221	19	987	81	3	0	1,211
19. Moorgreen	123	20	511	80	0	0	634
20. Moorgreen Workshops	83	19	364	81	0	0	447
21. Newstead	223	29	551	71	0	0	774
22. Ollerton	335	34	681	66	3	0	1,019
23. Pye Hill No.1	121	19	525	81	0	0	646
24. Pye Hill No.2	18	14	123	86	1	0	142
25. Rufford	409	34	760	64	0	1	1,170
26. Sherwood	330	40	494	60	2	0	826
27. Silverhill	248	24	788	76	1	0	1,037
28. S. Normanton Tran.	21	11	333	89	1	1	372
29. Sutton	107	20	455	80	2	0	564
30. Thoresby	314	24	1,003	76	3	0	1,320
31. Welbeck	324	29	801	71	2	1	1,128
Total	7,205	20.5	20,188	73.5	57	5	27,551

*Bolsover, although geographically, and as far as the NCB was concerned, situated in Derbyshire, was a Branch of the Nottinghamshire Area NUM, dating back to the NMA's battles against the Spencer Union.

77

For the strikers, the situation was beyond belief. Over eighty percent of their union nationally were out on strike, that majority uniting against the impending demise of their industry and with it every miner's job. Yet in their own backyard the strike-breakers thought they could carry on regardless? As if Nottinghamshire could somehow be an oasis of tranquillity for industrious working miners?

On the other side of the divide, the working miners were insistent that if the actions thus far had been Area actions, then they were under no obligation to join in. They'd had their ballot in Nottinghamshire and the decision was to work: all very democratic, above board and, they insisted, in stark contrast to the anti-democratic manoeuvrings and procedural sleights-of-hand of the leadership. The NEC couldn't have it both ways.

The Nottinghamshire loyalists scorned such thinking: their very jobs and livelihoods were under assault from the most hated Prime Minister in history. Here was the miners' natural class enemy, a Conservative Government, out to neuter the NUM and effective trade unionism, and if the Tories had to wreck the entire industry to get to the NUM, well, it was clearly a price they were more than willing to pay. Apart from anything else, the Nottinghamshire strikers asked, what about loyalty? What about solidarity? What about the ultimate working class commandment: thou shalt not cross a picket line? How could men turn their backs on their own comrades who were fighting for their jobs? How could anyone leave their mates to sink while coining it in themselves? In short: how could any man bear the shame of being a scab?

Eric Eaton, former Nottinghamshire Area President and today the Chair of Nottingham NUM Ex- and Retired Miners' Association, worked at Newstead. Eaton is dismissive of any noble motives on the part of the working miners. "As far back as the overtime ban, the year before the strike started, there were men saying *then* that they'd be crossing picket lines if we went on strike whereas I'm arguing that the first law of trade unionism is that you don't cross a picket line. So the seeds were starting to be set even *before* we went on strike."

Certainly, the feeling among the striking miners was that money was the only consideration for the majority: that and their conviction that Nottinghamshire's pits were safe from closure. "It were simply a case of 'I'm all right, Jack. Sod you.',"

78

says Eaton. "I had a mate who was out for about six months and then he went back. He said to me, 'Come back to work, youth! It's like a black river down here! They'll *never* shut this pit!' Well, they did, didn't they?" Indeed. Newstead colliery was closed just two years after the end of the strike, in 1987.

Keith Stanley's disgust is still palpable, nearly thirty years later. "In 1980, when they announced they [NCB] were shutting Teversal pit, the lads there went on strike and got permission from the NEC, all above aboard, and the Notts Area balloted on strike action. Not one single pit voted to strike! Not one. Apart from Teversal itself. If they weren't even going to strike to save one of their own pits, in their own back yard, what chance was there of them striking to save someone else's?"

A rank-and-file meeting was held at the Area Headquarters on 31st March, where attendees were given the report from the Area's NEC members, Richardson and Chadburn. Those present were overwhelmingly anti-strike and Richardson, despite his decidedly minority status, remained defiant in his support for strike action. He warned that Nottinghamshire would not be exempt from the closure programme. The assembly then descended into acrimonious bickering with the pro-strike minority shouted down by the strike-breaking majority. Keith Stanley, in his own account of the dispute, recalls feeling isolated and alone. "... we, as striking miners in Nottinghamshire, were in absolute no-man's land."

Nationally, much else was happening that month. Kent pickets, who had previously been stopped at the Dartford Tunnel on their way to Nottinghamshire, lost their legal action against the police blockade. NACODS, the pit deputies' union responsible for safety in the pits, voted to accept their recent pay offer and an assortment of right-wing NUM officials, led by Power Group leader, Ray Ottey, issued a press release demanding a national ballot, the immediate cessation of flying pickets and a return to work (an NCB official had contacted Chadburn on behalf of the organisers, assuming he'd be a willing participant, and invited him to the meeting to be held in Leicester. The Nottinghamshire President was in court that day on business concerning NUM pensions. He declined the invitation, suggesting Roy Lynk would be a more fitting attendee). Eric Hammond, right-wing leader of the EETPU, advised his members to defy the miners and cross NUM picket lines. At the tail end of the month, however, in the strikers' favour, were the instructions from the transport, maritime and rail unions to their members not to handle or move coal or coke stocks.

Henry Richardson certainly had a month to remember, with his friends and comrades in other Areas unaware of the fine detail of the Nottinghamshire situation only adding to the pressure. Fiery Jack Collins, the Kent leader, dashed off a furious letter to Richardson castigating him for Nottinghamshire's treachery.

NATIONAL UNION OF MINEWORKERS

Miners Offices: Waterside House . Cherry Tree Avenue . Dover CT16 2NJ

Telephone 0304 206661
206271

MALCOLM PITT, President
JACK COLLINS, Secretary

JC/SAS

24th March, 1984.

Mr. H. Richardson,
N.U.M. (Notts) Area,
Miners' Offices,
Berry Hill Lane,
Mansfield, NOTTS.

Dear Mr. Richardson,

I am writing to let you know that I have, with a heavy heart, been compelled to cancel my acceptance to attend the 1984 Nottingham Miners Gala.

Since I am employed by the finest people in the world, the miners, they have the right to place a cross on a piece of paper and thereby determine my future but no one, no fellow miner has the moral right to place a cross on paper and in doing so take it upon themselves to sack another miner employed, not by them, but by the Coal Board. That which cannot be justified morally cannot be justified at all, so please, don't make a fool of yourself trying to do so.

You, by advocating a ballot, are assuming that your members have some kind of authority over the future of my two sons and their families together with the future of others in this coalfield. Such an assumption is dangerous claptrap and a betrayal of other workers who are demanding the right to work, it is also, needless to say, an attitude in support of the bosses. Voting another's job away has nothing to do with democracy but is the ethics of the rat cage.

Further, to believe that breaking a picket line that is cordoned off by the police, should be a free choice of brother miners has your approval really amazes me, thousand of non-miners are heeding our call for survival whilst you line up against us. I hope when you next look at a Kent miner you will be able to hold your head up.

You can sleep well in the knowledge that my grandchildren could grow up in an unemployed household, at least their father had the guts to fight the bosses.

Remember the quote "First they came for the communists.........
then they came for the Jews ...."

Yours sincerely,

JACK COLLINS
Secretary.

80

"It really hurt me, at the time," says Richardson. "Me and Jack were great friends and to receive that, at that time, with all that was going off, cut me to the quick. It really did. We made it up, though, and Jack apologised. He couldn't have been sorrier; he just wasn't aware of the full facts, at the time. He knew we were on the same side and we put it behind us."

April saw significant events which would impact on both strikers and strike-breakers alike, both in Nottingham and nationally. The first of these was the meeting of the National Executive Committee in Sheffield on 12th April. The question of a national ballot was the central issue. The Right demanded a ballot, convinced that without one the strike was lost. Henry Richardson and Ray Chadburn supported the Right in their call, albeit for entirely different reasons. With a divided membership and a lost Area ballot behind them, Richardson and Chadburn saw a national ballot as the only mechanism by which pressure could be brought to bear on the Nottingham strike-breakers. (In any case, they were constitutionally mandated to press for a national ballot by their predominantly anti-strike membership.) For some, the subtlety of the Notts leaders' position was missed, with both Richardson and Chadburn jostled and jeered by inflamed Yorkshire men. Richardson remained unmoved. "The longer we go on, the bigger the split. Our men who are striking are getting nothing. The majority of Notts miners are saying, 'We shall not move without a ballot.' We are destroying trade unionism in Nottinghamshire."

Scargill, as President, chaired the meeting and was unable to speak either for or against any of the motions and propositions; an inconvenient truth for his and the miners' detractors. Ruling only on procedural matters, he ruled a motion for a national ballot out of order as the same motion had already been defeated at the previous NEC meeting of 8th March. Instead, a full discussion and vote on this, and related matters, would take place at a Special Delegates' Conference which was called for the following week, 19th April.

The day of the Conference saw a mass rally and lobby of pro-strike miners many of whom, ironically, were convinced the whole affair was merely a ruse of the NEC's to get themselves off the hook and sell-out the members already on strike. Amidst noisy scenes, a replay of those that had taken place at the Yorkshire Area Council meeting of March 12th, some 4000 rank-and-file miners gathered outside Sheffield's City Hall bellowing 'Stick your ballot up your arse' while inside the Conference convened to consider the question.

It wasn't the only matter. First, a proposed rule change to lower the majority needed for strike action was considered: from its existing fifty-five percent to a simple majority. The Left argued that such a proposal, as it stood under current rules, would need to beat 18,000 votes against simply to arrive at square one. The Right, on the other hand, not least Roy Lynk, argued quite the other: that a majority of one was insufficient to make such matters of import as a national strike official and credible. The Right lost with fifty-nine votes to the Left's 187, with two abstentions.

On the question of a national ballot, an exhaustive and wide-ranging debate took place regarding some half-a-dozen different motions upon which the delegates would vote. At the end of the process, the *delegates,* not Scargill, not the NEC, mandated as they were by their respective Area memberships, voted *not* to have a national ballot. Against all the prevailing mythology that has endured since the beginning of the strike, the facts speak for themselves; the *members themselves* over-whelmingly and democratically voted *not* to hold a national ballot.[24]

The reasons were many: why should those in 'safe' Areas be given the option of voting men in threatened areas out of their jobs? There already *was* a strike and over eighty percent of the membership supported it by, well, *being* on strike: who needed another ballot? The miners were under a concerted attack by the Government and the NCB with all the resources of the state at their disposal and, in Mick McGahey's famous words, the NUM were not going to allow anyone to "...constitutionalise us out of our jobs."

In addition to all that, loyalists asked, what about the ballot for the Area Incentive Scheme which had been flouted by Nottinghamshire? Why was it OK to ignore that ballot but insist on one in this instance?

Where this left the Areas like Nottinghamshire, which had previously voted against strike action at a local level, was tech-nically complex but morally simple: Nottinghamshire's working miners were breaking no rules. There was no national strike and an Area ballot had rejected a call to join the domino-action.

On the other hand, the Special Delegates' Conference had rejected a national ballot so Nottingham, under Rule 30, had to accept that decision. In a conflict between an Area rule and a National rule, the National rule took precedence. Much to the strike-breakers' chagrin, the Nottinghamshire Area Rule Book even contained in Rule 30 an explicit acceptance of subordination to the National Rule Book:

> *30. — In all matters in which the rules of this Union [Nottinghamshire Area NUM] and those of the National Union conflict, the rules of the National Union shall apply and in all cases of doubt or dispute the matter shall be decided by the National Executive Committee of the National Union.*

The working miners' position was, well, that's fine then. We've had our own ballot and we're not striking in our Area and that doesn't conflict with a national rule because there is no national strike.

When instructed not to cross picket lines by their elected Area Officials, their position was that the Area had voted to work and that pickets had no business being anywhere in the Nottinghamshire coalfield anyway.

The loyalists countered that Nottinghamshire was bound by Rule 30 *not* to cross picket lines because the instruction had come not just from their own Area Officials (or at least fifty percent of them) but from the NEC as well (later, Nottinghamshire, prior to the majority breaking away to form the UDM, avoided this thorny question by simply ditching any Area *and* National Rules it didn't care for, with Rule 30 among the first to go).

As far as the strikers were concerned, all such debates were irrelevant and the fact that they were being held at all, under the circumstances, was incomprehensible. *How* the strike had started was only ever a purely tactical consideration; the *real* issue was to stop pit closures, save jobs and to stop the Conservative Government dead in its tracks as it attempted to destroy the NUM, the mining industry and trade unionism throughout the UK. In any event, Conference had spoken and as Arthur Scargill emerged onto the balcony of City Hall to announce the news, the miners outside cheered and celebrated and sang, 'Here we go, here we go, here we go.'

The strike was now official. There would be no turning back.

Chapter 5:
Two Tribes

"How easy it is, treachery.
You just slide into it"
MARGARET ATWOOD

In March 1984 David Amos was twenty-seven. He had been at Annesley colliery for ten years. The year before that, he'd been elected to his NUM Branch's committee.

Although he voted to strike in the Nottinghamshire Area ballot, Amos decided to support the majority in his Area and return to work once the ballot result was in. He describes himself as a moderate and in a very conscious sense: he deliberately aligned himself with a strand of trade unionism that he still feels is as valid in the NUM as the militancy of the majority.

"I think it would be fair to say that my views on the subject come from direct experience of being a NUM Committee member at the time and not a rank-and-file NUM member. Also you will find people like myself are not, and never have been, extreme critics of strikes in general, or anti-NUM. One of the main issues in 1984/85 was about how the strike was conducted."

This view was widespread among Nottinghamshire strike-breakers. Somehow the intricacies and mechanics of ballots and internal NUM procedures were elevated to a principle that overshadowed the question of the pit closure programme itself. Amos disagrees but then goes on to prove the point.

"No, it was about the order you do things in: the procedure. That's what the argument was about. You had picket lines but the problem with that was when is a picket line official or not official? You see, it's well known that in Yorkshire, particularly South Yorkshire, Doncaster particularly, a very militant area, they've used that for secondary support for a long time. They used it in 1969 and 1970, which were classified as unofficial strikes. In Nottinghamshire, that was never the case. Your moderate areas were always sticklers for what they considered the proper procedure."

For the striking miners, this was widely seen as a fig-leaf behind which scabs hid and justified shameless 'money-grabbing' while their comrades faced the dole queue. Amos sees things very differently.

"Moderate trade unionism is as *bona-fide* as militant trade unionism. With the NUM being a loose federation of area and craft organisations, the issue was very much about managing diversity. How people determine what a mandate actually consists of is always very interesting."

Indeed. What *does* constitute a democratic mandate? For the establishment it is only and always a secret ballot that counts (unless, of course, one happens to be Joe Gormley seeking to subvert the wishes of your left-wing majority). Mass meetings, open and exhaustive debate, on the other hand, are only ever opportunities for 'bully-boys' and 'thugs' to intimidate the 'moderate' and 'reasonable' majority — a view to which Amos himself subscribes.

Although it has now been thirty years since the strike, with countless volumes dedicated to its study, no one has yet satisfactorily explained how a couple of thousand Nottinghamshire strikers managed to intimidate over 20,000 working miners: over 20,000 working miners who were backed by the combined might of the Government and State...

Regarding Nottinghamshire's reaction to the Yorkshire pickets, in one sense it seems quite extraordinary. Picketing is almost as old and established a custom as trade unionism itself. Virtually every trade dispute of any substance features a picket line and yet Nottinghamshire reacted badly. Amos, again, disagrees.

"Well, it is in some areas and in some it isn't. In Nottingham, of course, it didn't; it clashed with the culture where, basically, whatever the issue is, we have a meeting and then once the debate's took place, if it's a hot potato, it went for a ballot: wage-rises, elections of officials and so on. And why that happened, in this instance, was that it allowed every man, *every man,* to have a vote. And bear in mind a lot were travelling in from former mining communities, in from outside the area but, over twenty-four hours, it gave them that option to have a say on that issue, whereas a Branch meeting on a Saturday night don't. Even though you might argue, technically, everybody can get to that, they can't always."

The two things aren't mutually exclusive. A picket line is a medium whereby workers in dispute can put their views to their fellow-workers and appeal for support. One might even argue that picketing is an essential component of the demo-cratic process as any subsequent meetings are at least informed by having heard the striking workers' case first hand, not solely the media's distorted interpretation of that case.

Despite the hostile feelings provoked by Yorkshire pickets, Amos says, "...at the time, ironically, them first few weeks, I was *pro*-strike and *voted* to strike." What changed his mind? "...It was explained to me, because they'd had the ballot vote, 'Look, this is how things work in the NUM: it works from the bottom up.' We had the meeting and the Annesley vote, same as all Nottingham, was seventy-four percent to twenty-six percent. 'Your job as a committee man, elected, is not your own. Once you've been mandated you take the mandate with you.'" Amos pauses and then adds, quietly, "And that's what I did."

With the subsequent annihilation of the British coal industry, and the parallel demise of not just the NUM but the effectiveness of the trade union movement in its entirety, even former working miners are hard-pressed to argue history was on their side. Says Amos, "Most people would agree now that the strike was a valid strike over a valid issue and I still would now." Bafflingly, though, he continues to cite the mechanics of the strike's origins as justification for breaking it.

"It wasn't just a case of disagreeing initially; you could see the way it got people's backs up. You see, you got to remember, also, that the Yorkshire NUM had been asked to keep pickets out 'til the Notts ballot. You see, you've got to remember that

86

officially when the NEC met that Saturday, they only authorised the strike, under Rule 41, in Yorkshire and Scotland.
They didn't authorise it nowhere else. Now, to get that domino
effect, what you had to do was, obviously you know, bring all
the other areas out but the problem is what do you suddenly do
then? Bear in mind that meeting of the NEC that authorised
strike action in Yorkshire and Scotland also authorised the
ballot in Nottinghamshire. Richardson and Chadburn asked for
it 'cause they knew there was no way they could come out of
there and say 'you're coming out on strike here.' That's what
history proves."

Quite. What history *also* proves is that a motion for a national
ballot was defeated at the 8th March NEC meeting. History
further proves that the Special Delegates' Conference decided,
democratically, *not* to have a national ballot. Yet Amos, along
with over 20,000 of his strike-breaking Nottinghamshire
colleagues, chose to ignore *that* democratic decision and, instead,
cite their Area ballot as having greater moral authority. Of
course, abiding by the Nottinghamshire Area ballot allowed those
so inclined to continue earning; one doesn't have to be an unreconstructed cynic to find that rather convenient.

Apart from anything else, the NEC didn't decide *only* to
make official the action in Scotland and Yorkshire. As early as
the meeting of 8th March, *before* the Nottingham Area ballot,
they *also* decided to make official, in advance, *any* strike action
other Areas might decide to take; as long as such action was in
accordance with Rule 41. The working miners faced an uphill
battle convincing anyone that they were motivated by a noble
commitment to democracy rather than a commitment to pound
notes.

Amos remains unmoved. "By 19th April 1984 various
members of the NUM NEC were not reflecting the views from
their members e.g. Lancashire, Notts, Power Group, Midlands,
Leicestershire, North Derbyshire, all of which had no mandate
for strike action in the various area ballots held during March
1984." One can imagine Henry Richardson feeling rather bitter
on this point, given the abuse he received for doing exactly what
Amos says he didn't: carrying out his Area's mandate, no
matter how much it conflicted with his personal principles.

"I think you will find out that Durham initially voted by four
pits to two against striking. If some of the NEC did not reflect

the various Areas' no-strike mandate what chance had a Special Delegates' Conference made up of mainly left-wing delegates got?" That hundreds of delegates, representing *every* Area of the NUM, were conniving left-wingers is not very convincing. That they further pulled the wool over the eyes of a combined membership of over 200,000, all of whom were too stupid and too apathetic to resist, is simply ridiculous. Apart from anything else, such a picture flies in the face of Amos' own assertion that democracy in the NUM flowed from "...the bottom up". As indeed it did. If Delegates, or indeed any officials, were not carrying out their Area's wishes, then they were replaced, as Nottinghamshire itself did in the June Branch elections and the July Area Council elections.

In reality, the Delegates present on 19th April *did* abide by their respective mandates. It's clearly a painful truth for the Nottinghamshire strike-breakers to admit, but the overwhelming majority of the membership *supported* the strike, *were* on strike and decided, democratically, *not* to hold a national ballot.

Amos does, though, concede that Arthur Scargill was neither the inept tactician nor the autocratic dictator of Conservative and Kinnock-led Labour propaganda, denying his men a democratic voice. "Technically, it wasn't a lot to do with Arthur Scargill, directly, 'cause it were Area-by-Area, it were men-led." Indeed.

For those mystified by the inner-workings of the NUM, it has to be said that the organisation's federal structure was not the easiest to understand. Immediately prior to the strike, the NUM comprised twenty-one Areas. Most of them were also independent trade unions in their own right and legally constituted, registered and certified as such. There were thirteen geographically-based Areas and seven trades-based Areas.

The composition of Areas and membership figures as of autumn 1983 broke down as follows:

88

Area	Number of members	N.E.C. delegates
Colliery officials and staff	17,246	1
Cokemen	4,822	1
Cumberland	661	1
North Derbyshire	11,221	1
South Derbyshire	3,160	1
Durham	13,294	1
Kent	2,538	1
Leicester	2,691	1
Midlands	12,996	1
Northumberland	5,761	1
North Wales	1,045	1
North Western	7,655	1
Nottingham	32,493	2
Scotland	13,010	1
South Wales	22,888	2
Yorkshire	59,643	3
Durham mechanics	5,799	1
Northumberland mechanics	2,049	1
Durham enginemen	619	1
Scottish enginemen	4,200	1
Power group	4,649	1
Total membership	**228,440**	**25**

Typical of most other trade unions, the National Executive Committee (NEC) oversaw the running and management of the Union's affairs in between Conferences: Conference being the highest authority (unless, of course, you happened to be a High Court Judge or Joe Gormley). The Areas contributed twenty-five members to the NEC: one for each Area with the bigger Areas entitled to more: Yorkshire had three with Nottingham and South Wales two each. Historically, these were elected every two years and were supplemented by the three national officials: President, Vice President and General Secretary. Of these three, only the Vice President had a full vote, with the President entitled to a casting vote only.

All the Areas were autonomous to a high degree and not only did many have their own finances, premises and staff but also their own rule books.

The larger of the Areas also had Agents. In Nottinghamshire, the coalfield was divided into four sections and each of the Area Officials assumed responsibility for the pits in their quarter, acting as Agents for their respective patches. Typically, this meant handling membership queries and involving themselves in disciplinary hearings and the day-to-day business of representing individual members when required.

The three larger Areas also had Area Councils upon which Delegates from each Branch sat. The Branches themselves had a full complement of lay officials, including Presidents, Secretaries, Treasurers and Delegates.

Adding to the complexity of the structure was local culture. Many Areas had distinct and specific local customs and traditions. These were fiercely guarded and often defended vigorously against any perceived attempt by 'National' to interfere, particularly so in Nottinghamshire. The Area's traditional rivalry with Yorkshire led to many convoluted justifications for strike-breaking. Somehow, the 'democratic' traditions of the Area and Nottinghamshire's unique culture and independence were justifiable reasons for continuing to work. The irony that a significant part of that 'unique culture' was strike-breaking and the creation of Spencerism seemed to escape many.

All eyes turned once again to Nottinghamshire when, on 25th April, the Area officials, along with Arthur Scargill and the Union's General Secretary, Peter Heathfield, attended the Area offices at Berry Hill in Mansfield. The purpose of the assembly was to underline the decisions taken at the Special Delegates' Conference of the preceding week. Of particular importance, that the strike was now official and, in accordance with the national rule book, that national decisions overruled any taken at an Area level.

Whatever the temperature inside Berry Hill, it was a reasonable bet that it was considerably higher outside. working miners faced off against strikers with the police forming a barrier between the two factions.

The following day, the Area Executive met and by eleven votes to two (the two against were Roy Lynk and David Prendergast) agreed to circulate a notice to all the Nottinghamshire Branches.

The instructions contained three key points: firstly, that the strike was now official and that all Branch Committees and Officers must abide by the decisions agreed at the Special Delegates' Conference. Secondly, that no NUM member would canvass against those decisions; and thirdly, provide facilities and support for those on strike.

Less than a week later, on 1st May, Berry Hill was again the focus of national media attention. The NCB laid on free buses and waived the usual seven-day notice period required for miners to take 'rest days' so that as many strike-breakers as possible could attend an anti-strike rally outside the Area HQ. Henry Richardson's lip curls as he recalls, "They even had the National Front there with them."

The adjacent field was soon filled with thousands of working miners and a smaller number of pro-strike supporters. The mood was ugly and volatile and as the Area officials appeared on the balcony to speak to the crowd their respective opponents booed and jeered.

On the working miners' side, a variety of placards with various slogans were brandished. Among them, 'Scargillism is Communism' 'Notts Voted to Work!' and 'For a Democratic NUM'. "Ah yes," remarks Dave Douglass dryly, "The 'moderates' with their gallows and their nooses." Indeed, the strike-breakers actually had constructed several makeshift nooses and gallows. Further underlining their commitment to the democratic process, they howled for Jimmy Hood to be hanged when he appeared on the balcony. Henry Richardson fared little better, greeted by a furious refrain of 'You're sacked! You're sacked! You're sacked!' As for Ray Chadburn, his repeated question, "Where will you go when your pit shuts?" was answered by thousands of working miners screaming, 'Resign! Resign! Resign!' Roy Lynk, though, was applauded by the anti-strikers as he stated, "You voted to work, so carry on working!"

The gathering descended into chaos with pitched battles breaking out as both sides hurled stones at each other, all the while bellowing abuse. The police waded in and made a number of arrests, earning the hatred of the strikers as only their number was targeted with not a single strike-breaker arrested. Instead, working miners laughed and jeered as strikers were kicked, punched and hauled away by policemen displaying a commendable respect for democracy and due process.

In the same month, the nation was introduced to 'Silver Birch', a miner from Bevercotes colliery. A thirty-four-year-old blacksmith, Chris Butcher wasn't content to simply cross picket lines and continue working. He decided to actively campaign to undermine his Union's defence of jobs and pits and to convince his fellow miners to return to work. Initially, he handed out his contact details on printed slips of paper to any miners he felt might be interested in organising coordinated action against the strike. Once sufficient interest had been generated, he organised a meeting at the Victoria Hotel in Stanton Hill, a small village a few miles from the NUM's Area Offices at Berry Hill.

The Notts Working Miners' Committee was formed at this meeting and its elected officers comprised Mick Smith from Bevercotes as Chair, John Blessington, also from Bevercotes, as secretary, Graham Taverner from Gedling as Treasurer and Ken Duckworth from Babbington as Vice-Chair. The Committee was rounded out with Butcher himself and fellow Bevercotes miner, Geoff Porter, along with Steve Williams from Annesley.

Also in attendance were Colin Clarke from Pye Hill No.1 pit and John Liptrott from Sherwood. These two had already held meetings with a London-based barrister with a view to taking the NUM to court. The basis of their action was spelled out in a leaflet they'd circulated to every pit. It read:

There will be a collection on Friday 18th May 1984. To pay for legal action being sought for the following:

I. *A declaration that no official strike exists in the Nottinghamshire Area.*

II. *That accordingly any instructions with regards to part (I.) given by any National, Area or Local Official of the Union is void and must be withdrawn.*

III. *Furthermore the Branch Committee are instructed to lend the name of this Branch as additional plaintiffs to any action as Pye Hill No.1 Branch may, upon proper legal advice, henceforth institute.*

IV. *If possible please donate £1 per man. This is a reasonable price to pay for democracy.*

[Insert name of] N.U.M. Branch Committee

The duo lacked the necessary funds to finance their legal offensive: some £5000. One of the first duties of the newly-formed committee was to organise a bank account and fighting fund to assist Clarke and Liptrott. The agreed aims of the strike-breakers were:

— *To form a link-up of all 25* Notts pits. To stop rumours spreading through the Notts coalfield.*

— *To assist mineworkers who are still working for the sake of democracy, who may be being intimidated.*

— *To reaffirm democracy within the NUM, but not to break or replace it.*

*There were actually twenty-seven pits in the County, at the time, and a total of thirty-one NUM Branches.

The last point was particularly astonishing. What, one imagines, did the working miners think their actions would achieve if not to facilitate precisely that breaking of their Union which they claimed to oppose?

With either an ignorance of labour and trade union principles or remarkable effrontery, the Notts Working Miners' Committee then wrote to all the local Constituency Labour Parties (CLPs) appealing for funds. The responses uniformly expressed the respective CLPs' disgust at the activities of the strike-breakers. Newark CLP's reply was typical. "For NUM members to cross picket lines in this dispute, following the decision at the Special Delegates' Conference — an integral part of your Union's structure; which you ought to understand — is a betrayal of fellow workers, their families and communities of the worst kind. Continuing to go to work is an act which can only serve to lengthen the dispute and which any thinking and caring human being would be ashamed even to contemplate."[25]

Demonstrating a singularly novel understanding of the principles of working class loyalty, John Liptrott, on behalf of the Committee, wrote to local Conservative Associations soliciting Tory aid and financial support. Following the objections of some members, this practice was abandoned. Apparently, some were concerned such actions might be perceived as aiding Thatcher and the Government against their own Union. The very idea...

Soon, the Notts Working Miners' Committee saw donations flowing in from businessmen, individual Conservatives and others opposed not just to the strike but to the existence of trade unions in any sort of capacity. A part of their funds was used for financing legal actions against the NUM by those in other coalfields.

Butcher rose to national prominence as, under the cloak of anonymity provided by the alias given him by a fellow strike-breaker, 'Silver Birch' travelled the coalfields of England, Scotland and Wales. Promoting strike-breaking and encouraging, funding and assisting other areas to set up their own working miners' committees, he soon became an establishment *cause célèbre*: eagerly championed by the Tory press and lauded for his 'bravery' and struggle for trade union 'democracy'. *The Mail on Sunday* dispatched one of its reporters, Chris Leake, to get the inside-track and he and Butcher toured the coalfields while *Mail* readers thrilled to first-hand accounts of the intrepid Silver Birch's heroic crusade.

Eventually, there were a number of working miners' committees spread across the UK, all operating under the auspices of the umbrella, the National Working Miners' Committee. In most cases their usefulness was limited given that many of their members weren't actually working but on strike, and were fearful of returning to work. One of Butcher's key tasks was to stiffen the spines of his fellow oppositionists and devise means and ways, aided by the NCB, of smoothing their return to work in as painless a manner as possible. The real damage done by the Working Miners' Committee was felt after the strike, when its ringleaders had provided the impetus and motivation, with Lynk and Prendergast, towards a breakaway union.

By mid-May the working miners were well under way to being co-opted by the Conservatives as a central weapon in their efforts to break the NUM in Nottinghamshire. Some feel the creation of the Committee was a conscious construct of the State, possibly even predating the strike itself. Certainly, some of its leaders were already colluding directly with the Government and shadowy figures attached to the security services. In the years since the strike, much has emerged to confirm that some of the strike-breakers weren't misguided pawns used by Thatcher's emissaries, but conscious and willing participants in the security services' campaign to destabilise the NUM. Silver Birch himself ('Silver Berk' or 'Dutch Elm' as loyalist wags christened him) was confirmed as a state asset in 2009. Papers released to *Morning Star* reporter, Solomon Hughes, under the Freedom of Information Act, revealed that Butcher reported to his handler, "a detective inspector in the

Intelligence Office at Nottinghamshire Police Headquarters," on a regular and frequent basis.[26]

Set against such revelations, Butcher's links to Ian MacGregor appear unsurprising and almost humdrum. Butcher happily admits discussing his strike-breaking plans with Ian MacGregor and enlisting his help. Indeed, the NCB boss personally instructed his Area Industrial Relations Officer to put Butcher in touch with Newark solicitors, Hodgkinson and Tallents, to further the working miners' efforts to bring down their own Union.[27]

Perhaps the definitive insight into the character, integrity and motivation of Silver Birch comes from Butcher himself; speaking to *The Guardian* in 2004, he reflected, "... If I regret one thing, at the time Silver Birch was running round the country, is that I didn't know what the story was worth." Lest there be any remaining doubt regarding his feelings about his part in wrecking the strike and the NUM, he went on to add, "I'm sorry if I sound bitter and I'm not bitter. I made a promise to my family quite a few years ago, I don't speak to the press, there's nothing to gain from it, all I can do is lose. You're not offering me £10,000 for my story, are you?"[28]

Butcher's plans eventually crashed and burned when a falling-out with Clarke and Liptrott saw him expelled from the organisation he'd set up in the first place. This development contained a degree of irony and poetic justice the strikers were not averse to savouring.

Meanwhile, the rest of the Notts Working Miners' Committee were being wined, dined and funded by one David Hart. The Eton-educated millionaire was on the hard right of the Tory party and had previously advised Thatcher during her 'Star Wars' negotiations with US President, Ronald Reagan. The Prime Minister was enthusiastic about Hart's involvement with the Nottinghamshire strike-breakers and instructed MacGregor to afford Hart any assistance he might request.

Hart's links to the intelligence services and dubious counter-insurgency types, on both sides of the Atlantic, appeared to present no problem to Clarke, Liptrott and the rest; such was their hatred of Arthur Scargill and the NUM Left. They and Hart shared exactly the same goal.

Hart threw money at the working miners and, using press credentials to initially explain his presence in Nottingham-shire, set out to woo the strike-breakers. He didn't have to work particularly hard and soon various legal actions against the NUM were launched by Clarke, Liptrott and company, on the back of funds provided by Hart. Intelligence reports sent back to Downing Street and Hobart House, the NCB's headquarters, were received with delight.

This was an essential feature of the Government's plans: the establishment of a scab-labour force to break the strike, and Hart's Nottinghamshire miners fitted the Tory bill perfectly. Having said that, the effectiveness of the working miners' committees' contribution to the Government and NCB war-effort was limited and consisted mainly of propaganda value: on the one hand, the legal actions and resulting red-tape undoubtedly damaged the NUM considerably. On the other, despite the triumphalist crowing regarding the 'droves' of men 'flooding' back to work, production, at least in the first few months, was seriously impaired. Hart's Nottinghamshire quislings were no match for the thousands of pickets who really did 'flood' the County and seriously hampered the NCB's attempts to keep pits working normally.

At Harworth colliery, for example, the most northerly of the Nottinghamshire pits and the historic site of the Nottingham Miners' Association's battle against Spencerism, a genuinely mass picket took place on 2nd May. Around 8,000 miners blockaded the pit and could only be dispersed by a virtual rerun of the legendary 'Harworth Riot.' The police ran amok, truncheoning and bludgeoning indiscriminately and the injured ran into the hundreds. Even those scenes were eclipsed by events in Mansfield on 14th May.

40,000 striking miners and their supporters, from all over the UK, had converged on the north Nottinghamshire town to attend a mass rally. A glorious late spring-early summer's day, of the type all-too rarely seen in England, provided an idyllic backdrop. As usual, at such events, the attendees listened to barnstorming speeches from the platform speakers. Not least by Scargill himself who, on appearing, was greeted by deafening roars of approval. The NUM President attempted to quieten the crowds by waving both his arms in a downwards motion.

The Sun then attempted to run a photograph of the scene; but with one difference. The paper deliberately cut out one of Scargill's arms to leave the remaining arm looking for all the world as though it was raised in a Nazi salute. Even by the *The Sun's* low standards, this was a particularly spiteful attempt to smear a prominent trade union leader. The printers refused to publish the offending image. The tabloid was forced to run a blank front page and, rather than the doctored photograph, a mealy-mouthed explanation for its ruined front page was substituted in its stead.

This was merely a diversion, though. The real drama occurred at the end of the rally as the strikers were making their way back to their coaches and cars to travel home. Mounted police suddenly appeared from several different junctions and charged the departing miners and their families. The unprovoked police attack left dozens injured and in need of hospital treatment.

Striking miner, Bobby Girvan, in his famous account, first published in *The Enemy Within: Pit villages and the Miners' Strike of 1984-5,* spoke of seeing a young man of around eighteen lying on the road while half-a-dozen policemen administered a savage kicking. The sickened Girvan described it as, "... like one of these African executions. He got his stick out, about a yard long, and whacked him across the face and the ambulance men was angry and was effing and blinding to the police and they had to put that young lad in an oxygen tank for about twenty minutes before they even moved him and I've never seen a sight like it."

Sixty-one miners were arrested on charges of rioting, affray and conspiracy. This was serious stuff indeed: the average sentence of anyone convicted would be in the region of ten years. That most of the cases would eventually collapse, be abandoned or commuted to lesser charges was of little consolation to anyone. While many found it incredible that good old British 'Bobbies' could behave in such a manner, such scenes were the norm, rather than the exception, in Nottinghamshire. During the notorious 'Siege of Blidworth' police occupied the village and assaulted miners and their families for 'harbouring Yorkshire pickets.'

Why Yorkshire pickets were still in the county in such vast numbers, was partially the responsibility of Arthur Scargill. As Dave Douglass recalls, "Once in Mansfield he had made the call for everyone just to stay there and picket the Notts pits. This too was taken up by the left papers and by word of mouth. But pickets assumed this was an official 'commandment' and that some organization lay behind it. There wasn't. Men ended up sleeping in hedgerows and without money and transport and a clue what to do and where to go. We had to try and tour the area afterward picking up stragglers and waifs and strays. It had been a most undisciplined and ill-thought-out call."

In Rainworth, miners were choked, punched and kicked on leaving the Miners' Institute at 10.30pm on the day of the Mansfield rally. Several officers, in clear view of stunned residents, delivered a vicious beating to a prone and defenceless miner, jumped repeatedly on the chest of another and choked a third with a truncheon before effecting wholesale arrests.

At Tuxford Junction, near Bevercotes colliery, pickets from Grimethorpe pit were beaten with truncheons and batons for the crime of challenging the officer in charge for illegally denying them access. One young miner needed several stitches for a serious head injury and even while in hospital, concussed and frightened, was intimidated by police who had followed his ambulance from the junction at Tuxford.

For many miners, the shattered illusions of seeing British police behave in such a manner were comparable to the physical pain of their injuries. Les Dennis spoke for many when he said, "I was brought up to respect the police and the law. I'd never committed a crime in my life before the strike. But what I saw that year changed my views forever. Now, I'll never trust a copper again."

While the media onslaught against the striking miners left viewers and readers with the certainty that miners were blood-thirsty hooligans, hell-bent on mob rule, the vast majority were simply ordinary family men thrust into extraordinary circumstances. Dennis continues, "I used to be proud of my country. I used to be patriotic but to hear us described as 'the Enemy Within' just because we stood up for our jobs and our industry, well, that sickened me to my stomach."

'Bob' (not his real name and as the only striker in a family of four former working miners he wishes to remain anonymous) observes, "I remember watching the police on the news getting stuck into, I used to call 'em, 'Wogs' and 'Pakis' at the Brixton riots and thinking, 'You must've done summat to deserve it. The police don't act like that without a reason.' I know bloody well different now, after what them bastards did to us! I met lots of coloureds during the strike and they were lovely people and the things they told me about what they had to put up with was a proper eye-opener."

A significant sociological feature of the strike was how the miners' experiences changed their views on a range of issues; the role of the state, feminism, racism, sexism and other forms of discrimination. Support came from the Black and Asian communities, as well as the Gay and Feminist movements. Exposure to these people revealed to many miners the struggles other minorities faced. Early on in the strike, Nottinghamshire miners had marched in the City with some chanting 'get your tits out for the lads.' By the end of the dispute, many of those same men had attended the women's peace camps at Greenham Common and spoken on Feminist and Gay platforms as well as those hosted by Black and Asian organisations.

Lenin is reputed (probably incorrectly) to have said that 'an ounce of experience is worth a tonne of theory', and for Nottinghamshire's striking miners that was certainly the case. One doesn't wish to romanticise them: after all, these were hardened working class men, not the Vienna Boys' Choir, and it would be foolish to suggest the strikers weren't guilty of violence themselves. Equally ridiculous would be any attempt to present post-strike miners as paragons of bleeding-heart liberal sensitivity. However, to feel the full force of the supposedly neutral state: government, police, judiciary and media; bearing down on men intent only on saving their jobs, was a life-changing experience. Certainly, many never returned to their previously-held opinions on class, race and gender and that British democracy and justice were things of which they should be proud.

The rest of May was equally eventful. In Barnsley on the 12th, the Women Against Pit Closures Support Groups held a mass rally with 10,000 asserting their opposition to the Government and NCB. On the 16th Scargill's wife, Anne, was arrested for 'obstruction' while picketing and on the 17th, the Home Secretary, Leon Brittan, was forced to admit to Parliament that 'plain-clothes' police officers were operating in Nottinghamshire. This was no surprise to the strikers, by then wearily accustomed to police *agent provocateurs* inciting violence and illegality, intended to discredit the NUM and trigger mass arrests.

On the 23rd, the NUM leadership met with MacGregor and his NCB team only for talks to collapse on the first day, and the

25th brought further unwelcome developments: the High Court ruled the NUM was not permitted to discipline strike-breakers. Still the hits kept on coming. On the 29th, the biggest picket so far at Orgreave coking plant saw 7000 miners trounced by riot police in full battle-kit. Over eighty pickets were arrested and nearly seventy injured, with some requiring extended medical attention. A tumultuous month drew to a close with Arthur Scargill's arrest at Orgreave as police deployed a huge mounted operation with horses charging fleeing strikers.

The strike was barely three months old. The miners faced a long hot summer.

Chapter 6: Sisters Are Doing It For Themselves

"The thing women have yet to learn is nobody gives you power. You just take it."
ROSEANNE BARR

In one sense, Iris Wake's story is unremarkable. Unremarkable, that is, compared to those of the tens of thousands of other miners' wives who backed their striking husbands. Their individual stories were often so similar as to be almost indistinguishable one from another. That, however, is only when viewed from within the narrow context of the strike itself. Take Iris's story out of the strike and place it in the wider cultural and social context of the time and it becomes remarkable, as well as inspiring.

She was forty-six when the strike started. A mother to her three daughters and one son, Karen, Julie, Susan and Alan, she also worked as a 'Domestic' at the Nottingham City Hospital, just a couple of miles along Hucknall Road from her home in Bestwood Village (*not* Bestwood Park, a large nearby housing estate with a similar name. The residents of the traditional mining village were *very* keen on ensuring no one confused the two). Iris supervised a number of other Domestics or cleaners, having worked her way up from that position herself.

When spared some time from her job and family, she liked to indulge her creative side. She was an expert knitter and highly proficient in crocheting. Along with weekly trips to play bingo, this was, largely, the life Iris enjoyed up to March 1984.

From that moment on her life and outlook would undergo a change of such proportions that, in Iris's words, "If I'd known at the start what was going to happen, I'd have laughed, and then run a mile!"

Iris was, initially, firmly behind her striking husband. Later, she might even have been in *front* of him, such was the enthusiasm and commitment with which she embraced the miners' cause. Her husband, Maurice (or 'Mog' to most who knew him), had come out on strike from his pit at Linby, and Iris soon found herself involved in every aspect of the dispute as a member of the Hucknall and Linby Women's Action Group.

The two pits were only a couple of miles apart and the women decided to combine their forces. Linby had a reputation as a militant pit with over 500 of its 845-strong workforce out at one point. In Nottinghamshire, though, 'militant' was a relative term: ultimately, only 103 miners were 'loyal to the last', staying out for the full duration of the strike. Linby's neighbour, Hucknall, was even worse from a striker's point of view: according to Linby Picket Manager, Les Dennis, only forty-two from 927 stuck it out to the end. Nevertheless, the Hucknall and Linby women adopted the appellation 'Action' not just to underscore the pits' reputation for militancy but also to underline that playing a merely supportive role wasn't going to be sufficient for them. (In fairness to the hundreds of Women's Support Groups around the UK, these hardly consisted of docile little *hausfraus*, waiting patiently on the return of their men-folk.)

Iris raised funds, prepared food and all the other activities typical of a miner's wife during the strike. Like thousands of other women undergoing a similar metamorphosis, the strike transformed her. As her youngest daughter, Susan, put it, "My mum went into the strike as one woman, and then came of out it a completely different one."

Travelling all over the UK, speaking to hundreds of sympathisers on dozens of different platforms was a liberating, sometimes frightening, experience. Fortunately, Iris and Mog had a strong marriage and, with both convinced of the justice of their fight, they were largely spared the strains and stresses under which many mining marriages sometimes laboured. "Sometimes one of us would arrive home as the other was leaving!" said Iris. "But we believed in what we were doing."

Normally camera-shy to the point of phobia, Iris amazed herself by appearing in several accounts of the strike and posing for photographs, either *en route* or at various strike-related activities. "Oh, it was hard, at times," she says, "but I wouldn't have changed a thing; I had the time of my life. I went to Greenham Common, spoke at meetings next to MPs and all sorts of things."

It wasn't always fun, though. Like thousands of miners and their families, particularly in Nottinghamshire, Iris and Mog saw a very different side to the Police. The comforting Dixon-of-Dock-Green image, with which both had grown up, was shattered by the reality of the picket line. On one occasion, joining Mog on a local picket, Iris was "disgusted" by the behaviour of the 'Met'.

"I was just standing there when this policeman came right up behind me and started kicking my ankles," explained Iris. "When I refused to react, he put his head on my shoulder and starting whispering in my ear. I couldn't believe what he was saying! 'Miner's whore, effing slag, scum' and things like that. Then a working miner, crossing the picket said, 'I hope your effing kids die of cancer.' The police never said anything to him, though. I never would have believed it if I hadn't heard it myself."

The Metropolitan Police Force was hated with a passion throughout the county, earning a reputation for thuggery and violence that outstripped that of any other force, against frequently stiff competition. Often behaving more like football hooligans than upholders of the law, the Met regularly issued beatings to Nottinghamshire miners and then affixed little stickers to their victims' bodies, which read, 'I've met The Met.' This quaint custom was not reserved for just Nottinghamshire miners. Dave Douglass says, "We used to park our cars outside the villages we were picketing so as not to have them attacked

103

by scabs. More than once we returned to wrecked cars and the stickers 'I've met the Met' stuck on them."

Why the Metropolitan Police were even in Nottinghamshire, in the first place, over a hundred miles from London, was one of the most contentious aspects of the dispute. The origins of their deployment in other Forces' jurisdictions, like so much else in the Government's handling of the dispute, lay in the Ridley Plan.

The creation of the National Reporting Centre (NRC) was central to dealing with policing in the coalfields. Operating from a room on the thirteenth floor of Scotland Yard, its purpose was revealed by Douglas Hurd to Parliament on 5th April 1984. "Arrangements for a national reporting centre were first made in 1972. Its main purposes were and are to help in the national co-ordination of aid between chief officers of police in England and Wales, under Section 14 of the Police Act 1964, so that the best use is made of manpower and to provide the Home Secretary with information, in the same way as he receives reports from individual chief officers, to help him discharge his responsibilities for law and order."

This bland description, while accurate, was hardly the full story. In reality, the NRC became the management body of an effectively national police force, as the paramilitary wing of the Conservative Party. In seeking to combat picketing and deal with an industrial dispute in this way, rather than by simply applying civil law, the police UK-wide, enthusiastically spearheaded by the Met, became a partisan body, forcibly imposing acts of political policy rather than simply upholding the law. Hurd continued, "Since 14 March this year, the centre has co-ordinated the responses to requests from chief officers for assistance from their colleagues in policing related to the miners' dispute."

If the pro-strike women in Nottinghamshire expected chivalrous treatment by police officers and allowances to be made for their gender, they were quickly disabused. Assaulted, arrested, illegally held without charge and when legally charged, appearing in court, just like the men, they soon realised war had been declared on them and their communities.

For the Nottinghamshire women, the situation was considerably tougher than that of their counterparts in other coalfields. With the Union's Area finances under the control of the pro-working miners' leaders, Lynk and Prendergast, official funds were denied the women's support groups. As working class women down the ages have done, Nottinghamshire women were forced to draw on reserves of ingenuity and courage they'd never known existed.

Each pit soon had its own Women's Support Group attached to it, no matter how few strikers the pit might have had. Eventually, these autonomous bodies fed into a county-wide organisation, the Nottinghamshire Women's Support Group, which acted as a network and source of help, advice and support for its constituent parts. Each pit Group sent its elected Delegates to the regular meetings of 'Central' as it was known. Legal advice, mutual support campaigns, activities and advice on a whole range of issues were debated and exchanged.

'Central' was launched by Julie Wilkinson and local legend, Ida Hackett. Ida was a lifelong Communist Party member and trade union activist. At the start of the strike she was seventy, and had vivid memories of working class resistance during the General Strike when she was just eleven years old. Known throughout the county for her tireless activism, Ida was a much-admired and respected figure among mining communities. Aided by Ernie Dalglish and Andy Miller, the quartet quickly saw their initiative mushroom and soon the men bowed out and were replaced by women. Joining Ida on the Committee were Audrey Mulholland, Rita Abbott, Liz Hollis,[28] Margaret Brown, Pam Oldfield and Jackie Naylor.

One of the Group's most important areas of work was fundraising. Unlike the solidly pro-strike areas, Nottinghamshire women faced many obstacles in their attempts to keep their war chest well-stocked. The collections and attempts to establish street-stalls were frequently hampered. The women faced abuse, hostility and, sometimes, violence from members of the public — many of whom swallowed the anti-strike propaganda which poured from the nation's television sets and newspapers — as well as from those ideologically opposed to the dispute and the women's campaign to support their striking men.

Every Saturday, under the banner of the Nottinghamshire Women's Support Group, the women ran a stall outside St Peter's Church, a few yards away from Marks and Spencer's in Nottingham City centre. Braving police harassment, obscenities and unwelcome approaches from drunks, the women on the stall raised money and sold strike souvenirs and memorabilia to aid the miners' fight. However noble and worthwhile the efforts of the women involved, the money raised was insufficient to sustain the cause and they started to venture further afield. Travelling to towns and cities all over the UK, many found the friendly and supportive reception afforded them to be in stark contrast to the hostile and unpleasant reaction from many of Nottingham's shoppers.

Like the miners, such trips often widened the women's views of the world. This enabled them to place their struggle into the wider context of how the UK was really governed. Women from Mansfield Ladybrook Support Group travelled to Detroit where they saw the impact of privatisation first-hand. Friends of Iris Wake's from Hucknall and Linby went to Ohio, where $10,000 was raised for the strikers by American miners, who were themselves on strike at the time. Others from the Welbeck group went to Northern Ireland and saw similarities between the policing of the Nationalist areas and their own coalfields back home. All the time Nottinghamshire women were learning, evaluating and questioning.[29]

By nature, proud women whose priority was the feeding and clothing of their children, Nottinghamshire women were appalled at their treatment by the 'Social'. Thatcher had instructed benefits be stopped to striking miners on the assumption they were receiving strike pay. They weren't, of course, and the Government knew it. Miners who picketed got £1 per day and at many pits even this paltry amount was only paid to pickets who attended every day: miss one shift out of the week and many got nothing at all.

This spiteful move by the Government was introduced with the express intention of starving the miners back to work and increasing the moral pressure on men who would be forced to watch their children go hungry. Like most measures of this kind, all it did was consolidate resistance and ensure the women were even more determined not to be beaten. "It was awful, though, really," said Iris. "We were lucky because I still had my job but some families had nothing except what the women could claim from the Social for their kiddies. Single men were even worse off because they got nothing at all."

There can be little doubt that the strike would have been over in a matter of weeks if not for the commitment, support and bravery of the miners' wives, partners and families. Despite the machismo of miners, many were from matriarchal families. The women might well have carried out the traditionally-expected 'women's work' but many of them also called the shots. Substantial numbers of Nottinghamshire miners knew they would have crumbled without the unstinting support of their women. As one miner, who'd moved south from the North East during the pit closure programme of the 60s to find work at Gedling colliery, put it, "It were a piece of piss standing up to the Polis and Thatcher, compared to crossing wor lass! She were brilliant but if she'd been against the strike, I honestly don't know how long I would've lasted."

June was a particularly worrying month for Iris and many Nottinghamshire women, as husbands, sons and brothers set off for the 'Battle of Orgreave'. The confrontation at the South Yorkshire coking plant had been brewing since the beginning of the strike and had already seen periodic clashes between pickets and police. Offensives culminated on the 18th June.

Tactically, picketing Orgreave had been a contentious issue for the miners' leaders and opinions were split. For some, like Dave Douglass, Orgreave was a diversion, sucking badly-needed forces out of the Nottinghamshire coalfield. Stopping, or at least seriously hampering, production in Nottinghamshire was the key task and one that wounded the NCB and the Government the most. As far as Douglass was concerned, the Government and MacGregor would be only too delighted to engage several thousand pickets in a pointless push-and-shove while Nottinghamshire, unmolested, got on with the serious business of shipping coal.

Prior to the final confrontation, picketing Orgreave had been widely viewed as a Plan B for pickets unable to get into Nottinghamshire. Soon it became little more than a fall-back option for those whom the police had successfully prevented entering the County. Some of the NEC also saw Scargill's call for a mass blockade of the plant as little more than an ego-tripping quest to replay the triumph of Saltley Gate. Scargill vehemently disagreed. The former NUM President insisted, "My passionate conviction that the Orgreave coking plant in South Yorkshire should be selected as a main target was rubbished at the time. Yet, it has now been revealed from official sources that show coal stocks at steel plants — particularly

Scunthorpe in Yorkshire, Ravenscraig in Scotland and Llanwern in Wales — were so low that these works could only continue in production for a matter of weeks, with Scunthorpe (where British Steel had already laid off 160 workers due to coal shortages) actually earmarked for closure by 18 June 1984."[30]

At the heart of the debate was the question of NUM-approved 'dispensations'. Scargill stated, "The issue of dispensations that would allow provision of coal supplies created divisions among the most militant sections of the NUM. I had argued passionately that there should be no dispensations for power stations, cement works, steelworks or coking plants, whose coal stocks were extremely low."[31]

This was a highly controversial stance to adopt and Scargill's colleagues were fiercely opposed. Scargill remains unrepentant. "Many on the Union's left — particularly those in the Communist Party — argued that the union had a responsibility to ensure that a minimal amount of coal could be delivered in order to keep the giant furnaces and ovens 'ticking over'. Heathfield and a number of others on the NUM left agreed with me that there should be no dispensations and that if steelworks had to close down, as British Steel's chairman, Bob Haslam, warned was inevitable, then the responsibility lay firmly at the door of the government, not the NUM."[32]

Eventually Scargill was overruled. "Despite the passionate arguments made by Heathfield and myself, areas *did* give dispensations. Two months went by before it dawned on Yorkshire, South Wales and Scotland that they had been outmanoeuvred by British Steel, and the leadership of the steelworkers' union, and that British Steel was moving far more coal than the dispensations agreed with NUM areas. Yet there was still time to stop all those giant steelworks, and if the steelworkers' union would not cooperate with the NUM to stop all deliveries of coal to the steelworks then the National Union of Seamen and rail unions ASLEF and NUR had already demonstrated that they would stop all deliveries."[33]

To the anger of the NEC, Scargill, in typical fashion, went ahead anyway with his call for a mass picket and publicly demanded that pickets and sympathetic trade unionists converge on the plant on the 18th and shut it down.

Dave Douglass disagrees with his former President's interpretation. "Arthur's version of events just can't be allowed to stand unchallenged. Neither Arthur nor the NEC had overall direction of pickets or targets, the targets based on the experience of '72 and '74 were obvious and unchanging. Areas deployed their own pickets and chose their own priorities. He couldn't have argued for Orgreave to be a priority at this stage because Orgreave wasn't a target in any shape or form at that time. He was not overruled at this stage because he didn't have control of picketing and who we — the Areas — granted dispensations to because he didn't have that power then. What he means is we disagreed with him.

"It only became a target because he gained control of dispensations granted on safety and social responsibility and PR grounds, and tore up unilaterally the agreements we had with ISTC, GMBU and BSC. This created the situation at Orgreave, which didn't have to exist in the first place.

"The disagreement over tactical dispensations etc predates the creation of a crisis with BSC and the process which then leads on to Orgreave. His 'now revealed from official sources about low stocks of coal (actually coke) at steel plants' is just so much bollocks.

"Coke stocks were low at all the steel plants because *we* in Yorkshire, South Wales and Scotland in agreement with ISTC in those regions (but not with the agreement of Sirs or Arthur) had kept them that way. At Scunthorpe the only coke on site was delivered by ASLEF driven trains, with NUM members riding shotgun, with specific dispensations to strict amounts needed only to keep the boilers and furnaces intact, but not enough to produce steel. The point of the exercise was not to destroy the plant, wipe it out, play bluff with the Government or take BSC as lethal hostage: 'surrender or the plant gets it', *but to stop the production of steel*. We had stopped the production of steel from the beginning of the strike. No steel was being produced. This was the agreement with BSC. That pocket was covered.

Amounts of coke on premises wasn't a big secret because we, in the case of Yorkshire, Sammy Thompson, the Area Vice President and well known left member of the union — and Bill Ronskley Yorkshire Regional President of ASLEF and President of Yorkshire and Humberside TUC — held weekly inspections to check that no other coke was on site, how much had been used and to ensure no steel was being produced as per agreement. *This* is why men were being paid off (on full wages): the rank-and-file of ISTC were supporting us.

"I just don't know how you can say it any clearer: it wasn't broken, it didn't need fixing or interfering with. It is simply untrue to say 'production couldn't continue' because there was *no* production since March. What he is referring to is the request from Scunthorpe steel unions and management for an additional influx of NUM-approved coke to save the walls of the furnaces from cooling and collapse. In the intervening period he had wrested control of dispensations from Area Planning Committees, quite without our support or knowledge really, and was overlooking these himself. He refused the request and was ready to let the plant be written off or the Government cave in irrespective of the effects on steel workers' jobs and our market for coal/coke in steel making.

"Now while this was perfectly good dog-eat-dog-strategy in the case of a steel works scabbing and producing steel with scab coke, they weren't. They had an operating agreement with us *not* to produce steel but to operate safety cover. We had *never* allowed dispensations to power stations and asked only that they accepted no new coal onto the premises as they had done in '72 and '74.

"We did allow dispensations for coke works, and since we could only do this by allowing the production of some coke, it was done on the agreement that *all* of that coke went to miners, pensioners and DSS hardship cases, and mothers with new born babies etc. Again, not to do so meant writing off the coke works which were major customers, *and* alienating the public. This coal was provided only by *union* miners working for the same rate as the pickets, and only producing enough coke to keep the oven walls intact, and only then distributed to the people we said they could deliver to.

"We were operating the self-same systems which we used and won with in '72 and '74 and exercising our complete control over the process and with agreements. The coke works were operated by *our* members. To try and kick this all in the air was short-sighted counterproductive stupidity. *We* allowed safety men to operate at pits, we did this to stop the mine caving in, flooding or blowing up, and we allowed our own NUM members to provide safety cover. We only withdrew them the minute a scab came down the lane. The management could have safety men or scabs but not both.

"In Yorkshire the first scabs didn't appear until August because the management knew a few scabs could jeopardize the safety of the mine. But here's the point: to allow safety men to operate at pits to save the fabric of the pit so we had a pit to go back to, and *that's* what we were fighting for, but to *not* allow the same consideration to coke works and steel works meant you were making other workers pay a higher price for our strike than we were. That couldn't be fair and it turned a lot of support and comradeship and solidarity from our door and made us look strictly self-interested and not bothered about other workers."

In a dispute filled with violence, the final showdown at Orgreave produced the most appalling scenes thus far. Even thirty years later, the footage has the power to shock. Pickets in trainers and T-shirts, some entirely shirtless on that beautiful summer's day, were mercilessly battered by police officers in full riot gear, flailing away indiscriminately with truncheons, while mounted officers charged fleeing bands of men, desperate to escape. On the miners' side, barricades were erected and bricks and stones were hurled into the *mêlée*. A car from a nearby scrap-yard was dragged into the middle of the road and set alight and police pursued the miners into the nearby village, through gardens and houses, hammering down all they caught.

The numbers were formidable. Accounts vary but around 6,000–7,000 pickets to 10,000 police is a generally accepted figure. The police deployed around sixty mounted officers, sixty attack-dogs and several thousand officers with short-shield riot-gear and the remainder sporting long-shield issue.

There remains little doubt that the violence meted out to the miners was pre-planned, deliberate and sanctioned at the highest level of the South Yorkshire force (if not directly from the Prime Minister's office).

Miners *en route* to the plant were amazed to see signs directing them to convenient car parks, smiling officers help-fully pointing the way and guiding them in with no attempts whatsoever to dissuade or turn back the thousands of pickets who had heeded Scargill's call. Such behaviour stood in contrast to the manner in which all police forces had handled flying pickets up to that point.

For the Nottinghamshire miners, their experiences confirmed suspicions that 'The Battle of Orgreave' was a set-up orchestrated by the police. Years later, Margaret Thatcher's man David Hart would boast that The Battle of Orgreave had been a "... set-up by us. It was a battleground of our choosing on grounds of our choosing... the fact is that it was a set-up and it worked brilliantly."[34]

Les Dennis recalls, "As we pulled up and parked up there was this pit-tip and there must've been about a thousand Notts men, all coming over the top of this pit-tip. You looked back and all you could see were us trailing down this pit-tip and we ended up at the back-end of the depot. We were *behind* police lines and about half a mile from the main picket line where all the action was, where they were smashing lads to bits with truncheons, so we were determined to get there. As we approached the depot from the back, we took 'em [police] by surprise. Anyway, we get around the corner of the coke plant, onto the main road that led up to the picket line, and we saw a line of police across the road, from one side to the other with their truncheons and shields, and there's us in our trainers and shorts, so we gave 'em a charge; 'come on!' Anyway, they're all stood there, grinning, and they just opened up and let us through! So we're through but there's *another* police line so, same again, 'come on!' and we charged at that line and we got through again. Well, we're all laughing and thinking 'it's a piece of piss, this is!'

"As we got through that second line of coppers, we heard the noise: clip-clop, clip-clop, and across the road I counted fourteen police horses, side-by-side, filling the road, and they came charging towards us so we turn round and who's behind us? The two lines of coppers! Advancing with truncheons and shields ready to clatter us as we ran back. We were diving off the road, into corn-fields, just running for our lives, really.

"We eventually made our way back around, behind. We never made it to the main picket line, never got there, but we did us bit from behind the lines; we were like the rear offensive. We fended 'em off, chucked a few stones, made life hard for 'em.

"Eventually, we broke off and went for a bit of a rest and all you could see, looking down, was this massive swirling cloud of dust as the horses were charging into our lads and battering 'em."

The fall-out from Orgreave was considerable, although it would be many years before its full truth was revealed. TV viewers were treated to scenes of mobs of violent thugs hurling bricks and stones before embattled mounted police moved in to disperse the offenders. Only it wasn't like that at all. As *Red Pepper* reported, nearly thirty years after the event, "When broadcasting footage of Orgreave, the BBC, incredibly, transposed the sequence of events, making it appear that police cavalry charges had been a defensive response to antagonism by stone-throwing pickets rather than an act of aggression. Only in 1991 did the BBC issue an apology for this, claiming that its action footage had been "inadvertently reversed."[35]

The publicly-funded, 'neutral' state broadcaster had *reversed* footage which, in its original form, showed cowering pickets with nowhere to run, desperately fending off charging police with whatever they had to hand. Given the pre-digital era of 1984, with physical tape being used for filming, which required conscious human cutting, splicing and chopping for editing purposes, one can view the BBC's claims of the footage being "inadvertently reversed" with a degree of contempt.

The South Yorkshire Police didn't stop at merely bludgeoning defenceless men, either. Ninety-five pickets were arrested and charged with a number of offences, the most serious being charges of rioting and affray which carried sentences of upwards of ten years. In 1987 the trials soon collapsed in a welter of conflicting police evidence, fabricated statements and embarrassing inconsistencies. Although described by renowned QC, Michael Mansfield, as "the biggest frame-up ever," no officers were ever investigated or charged. This was despite South Yorkshire Police being forced to hand over nearly half-a-million pounds in compensation to thirty-nine of the arrested pickets and incurring costs of over £100,000.

In light of the Hillsborough cover-up, it's possible that an independent enquiry into Orgreave might yet bring further humiliation to a force that was institutionally corrupt. The Orgreave Truth and Justice Campaign, Justice for Mineworkers and other organisations continue to press the case.

The furore over Orgreave hadn't even begun to subside, when, on 21st June, Iris Wake and her family received another shock. Mog was arrested on the picket line at his own pit,

Linby. By the fourth month of the strike, both he and Iris had few remaining illusions regarding the state's efforts to crush their fight, but still the arrest was a painful experience. They worked hard, were law abiding, paid their bills on time and refused all credit and debt; if they couldn't afford it they went without or saved hard. As their daughter Susan recalls, "Dad would save up for the first few months of every year to take us all on holiday and then as soon as we were back, he'd start again, saving for Christmas." Mog was to be arrested three times during the course of the strike, but the first hit home the hardest, possibly because of its shock value.

The picket that day had started early, at around 5.15am, to catch strike-breakers going in on the morning shift. Mog had been picketing for about twenty minutes when fellow picket, Bryan Plenty, was arrested without warning and, seemingly, with no cause. As Mog's official statement read, "... I approached a police officer and asked why my colleague had been arrested. His response was to remove a printed card from his pocket and read from it. This response surprised me and, not understanding what he had read out, I again asked why my colleague had been arrested. Once again, he read to me from his printed card. I tried a third time to understand what was happening but the only information offered was the card being read repetitiously."

Giving up on the police officer, Mog turned his attention to three working miners breaching the picket line and shouted, "Aren't you ashamed of yourselves?" The response from one of the strike-breakers was, "Aren't you ashamed about last night on the 'Black Pad'?" [a footpath on the way into Linby village]. It was alleged that two working miners had been assaulted on the footpath. Despite there being no arrests, no witnesses and no exchange between the alleged attacker and the alleged victims, or any indication of any kind that the assault had anything at all to do with the strike, it was accepted unquestioningly by the working miners that the assault had been carried out by strikers.

Mog replied, "There are hundreds of our lads getting their heads banged every day on this job!" The exchange continued, "Who's doing it then? You lot!" to which Mog, somewhat unwisely, responded "I wouldn't mind banging *your* head!" He was promptly arrested and charged with using 'abusive language and threatening behaviour liable to cause a breach of the peace' under

Section 5.5 of the Public Order Act 1936. Ironically, the Act was introduced to combat Moseley's Blackshirts and prevent quasi-military and uniformed public demonstrations. It was the popular weapon of choice for arresting officers all over England and Wales during the dispute.

To add to the Wake family's humiliation, Mog was granted only conditional bail as, according to his charge-sheet, he "will commit fresh offences on bail." The conditions were so frequently imposed on arrestees that the police had printed them out onto little squares which were then stapled to the

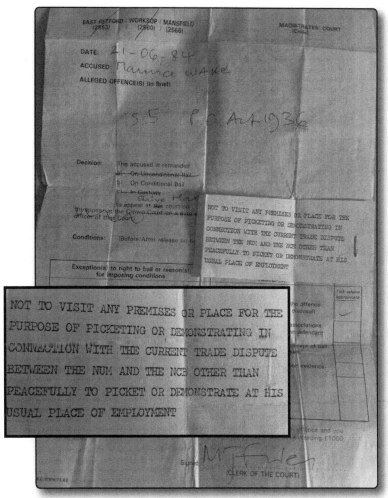

charge-sheet. The conditions were "Not to visit any premises or place for the purposes of picketing or demonstrating in connection with the current trade dispute between the NUM and the NCB other than peacefully to picket or demonstrate at his usual place of employment."

This was a favoured tactic by the police, to render the strikers impotent and prevent them from attending picket lines. But mass arrests clogged up the Magistrates' Court in Mansfield and evening and weekend sittings soon had to be introduced to deal with the backlog, a task which saw local Tory Magistrates rising manfully to the occasion.

The commanding officer on duty at Linby that day was a Metropolitan Police Inspector, Police Inspector Peter Crooks, number 158898. Typical of the favoured Police Support Unit (PSU) formation deployed during the strike, he had two sergeants and twenty constables under his command, and while his statement doesn't differ significantly from Wake's, it does contain an assertion that Mog struggled and resisted arrest, an additional offence in itself and one that could have easily resulted in a custodial sentence. Fortunately for the Wake family, when the case eventually came to court the judge dismissed the charges. The police witnesses contradicted each other and, in a particularly embarrassing *faux pas,* it transpired that one of the officers who gave eyewitness testimony wasn't even at the colliery on the day in question. No police officers were ever charged with perjury, attempting to pervert the course of justice or malicious prosecution.

Tragedy struck the striking miners again when, on 15th June, the dispute claimed its second casualty in the form of Yorkshire picket, Joe Green. He was hit and killed by a lorry while picketing Ferrybridge power station. As with David Jones, no arrests were ever made and no charges were ever brought.

Earlier in the month, on the 7th, a national demonstration in London and lobby of Parliament had been extremely well-attended. Unfortunately the good spirits were shattered as the police waded in, yet again, effecting mass arrests and truncheoning the attendees. Iris and Mog had taken their youngest daughter, Susan, then aged twelve, with them and had to shield her as mounted police thundered by bludgeoning the marchers. Many of those arrested were held overnight only to

116

Linby miners, families and supporters. March and lobby of parliament, 7th June 1984. Iris Wake, far right of photo.

be released the following morning with no money or means to make it back to Nottinghamshire.

Once safely back in the county, further bad news awaited. Despite Lynk and Prendergast holding the union's purse strings in the Area and consciously cutting off funds to their striking members, many of the Branch Committees had strikers holding lay positions. The paltry amounts the loyalist Committee men managed to prise from Branch coffers were nevertheless thankfully received by their poverty-stricken comrades. All that was to change, though, as Branch Committee elections were held throughout the Area. With few exceptions, like Keith Stanley's election to the Newstead Committee, the strikers were wiped out *en masse*. The working miners undertook a successful campaign to unseat every pro-strike Branch official. With over 20,000 of the Area's members having voted to continue working, the results, although depressing, surprised no one. When the numbers were eventually in, the result was clear: the strike-breakers had taken full control of every Branch in the coalfield.

Chapter 7:
Cruel Summer

*"Think of the press as a great keyboard
on which the government can play."*
GOEBBELS

It was July 1984 and Nottinghamshire was hot and sunny. The average temperature for the month was around twenty degrees. While this made life a bit easier for those on strike, and meant precious coal reserves could be saved for the harsher climes ahead, it did little to help erode the coal stocks held at power stations.

Controversial Merseysiders, Frankie Goes to Hollywood, held the number one singles spot for the entire month and Labour leader Neil Kinnock enjoyed a brief lead over the Tories in a MORI poll which put Labour at 40 percent, three percent ahead of the Conservatives

Of rather greater significance for the NUM, however, was Robert Maxwell's purchase of the *Daily Mirror* on 12th July for £93 million.

The *Mirror* had adopted a typically fence-straddling position, prior to Maxwell's acquisition of the tabloid. On the one hand, the Labour-supporting daily championed the miners' fight to keep their pits from closing, with many an editorial berating the Government. It then rendered such support largely useless by siding with its Tory counterparts: making the absence of a national ballot the central issue. While it was marginally more balanced in reporting police violence, it rarely missed an opportunity to condemn violence by the miners, irrespective of its defensive character or evidence pointing to police *agent provocateurs*.

Under Maxwell's ownership the paper gradually moved towards outright opposition to the strike. On more than one occasion, the proprietor rewrote copy submitted by his journalists to better reflect his own view of the dispute. That is, unless such articles were written by the Mirror Group's Political Editor, Joe Haines. The former press secretary to Harold Wilson was on the hard right of the Labour movement and was no fan of Arthur Scargill. He was also slavishly loyal to Maxwell, often embarrassingly so. Commissioned by Maxwell to write his official biography, Haines' account was so hagiographic that Fleet Street comedians insisted Maxwell would give guests copies of the book rather than business cards.

Maxwell, the future pension-thief, would go on to preside over the smear-campaign against Arthur Scargill and Peter Heathfield in 1990. His proven links to various intelligence services around the world, including MI5, MI6 and Mossad, were undoubtedly very useful to the state in its use of the *Daily Mirror* to smear the miners' leaders.

With the rest of the largely Conservative-supporting national newspapers lined up against the NUM, the miners had little chance of their case receiving a sympathetic hearing. It had one National Press Officer, Nell Myers, who doubled as Scargill's PA. From the outset, Myers and the NUM President decided journalists of almost any stripe were not to be trusted and scorned their advances and overtures. By contrast, the Conservatives decided also that the press was not to be trusted but, instead, under the guidance of the Energy Secretary, Peter Walker, set out to flatter and court Fleet Street. It would be foolish to deny that the Government started from a position of considerable strength, compared to the miners, in the year-long media war. Almost all the national dailies were allies of the Conservative Party anyway and while the NUM's intransigent and defensive approach hardly helped its efforts in waging a propaganda counter-offensive, it was understandable.

Myers' and Scargill's view left little room for doubt where the press was concerned: "The industrial correspondents, along with broadcasting technicians, are basically our enemies' front-line troops." The assertion that the media in general generated "a cyclone of vilification, distortion and untruth" was justified: the miners and Scargill in particular, were subjected to an almost continuous stream of invective, vituperation and outright lies.

At a local level, away from Fleet Street, the situation, while slightly more complex and nuanced, still resulted in similarly biased coverage. By and large the striking miners were still treated appallingly by the regional press but there were important factors for the provincial press bosses to consider. In places like South Wales and parts of Yorkshire, where the strike was solid and enjoyed support from the wider community, local editors faced a dilemma: although politically and instinctively inclined to supporting the Government, they had their sales and circulation figures to consider. Alienating huge swathes of their readership by hysterical condemnations of striking miners would hardly serve their commercial interests. Like Maxwell at the *Daily Mirror,* these circles were often squared by editorials ostensibly supporting the miners' cause while attacking picket 'violence' and the absence of 'democracy' within the NUM.

Nottinghamshire had many local journals and one of the UK's biggest regional papers in the *Nottingham Evening Post* (now the *Nottingham Post*). Town and village-oriented publications like the *Hucknall Dispatch, Mansfield Chad* and the *Eastwood and Kimberley Gazette* opened up the letters pages to strikers and working miners alike and the debates raged throughout their pages for the course of the dispute.

Typical of the coverage and exchanges between readers, and tho careful positioning by some editors, was the letters page of the *Hucknall Dispatch* from one of its May issues. A pro-striker's letter was headed, "Nonsense to Say Pits Are Working Normally" while the strike-breakers' position was represented by an alternative heading entitled, "Three-Quarters Of Linby Miners Are Working." The hapless editor rounded off the exchange by stating that "The figures between Coal Board and Union vary so widely that we are quite frankly baffled. But we can only print what we are told."

On the same page, a letter from an anti-strike miner's wife urged older miners to take redundancy to 'make room' for younger men coming into the industry. The editor responded by asking, "But will it make room for a younger man — or will that job disappear?" And so it continued.

The *Mansfield Chad* had no such concerns. Implacably anti-strike and hostile to the NUM from the very start, its owner, Ian Linney, was an ideologically-committed free marketeer and placed his newspaper at the service of the Government and NCB. The *Chad* attracted particular loathing from strikers for its bias and the complete absence of balance in its coverage of the dispute.

Freelance cartoonist, John Clark, AKA 'Brick', who worked for the paper during the strike and was eventually sacked for his pro-strike artwork, says of the influential Linney clan, "They are bastards and still powerful in the county. As their weekly pocket cartoonist, I was a freelancer and wrongly presumed that, whatever anybody thought about Scargill's handling of the ballot issue, the paper would be perceptive enough to at least support the striking communities. After all, they were the *Chad's* readers and buyers. WRONG! I had complete editorial control of my cartoons, producing four possible ideas for selection every week, but during the build-up and strike, I offered them nothing but cartoon ideas around the issues. The one that finally got me sacked now seems limp, but it is the only one I still have a record of."

The *Nottingham Evening Post* took anti-strike propaganda to an even greater level. Its Managing Director, Christopher Pole-Carew, was a notorious anti-union figure. He was despised by trade unionists throughout the county for his sacking of twenty-eight *Post* journalists during the National Union of Journalists' (NUJ) strike of 1978. The NUJ had called the strike in defence of poorly-paid journalists on other newspapers in the north. Although the *Post* reporters were, apparently, satisfied with their own pay, they decided to show solidarity with their fellow members by joining the strike. As former *Post* editor and biographer of Pole-Carew, Barry Williams, put it, summing up the *Post* strikers' position in his admiring account of his boss, "What else was a trades union for but to fight for the less fortunate and exploited among its membership and how could that battle be won without total support, solidarity and absolute loyalty to your union?"

'THEY RUSHED US UP HERE THAT QUICKLY, SARGE, I THINK HE'S GONE DOWN WITH A TOUCH OF COACH-LAG....'

Williams was close to Pole-Carew. Indeed it was the union-busting executive who had brought Williams back to the *Post* as its editor, and in Williams' biography of Pole-Carew, he went on to say, "What on earth was the point in going on strike for £1200-a-year less than you were already being paid and why would you repay the goodwill and generosity of the best employer in your industry by withdrawing your labour when you had no quarrel whatsoever with your own bosses?"

Nevertheless the *Post* journalists stuck by their union, came out on strike and were immediately dismissed by Pole-Carew. The aftermath saw the NUJ derecognised at the *Post,* with the pro-strike Nottinghamshire NUM crying in vain, six years later, as it struggled to receive a fair hearing in the pages of the County's most widely-read newspaper.

There had always been a great deal more than just a whiff of Victorian paternalism about the *Nottingham Evening Post*: its people were relatively well-paid and enjoyed better conditions than many of their counterparts at other regional papers. In return, Pole-Carew demanded absolute and unconditional loyalty. A cowed and compliant workforce, with now no trade union to represent them, were ruthlessly managed by the unrepentant MD, and by the time the miners' strike arrived there was little chance of Nottinghamshire's NUM loyalists receiving a fair hearing.

Williams, as editor, retrospectively laid out his position, and the one which the *Post* would adopt, in his 2007 memoir, *Ink in the Blood*. "So who, now, did my paper support? The majority of the nation's miners who were striking for their survival or the minority in Nottinghamshire who were crossing picket lines to carry on working? It was a classic no-win situation. Whichever side I supported I was going to anger a lot of people and to experience the intensity of local feeling was to know that this would be no small matter of fleeting upset. Any stance I took was, for better or for worse, going to remain identified with the *Nottingham Evening Post* for many years to come.

"This was most definitely not to be rushed and for a while I sat unashamedly on the fence. I got to know the UDM leaders, Roy Lynk and David Prendergast — who had become national household names — really well. I listened very carefully to their arguments. I also listened very carefully to the arguments of Henry Richardson, the leader of the Nottinghamshire NUM. These were all decent, principled men — just as the miners they represented, from their different sides of the conflict, were decent, principled men."[36]

Williams is incorrect here; the UDM wasn't formed until the end of 1985, after the strike had finished, and while Lynk, Prendergast *et al*, were clearly agitating for the breakaway quite some time prior to its formation — despite indignant denials — they were, at the time of the strike and for its entire duration, officials of the NUM.

In any event, the strike-breakers were the side to receive the *Post's* favour and support, with Williams explaining, "Finally I was swayed by two points...

1. The [soon-to-be] UDM miners were exercising their fundamental human right to work in the face of appalling daily violence having taken a democratic local vote (which Arthur Scargill never did) to do so. Stripped of all the understandable emotion, right was *surely* on *their* side.

2. I agreed with Roy Lynk and David Prendergast that striking would only eventually weaken the miners and if they were going to stand up to Margaret Thatcher and fight to save their industry they had to be strong. She was, almost certainly, very pleased that they were striking and that they were being led by Arthur Scargill with his transparent ambition to bring her down because that allowed her to present the fight as good old British democracy versus alien Communist oppression and when push came to shove there was only one of those two horses that Joe Public would back."[37]

Possibly the passage of time addled Williams' memory somewhat because there was no discernible fence-sitting by the *Post*. As early as 6th March the paper was happy to place alleged violence by striking miners front and centre, irrespective of the wafer-thin evidence in support of its lurid claims. "Showdown!" screamed the front page headline of that day as a "Post Reporter" breathlessly reported on the erection of barriers outside Hobart House in response to an "alleged stoning incident at a police line." Unnamed NCB officials were quoted stating, "A deputy engineer was hit in the face by an object thrown by a picket outside the Yorkshire Main colliery, near Doncaster." Quite what the "police line" had to do with the "deputy engineer" was not apparent (unless it was a typo and was intended to read 'picket line'). Neither were there details of names, arrests or anything approaching proof. The tone was set and the *Nottingham Evening Post* was quite content to toe the line set by its Tory counterparts on Fleet Street.

Tucked away at the end of the piece was a brief comment by "NCB Officials" insisting that "no pits in the Nottinghamshire Area are under immediate threat." The next day, 7th March, Simon Greaves reported that "The threat of widespread strikes by miners loomed large today after the Coal Board's announcement of a new round of job and output cuts — including a 900,000 tonnes cutback in the South Notts coalfield." The last word went to NCB South Nottinghamshire Area Deputy

Director, Harold Taylor, who insisted there would be no pit closures in the Nottinghamshire and Derbyshire Areas, at least for the forthcoming year. There the matter rested.

One might imagine any self-respecting newsman would contrast the information in his possession with the statements from the relevant officials and ask searching and probing questions. This was typical of the *Post's* reporting during the strike: reports of violence by pickets went entirely unchallenged as did NCB statements on the Area's future, no matter how contradictory or incompatible with the facts they might be.

Williams and his intrepid band of provincial reporters weren't above lending support to any quarter and indulging in astonishing hype, no matter how unlikely or insubstantial, as long as such parties were firmly on the side of the working miners. Thus on Saturday 10th March, the paper led off with the headline "Petticoat Pickets" and a story about the wives of working miners who were prepared to "... take on Scargill's men." The wife of a working miner from Moorgreen pit, Jane Paxton, was photographed in suitably defiant pose, with child on hip, speaking of her determination to form a "women's cooperative" to face down the pickets intimidating and bullying their beleaguered husbands. The no doubt formidable Mrs. Paxton, displaying an impressive grasp of the substantive issues and long-term implications of the strike, complained, "Since the overtime ban started we've lost between £25.00 and £30.00 a week. If the men are forced out of work [by pickets], we'll have just £32.00 a week."

Readers would have searched in vain for a balancing story on the wives of striking miners and the very real social phenomenon of the Women's Support Groups. Tales of hardship that would outstrip anything the poor Mrs. Paxton could ever have imagined were plentiful but went entirely unreported.

Two days later, the *Post* had elevated Jane Paxton to the lofty heights of "Notts Miners' Wives Leader." The implication that she spoke for all Nottinghamshire's miners' wives was met with disgust by strikers and their wives alike. In a reference to the contemptuous nickname bestowed upon Nottinghamshire miners, during the General Strike of 1926, one striker's wife declared Paxton's working husband and his fellow strikebreakers, to be "Jelly Babies." In response to that day's headline, "More Join Petticoat Protest", strikers acidly commented on the calibre of men happy not only to betray their union and their class but to hide behind women's petticoats while doing so. Whatever such statements lacked in understanding of women's oppression and the patriarchal nature of class society, they lacked for nothing in conveying the disdain with which the working miners were viewed by their striking counterparts.

Finally, on the same day, the paper published its first official editorial comment on the strike. Considering the preceding fortnight's reports of the unfolding dispute, it contained few surprises. Headlined "Sad Day For Democracy In The Pits", the line was predictable. While grudgingly acknowledging the NUM's right to take action in defence of their members' jobs and futures — even going so far as to concede Scargill had been correct in his predictions around the 'hit-list' — the bulk of its fire was aimed squarely at the strikers' use of "disgraceful intimidation" and assorted crimes. Scargill, the readers were told, had "no right to shut down pits by sending in squads of intimidating pickets where the miners want to vote properly on the issue before them." The reality that Scargill had sent no miners anywhere and that from the very first moments of the strike, picketing had been, and continued to be, controlled and organised from below by the membership, didn't fit with the *Post's* anti-Scargill agenda. So it was ignored.

Twenty-three years later Williams had modified his anti-strike and anti-Scargill position. In *Ink in the Blood*, he wrote, "Ask me now, more than twenty years later, if I was right to support the UDM and I'd have to say honestly that I don't know.

"What did become clear, after those poor beaten strikers had crept like thrashed dogs back to work, was that on one crucial point the much-maligned Arthur Scargill *had* been right all along... Mrs. Thatcher's Government *had* been privately determined to rid Britain of the pits and of the coal miners who toiled so proudly in them and all the Conservatives' public protestations to the contrary had been bullshit." The most worthless currency of all, wisdom after the event, was something Williams would struggle to spend in Nottinghamshire.

In 1984, as far as the *Post* was concerned, the gloves were off: not a word of the violence carried out by police against strikers was to be found. Nor, for that matter, the lockdown of pit villages throughout the County or the false arrests and illegal stop-and-search of striking miners. The paper really hit its stride with its headline, "Siege Fury." Readers learned that "Police were pelted with bricks and lumps of wood and local miners [working miners, of course] were punched and kicked as more than 1000 flying pickets tried to close down the coalfield."

The sight of yet another newspaper attacking their struggle was soon forgotten by the strikers as 2nd July heralded another setback. In the Area Council elections, following the pattern set by the previous month's Branch elections, Nottinghamshire's pro-strike officials were wiped out. At Ollerton and Blidworth, for example, not a single striking miner had retained office. At both pits, the entire Committee was replaced by working miners. John Liptrott crowed with delight and again demanded the resignation of Richardson and Chadburn. Speaking to the *Mansfield Chad* on 5th July, he went on to say, "I think without a doubt they should resign now. People keep asking for Thatcher and MacGregor to be removed and probably justifiably, but they should also ask for Richardson and Chadburn to go. They are as removed from their membership."

Jimmy Hood, deposed Ollerton Branch Secretary, pointed the finger at the NCB for their "disgraceful interference" and claimed the Board had produced posters to oil a "propaganda machine" levelled against pro-strike officials. He raged, "The pit elections had nothing to do with democracy and nothing to do with fair play. The Coal Board propaganda machine meant the men at work were bombarded with this propaganda and it has been absolutely disgraceful. I think there are a number of reasons why men have voted the way they did but the influence of the NCB has been major."[38]

Hood lost with 330 votes to strike-breaker, Ernie Vallance, who polled 542.

Given the NCB's conduct throughout the dispute, it's likely Hood was correct in his accusations of interference and bias. However, he surely grossly overestimated its impact. The working miners were as committed to wrecking the strike as the strikers were to its success and the fact that they were working in the first place meant it was unlikely they would have voted for pro-strike officials anyway. The Notts Working Miners' Committee had worked tirelessly, as they had in the run-up to the Branch elections the preceding month, to convince their fellow strike-breakers that unseating the strikers was necessary if 'democracy' was to be 'restored' and the Area 'reclaimed' from the 'Scargillites'.

The results were replicated across the coalfield. Ollerton's Delegate, Pete Crawford, went down to Eric Flint by a margin of 246 votes, though the Branch President, Dennis Walker, ran his anti-strike opponent to the wire but still lost by seventy-four votes.

At Thoresby collicry, the Branch's striking President, Jim McGinley, was ousted by Ken Smalley by 423 votes. He was joined in exile by both the Branch Secretary and Delegate.

Rufford Colliery only had one striking miner who held office, Mick Walker, and he was slaughtered in his bid to win re-election, polling just eighty-one votes to his rival's 683. The rest of the officials, all of whom were working, were re-elected.

Blidworth, which had polled the highest percentage of votes in the Nottinghamshire Area in favour of strike in the March ballot, completed its swing to the right by seeing off its militant President, Doug Wood. He was toppled by Anthony Fox who polled 183 more votes than his outgoing President. As with Thoresby, both the Secretary and Delegate were ejected.

The carnage continued: Mansfield re-elected both their working President and working Secretary but swapped their striking Delegate, Gerry Todd, for a strike-breaker, and Bilsthorpe had the dubious distinction of boasting an entire Branch committee of strike-breakers, all of whom were re-elected by crushing margins.

The Area Council elections saw exactly the same picture emerge at twenty-nine of the Area's Branches. Twenty-nine of the Council's thirty-one seats were won by strike-breakers.

The implications and consequences were far-reaching. Of immediate impact was the damage done to the strikers' cause. No one attempted to put a positive spin on what was, by any criteria, a heavy defeat. The propaganda value alone was of immense worth to the working miners and they made the most of the changed situation: the pressure on Henry Richardson and Ray Chadburn to resign was ramped up and it was clear, even at that relatively early stage, that their dismissal or sanction was now only a matter of time.

On a practical level, this was bad news indeed for the rank-and-file strikers. Area funds were now in the hands of the strike-breakers and even the meagre sustenance they'd been able to count on from sympathetic Branch officials was, at least officially, now cut off. With the wholehearted support of Lynk and Prendergast, the balance of power in the coalfield had swung irrevocably in favour of the strike-breaking majority.

Of equal concern were the attempts by the new Area Council to deny strikers legal aid in the event of arrests. This took even the most hardened of loyalists by surprise: that representatives of a trade union body could even contemplate deliberately serving up their own members to the state's legal machinery was unprecedented. Fortunately for arrested miners, Chadburn's ruling, as President, that the strikers were indemnified and entitled to access to the Union's legal support was sufficiently thorough and by-the-book to beat off the vigorous challenges of the strike-breakers.

Possibly one of the most significant effects of the working miners' electoral landslide didn't really make itself felt until after the strike. Chadburn foresaw the problem at the time, when he scoffed that the new officials "couldn't negotiate a half-a-crown rise out of an idiot." What might have seemed a severe case of sour grapes was a shrewd assessment. A great many of those swept into office on the dual tides of anti-strike antipathy and anti-Scargill hatred were simply not up to the jobs they'd been elected to do. Many had never even attended a single NUM meeting and had shown little or no interest in their Union's affairs until caught up in the hysteria whipped up by the Notts Working Miners' Committee and their fellow travellers. The grassroots infrastructure of the Nottinghamshire NUM was severely damaged by the simultaneous election of so many new officials. These were men who not only had little or no idea of how to conduct themselves in their new roles, or best represent the men they aspired to lead — such was their towering inexperience — but some even struggled with the basic literacy and numeracy required to deal with the administrative minutiae that is often the union rep's tedious lot in life. With such an overwhelming number coming to office simultaneously, it was inevitable that the Area machinery would break down, and it frequently did.

Brian Evangelista, then the Deputy Manager of Moorgreen, says of the period after the formation of the UDM, "The big change was at Area level where people became leaders of a new union overnight, and who would probably have never reached that rank in the National Union of Mineworkers. And, I suppose, you could loosely term them opportunists. And that's being kind. You'd have lads who thought there was something to be made if they could get on in the Union. There are one or two names spring to mind who were absolutely utterly useless; useless at their jobs and useless as union officials. 'Oh, I'll go and tell the manager this! I'll go and tell the manger that!' By the time they'd finished, the men had less than they'd had before they went in. That's the sort of people they were."

There was also an unexpected backlash against the Notts Working Miners' Committee. Many of the strike-breakers, despite agreeing with the Committee's aims and objectives, had refused to become officially involved in its activities. Some, like David Amos, because they found something not quite right about an unofficial rival structure operating alongside their Union, and others deeply embarrassed by Butcher, Clarke and Liptrott's unashamed fraternising and collaborating with the miners' natural enemies: Conservatives, millionaire anti-union businessmen and questionable intelligence figures. Once the July elections had turfed the strikers from office, many strike-breakers simply saw no need for the NWMC. It had fulfilled its brief and helped deliver the Area back into the hands of the working majority. It was now redundant. While Clarke and Liptrott continued with their offensive against the striking miners, and their attempts to wreck the strike, if anything, intensified, the NWMC was now a busted flush. With little now to offer its Conservative backers, save for a residual propaganda value, its days as a potential rallying point for a mass return to work were over.

The publicity-hungry Butcher, something of a Walter Mitty character, continued his coalfield tours, but his acrimonious split with Clarke and Liptrott and his resulting departure from the Committee of which he had been the creator further diminished the effectiveness of the NWMC.

The strikers had a brief respite before the next act in the Nottinghamshire drama unfolded. On 8th July thousands of them and their families and supporters gathered on The Forest to relax in the sun, enjoy a pint or two and listen to bands at the 'Food for Victory' rally. A joint initiative by the two Nottinghamshire Strike Centres (Ollerton and Mansfield Road) and Sheffield Trades Council, the event saw a huge convoy of vehicles from Yorkshire travel down to the historic Goose Fair site to deliver hundreds of food parcels to the strikers and the their families.

At the same time, on the bank of the River Trent, Nottingham CND was holding its large annual peace festival and the two events, in a show of mutual solidarity, swapped speakers and sent delegations to the respective gatherings.

The following day, 8th July, saw extraordinary scenes at Berry Hill. The newly-constituted Area Council was scheduled to meet to discuss motions and proposals for the forthcoming Special Delegates' Conference. On arrival, the Council members were thwarted as dozens of striking miners occupied the building with an estimated 400 forming a blockade outside the Union's premises, intended to deny the strike-breakers access and prevent the Council meeting going ahead.

The move was a guerrilla action on the part of the strikers to prevent the Council mandating their Delegates and issuing voting instructions for the Special Delegates' Conference. This was a bold move by the loyalists: if the Council couldn't meet then no mandate could be imposed on the Delegates, all of whom were strikers and all of whom had been elected and chosen *prior* to the Area Council elections. In line with the NUM's rules, in such circumstances, the Delegates would then be free to mandate themselves and vote freely according to their personal convictions.

The most contentious issue to be debated at the Conference was a proposed rule change, designed to enable the NEC to discipline miners who had crossed picket lines and defied the NEC's ruling that the strike was official and should be supported by all its members.

Inevitably, the new Area Council would have mandated its Delegates to vote *against* such a change. The loyalist Delegates, however, would have baulked at such a prospect. The occupation was intended to free them from their mandate so that they could vote *for* the rule change, which would then have seen virtually all the Nottinghamshire Area's new Branch officers and Council members disciplined by the NEC. In terms of its limited objective, the blockade and occupation was a success. The police were forced to turn away the arriving Council members to maintain the peace and the Council meeting was abandoned. The *Nottingham*

Evening Post reported, in its 9th July issue, "A police spokesman said there had been no arrests and the men had been generally well behaved." Presumably this uncharacteristically accurate account was deemed insufficiently hostile to the strikers. The next day, with almost admirable *chutzpah,* the paper was back on form when it shamelessly contradicted itself and informed its readers that, "More than 300 angry strikers forced police to call for riot shields to protect them from bricks and other missiles being thrown."

The retaliation from the working Area Council members was swift. Just twenty-four hours later, seventeen signatories took an application for an injunction to the High Court. To the surprise of no one, the judge, Vice Chancellor Sir Robert Megarry, ruled that the postponed Area Council meeting must go ahead, prior to the special Delegates' Conference. The ruling further instructed that the meeting should take place in secret, if necessary, to avoid further disruption by striking miners.

In an unprecedented display of interference in the internal affairs of an independent trade union, Megarry went on to order that should the Area Council be unable to reconvene in time, and officially mandate its twelve Delegates, then the Delegation *must* vote *against* the proposed rule change.

To the astonishment of partisans on both sides of the divide, the imperious Vice Chancellor even threatened to ban the entire Sheffield Conference if the Area Council meeting didn't go ahead. Chadburn was staggered and protested that it would be "impossible" to recall the Council at such short notice but his pleas fell: the ruling stood.

In a parallel action, a second group of working miners also attended the High Court and won an order for possession of the Berry Hill Headquarters. In the end, it seemed that the occupation had been little more than a pyrrhic victory.

As usual, both Richardson and Chadburn found themselves condemned by both the Right and the Left. John Liptrott told the *Daily Telegraph* on 10th July that "These two officials have gone to ground. The situation is that the Area General Secretary and the President, I firmly believe, do not want this Area to have a vote at the Sheffield Conference." The supporters of many of the far-left journals, on the other hand, particularly *Socialist Worker*, accused the Area leadership of 'vacillating' and 'twisting and turning.' In reality, it was the attacks from the working miners that were accurate: neither Chadburn nor Richardson especially wanted the Delegation to vote against the rule change. As supporters of the strike, their sympathies lay with the occupiers of Berry Hill but as elected officials they felt they couldn't be seen to endorse such 'unconstitutional manoeuvres' and 'illegal stunts'. The armchair Trotskys screamed treachery and cowardice but Scargill knew exactly what he and his Nottinghamshire leaders were doing. As Richardson recounts, "Arthur told me time and time again, 'Henry, whatever you do, don't *ever* break your mandate or break any rules. The slightest excuse and they'll have you out.' He was right. Me and Ray had to tread a very fine line and with the majority of the Area calling for us to be sacked, we had to be careful or Notts would have ended up with not one single Official who supported the strike."

Regarding the occupation, both Chadburn and Richardson knew exactly what was planned. As Jimmy McDowall, a striker from Linby pit and one of the men involved in the action, recalled, chuckling, "We were in there and Henry was sneaking us in fish and chips through the window!" Had the working miners learned of this, Richardson would have been dismissed instantly for gross misconduct.

Richardson continues, "Arthur were brilliant. He knew it killed me to vote for scab mandates but he always said, 'we know you're on the right side but the rules are the rules; you *have* to carry out the mandate you've been given.' So that's the position I was in. It were all very tactical."

On 11th July, as NUM Delegates gathered in Sheffield, they found themselves in an unusual position; certainly one that no trade union had ever found itself in previously. Megarry had decided not to press ahead with his threat to ban the Special Delegates' Conference. What he had done, instead, was to rule that no discussion of, or change to, Rule 51, the leadership's proposed amendment to permit the disciplining of those working against the strike, be allowed.

Scargill was in typically defiant mood. "There has been a lot of talk about 'democracy.' I have noted that those who are most vociferous are editors of newspapers or non-elected judges. They include such public figures as Vice Chancellor Sir Robert Megarry, who is now openly trying to run the affairs of our organisation. I would hope that Conference rejects this blatant state interference." Conference did. Delegates backed their President, ignored the judge and the agenda proceeded as planned.

Once the agenda item to discuss Rule 51 arrived, the Delegates demonstrated their contempt for interfering judges, strike-breakers and those who sought to undermine the principals of collective trade union solidarity: on a card vote, the motion was passed by 166,000 to 62,000 to adopt the proposed changes. Henry Richardson and Ray Chadburn voted *against* the proposal. Hardliners were apoplectic and the Nottinghamshire leaders were once again savaged by the more unhinged elements of the Trotskyist left. Further accusations of scabbing, treachery and cowardice were cast down upon the Nottinghamshire General Secretary's head. As is all too often the case, it was left to the rather more sober commentators of capital's flagship journals to spell out to the ultra-left what had *really* happened.

In reality, Chadburn and Richardson, after full consultation with Scargill, had pulled off a brilliantly audacious piece of brinkmanship. As the *Financial Times* of 12th July explained, "The decision by the leaders of the Nottinghamshire Area, Mr. Ray Chadburn, the Area President, and Mr. Henry Richardson, the Area Secretary, to vote against the rule change proposed by the leadership, was acknowledged by all sides yesterday to be a shrewd tactical move.

"First, it cuts the ground from under the working miners' charge that they have been denied their democratic rights in the Union and effectively answers the case they [the working miners] put to the High Court.

"Second, it still got what many of the working miners thought the Notts Area Leaders in any case wanted. The rule-change went through. Though working Notts miners last night were insisting that the 166-62 vote, in favour of the rule-change, was too low.

"Thirdly, it effectively discharged the first order made by the High Court against Mr. Chadburn and Mr. Richardson: to hold a meeting of the Notts Area NUM Council in order that Delegates could be mandated to oppose the change."

While the fact that the rule change had been discussed at all meant that, technically, Richardson, Chadburn and the entire NEC were in contempt of court, the working miners had been completely wrong-footed and were now themselves in an awkward position. While judges have the power to act independently in cases of contempt, in practice they very rarely do so. The usual custom is for the plaintiffs, in this case the Nottinghamshire working miners, to return to Court and request the judge impose penalties. However, given that the strike-breakers' substantive complaint had been answered, to press on with clamours for fines or even imprisonment of the leaders of their own Union would be to hand a propaganda triumph to Richardson, Chadburn and the NUM leadership. Such a move would undoubtedly have been interpreted as an act of spite, contrary to all the principles and traditions of the labour and trade union movement. While all the actions of the strike-breakers, thus far, had certainly been 'contrary to all the principles and traditions of the labour and trade union movement', to press for contempt was felt to be a step too far and one that could well lose the working miners the support and goodwill they had, hitherto, enjoyed among a significant swathe of the public.

This was something their solicitor, David Negus, was forced to reluctantly acknowledge. In a statement following the vote, he said, to snorts and jeers of derision from strikers, "My clients are not interested in blowing the NUM apart, if that can be avoided." He continued, "The Notts leaders' move presents the working miners with a ticklish conundrum: do we press for contempt, given that our basic grievance has been settled, and that we genuinely don't want to worsen the situation? Or do we just let the NUM leadership off the hook?"

Negus and his clients decided that discretion was the better part of valour and decided to let the matter rest. In any case, they consoled themselves: the NUM could not enforce the new rule without falling foul of the Court and risking huge fines under the earlier ruling, delivered in response to Clarke and Liptrott's application, that no miner could be sanctioned by the NUM for crossing a picket line.

The general consensus was that the strikers had won a significant tactical victory. But the cruel summer of 1984 was still a long way from over.

Chapter 8:
State of Shock

"The likelihood that your acts of resistance cannot
stop the injustice does not exempt you from
acting in what you sincerely and reflectively
hold to be the best interests of your community."
SUSAN SONTAG

After nearly eighteen weeks on strike, Nottinghamshire's strikers remained as committed as they'd ever been. Ollerton militant Rob Wells spoke for many when he said, "We'll stay out until hell freezes over, if necessary. There's no way we'll ever give up."[39]

Equally, the position of the strike-breakers showed little chance of softening. While picketing continued at all Nottinghamshire's pits, even the most dedicated striker knew there was no chance of picketing bringing out the Nottinghamshire miners: things had gone too far for that ever now to be a realistic possibility and with the electoral landslides of June and July behind them, the mood of the strike-breakers was positively upbeat.

"They were totally brazen," says Keith Stanley, with a hint of amazement in his voice. "They were actually *proud* of scabbing. It was unbelievable." While there were still some who slunk shamefacedly into work and who would drop their heads and stare at the pavement if passing a striking colleague, there was definitely a pugnacious mood about the working miners; sometimes from the most unlikely quarters. "Mr. Denis Beeston, for one," remarks Jimmy McDowall, sardonically. Beeston had been a miner for most of his working life and came from a large family of fellow-miners. During the strike, he was based at Linby colliery and was fond of regaling people with tales of his militancy during the 1974 strike. "Oh aye," scoffs MacDowall, "He were supposed to have put windows through on scab lorries in '74 and he lived off that for years. He were a union man but I reckon Stacey-King and Fells [leading strike-breakers from Linby] got to him and he fell in with that lot."

Beeston was a good example of the sort of brazen attitude among the working miners to which Stanley refers. Happily waving his wage packet from the safety of the 'scab bus' as it wound its way through the Linby picket, Beeston mocked his workmates as they stood helplessly on the picket line, staring in disbelief. Had this been any other working miner, there wouldn't have been anything particularly remarkable about such behaviour; indeed such actions were commonplace among Nottinghamshire's working majority. What was unusual in Beeston's case was that he'd been a committed Labour Party member for decades. Since the early 70s, he'd represented Bestwood Village on Gedling Borough Council, to date serving an unbroken run of forty-one years, which makes him the County's longest-serving Labour councillor. In 2009 he was awarded the MBE, receiving his medal from Prince Charles. Beeston said of his trip to Buckingham Palace, "It was really exciting, visiting the Palace and meeting Prince Charles. And he was brilliant, a really nice bloke."[40]

Crossing a picket line was no cause for complaint in Kinnock's New Model Party and Beeston's political career continued on its merry way: untouched and undamaged by his conduct during the strike.

Beeston was contacted by this author for his further thoughts but declined to make any response.

Neil, or 'Kneel', Kinnock, as he was known to many miners, led a very different Labour Party to that which had existed in 1974. Following its electoral hammering in 1983, he was determined to rid the Party of all that he felt rendered it unelectable. To thousands of constituency activists and the Campaign

Group of MPs, this meant jettisoning the socialist principles which they believed constituted the Party's core base. In reality, Labour had always been 'capitalism's second XI.' Its 1945 Government was the closest the Party had ever come to anything even remotely socialist. The fabled 'broad church', Labour had always been a battleground between left and right and, in Kinnock, Party moderates felt they'd finally found the man to see off the Bennites and the hard-left: those it held responsible for the disaster of the 1983 election, its manifesto described by Gerald Kaufman as "The longest suicide note in history."

Nominally of the soft-left, those clustered around *Tribune,* the speed at which Kinnock hurtled to the right induced travel-sickness even among his most fervent supporters. The ferocity with which he tore into the Left, too, made many gasp.

The previous year, 1983, had seen the editorial board of the Trotskyist weekly, *Militant,* expelled from the Labour Party. *Militant,* as represented by the editorial quintet headed-up by Peter Taaffe, was deemed to be in breach of Clause II, Section 3 of the party's constitution: it was found to be a 'party-within-a-party', and as such was unconstitutional and ineligible for membership. The defence of Taaffe and his comrades was that *Militant* was only a newspaper and that he and the several thousand *Militant* 'supporters' inside the Labour Party, were merely that: supporters of a journal which reflected views perfectly compatible with Labour Party values.

Of course, on one level, this was nonsense. Militant was a great deal more than simply a weekly Trotskyist newspaper: by the time of the miners' strike its members, not 'supporters', not only controlled many District and Constituency Labour Parties throughout the UK, and it had also seen two of its number, Terry Fields and Dave Nellist, elected to Parliament as Labour MPs.

However, there was a huge degree of hypocrisy where the expulsion of *Militant's* editorial board and the subsequent Kinnock-led purge of its members was concerned: the Labour Party had many organisations, any of which could equally have been described as a 'party-within-a-party.' Right-wing group-ings, though, were perfectly acceptable, it seemed. Militant's *real* crime was to be unashamedly socialist and, worse, to wield an impressive degree of influence among the Party's hard-left, particularly where its Young Socialist section was concerned.

From then until 1987, Taaffe's Trots led a high-profile campaign against the Government's rate-capping policy and, with Liverpool City Council firmly under its control and supported by tens of thousands of the City's trade unionists and Labour Party members, presented an implacable opposition not just to Thatcher but to Kinnock and his attempts to 'modernise' the Party.

In a display of tactical ineptitude, eclipsing any of those of which he frequently accused Scargill, Kinnock chose not to place himself and the Labour Party at the head of the Liverpool Councillors' fight, or to link it to the miners' strike and forge a powerful working class opposition to Thatcher's attempts to both destroy the NUM and neuter left-wing Local Authorities. Instead, he preferred to split the Party and, egged on enthusiastically by the Government and the Conservative-supporting press, embarked on a highly damaging witch-hunt of the Left. As Militant predicted, such a campaign would not be confined to just its members but would be extended to take in other socialists deemed to be a threat. So it proved and supporters of *Socialist Organiser* and others were also hounded from the Party.

Against such a backdrop, it was inconceivable that the miners would receive anything more than barely lukewarm support from the Labour leadership, and Kinnock's feeble attempts to draw a distinction between the hated Arthur Scargill and the miners themselves was doomed to failure.

On a personal level, he detested Scargill and all he represented. Kinnock believed that Scargill, like Militant, was wrecking the Party's recovery and terrifying the voters. In reality, the miners, along with the Liverpool City Councillors, enjoyed huge public support, and had Kinnock thrown the Party's full weight behind their respective struggles a different outcome might have occurred in both cases.

There is little doubt that Kinnock's undermining of Scargill, his continual agreement with Thatcher in condemning picket line violence, while saying little or nothing about the ferocious police brutality meted out to pickets, was a significant factor in the miners' defeat. It also gave the green light to right-wing union leaders like Hammond, Lyons and Sirs to instruct their members to cross NUM picket lines.

It was to Kinnock that the working miners would turn for support, with Colin Clarke telling the *Daily Telegraph*, on 10th July, "Mr. Kinnock has clout and I feel it would count for something if he tried to restore democracy in Nottinghamshire."

At the grass roots, though, things were very different, and local Labour Parties and individual Party members played a significant supporting role. Even in Nottinghamshire, where the dispute threw up startling contrasts and saw councillors who were also striking miners, like Gordon Skinner, brother of Dennis, pitted against fellow Party members, like Denis Beeston, who crossed picket lines, the degree of support was impressive.

The County Council was led by Dennis Pettitt, a shrewd and canny political animal. While no socialist by the definition of most, he was an extremely astute tactician and during his stewardship the strikers saw him leading his ruling Labour group in skilfully steering through policies which were very much to their material benefit. For example, free school meals were provided for strikers' children, even during the school holidays, which aroused fierce opposition from the Conservatives.

Pettitt went on to explain, "Whatever the rights and wrongs of the strike and the way it is being operated, it is of paramount importance that we consider the welfare of the children. The majority of people in the county would not want the children to suffer."[41]

This was vintage Pettitt. The implied criticism of the strikers, a sop to the Group's right-wing, was balanced with an appeal on behalf of the miners' suffering children. Thus both Left and Right were placated and the 'non-political' language, which disguised an initiative favourable to the county's striking miners, was eased through.

For the Right, attacking or opposing such a move would have appeared mean-spirited and churlish in the extreme. After all, what politician, of either left or right, would wish to appear to be snatching food from the mouths of hungry children? Certainly not the Labour Right and its strike-breaking renegades. The Conservative Party, on the other hand, had no such scruples. The Leader of the Opposition, Caroline Minkley, slammed the move as a "dangerous precedent."[42] In an attempt to block Pettitt, she unsuccessfully tried to level a charge of political bias. "It is a dangerous area we are moving into when we involve children in a strongly political scene. No balanced adult would wish to see any child suffer because of a decision taken by his father. We have children who are provided, rightly so, with free meals because their parents will not shoulder their rightful responsibility and others who qualify for free meals because of low family income or unemployment.

"This County Council should be seen to represent the views of *all* ratepayers. To appear to be supporting one side of a national dispute is a dangerous precedent, even if a child is used as the innocent means."[43]

The crafty Pettitt's response was merely to shake his head sadly and reflect on the coldness of those who would seek to deprive innocent cherubs of grub for the sake of political capital.

In vivid contrast to Kinnock and the Party leadership nationally, Nottinghamshire's Labour Councillors also displayed little reticence in calling the police to account for their treatment of the county's strikers and residents. On 12th July, a specially convened meeting of the County Council's Police Committee was the scene of some extraordinary exchanges.

Labour Councillor Eric Carter ripped into Charles McLachlan with a venom that left Councillors on both sides of the chamber stunned. Carter had clearly spent considerable time in putting together a prepared statement from which he read. Opening with a spirited polemic directed at the Prime Minister and her Government, he went on to declare that the miners' strike had been engineered by the Tories for the express purpose of destroying the NUM as a prelude to wiping out British trade unionism. To outraged heckles from the Conservative benches, he went on to accuse McLachlan's Nottinghamshire force of being willing and conscious political agents of Thatcher. "A large police presence is probing into the everyday acts of ordinary citizens and a dangerous precedent has been set. The police are being shamefully used, not to catch criminals, but as a strike-breaking force."

To the fury of the Conservatives and McLachlan himself, the recalcitrant Carter thundered on. "When I see these roadblocks, my mind goes back to the Germany of the 1930s." Carter, though, had only just warmed up. Describing as "deplorable" the situation that had led to a "corruption" of the judicial system, he slammed the granting of injunctions given to the working miners' leaders as evidence of a grave "threat to British justice and British democracy."

Pointing the finger at the county's Chief Constable, he demanded McLachlan take full responsibility for the acts of violence and disruption occurring around the coalfield and for behaving irresponsibly with the policing budget as laid down by the Authority. The Nottinghamshire force was engaged in costly operations which were entirely unnecessary: policing the dispute was costing the ratepayers £150,000 per week, concluded Carter as the chamber descended into uproar.

To rub it in, all attempts by McLachlan and the pro-police Conservatives to respond to Carter's remarks were ruled out of order by Carter's Labour colleague, the Committee Chair, Frank Taylor. With either a highly-developed sense of gleeful irony, or its complete absence, Taylor instructed the committee that only the financial implications of the dispute were the Committee's business and, therefore, only remarks pertaining to that aspect would be permitted.

The gagged Tories fumed and blustered through the remainder of the meeting until they could vent some spleen afterwards. Councillor Peter Wright described Carter's diatribe as "quite distasteful" and, speaking on behalf of the Conservative members of the Committee, declared full support for McLachlan and his officers.

As for McLachlan himself, he argued that all operations were necessary, even those away from the picket lines, to prevent "intimidation". He was, he insisted, acting entirely on his own authority and had received no instructions from the Government. Perhaps reflecting the Nottinghamshire Force's preferred style of policing, the Chief Constable angrily retorted that Councillor Carter needed "A damn good kick up the arse!"

Nottingham City Councillors, too, were not averse to getting up Tory noses as they sought to do their bit for the strikers' cause. On 18th June, the Council's Licensing Sub-Committee granted the issuing of permits to striking miners for the purposes of street collections for "... the duration of the present trade dispute between the National Union of Mineworkers and the National Coal Board."

The permits were issued in response to an application from the strikers based at one of the coalfield's two strike centres: the 'Notts Central Strike Fund', based at Mansfield Road in the City.

143

In addition, a number of other permits were issued to the Nottingham NUM Strike Centre, the Women's Support Group, Hucknall and Linby Women's Action Group, Hucknall Miners' Hardship Fund, Sherwood Women's Support Group and the Forest Fields Striking Miners' Support Group.

Tory Councillor Bernard Bateman was singularly unimpressed, describing the decision as "ludicrous" in a statement to the *Nottingham Evening Post*. "They [strikers] are being treated better than a number of local charities. These permits were only granted on the strength of a political vote," harrumphed the Conservative member. Possibly the Nottinghamshire public felt that politicians making political decisions was not quite the scandalous outrage Councillor Bateman clearly felt it to be. He hadn't quite finished, though. "Even the Royal Midlands Institute for the Blind — the oldest charity in Nottingham — is only allowed one day per year for a street collection. Here we have a situation where the miners on strike, who do not represent a charity, can collect wherever they please! It's ludicrous."

The Councillor's ire was further roused when the nominal conditions imposed on the strikers, not to collect in certain areas of the City Centre, were routinely ignored by miners and a blind eye was turned by the Council's enforcement personnel. "I've seen collectors in the Broadmarsh Centre and in the Victoria Centre!" spluttered the angry Bateman.

The police, still smarting from the mauling doled out to their boss at the recent County Council Police Committee meeting, chipped in with support for the Tory Councillor. "Rather unusual" was how Superintendant Dennis Adams characterised the Council's decision. "The granting of these permits appears to indicate a degree of political judgement in a quasi-judicial function," he observed. In contrast, presumably, to the entirely non-political policing of picket lines and the granting of non-political injunctions to working miners.

Unfortunately, the Nottinghamshire strikers' small run of good luck was soon over. On 18th July, the seventeen working miners who had won the injunction from Vice Chancellor Megarry preventing the NUM's Special Delegates' Conference from discussing or amending Rule 51, had the last laugh.

After careful consideration, the strike-breakers, on the advice of their brief, David Negus, decided not to press for contempt charges to be brought against Richardson, Chadburn and

Scargill. Instead they returned to the High Court to argue that as Conference had discussed matters in defiance of Megarry's previous ruling then the resulting rule change was illegal. Megarry agreed and ordered the NUM to desist from disciplining any of its members under the new amendment. It was, he declared, "Void and of no effect. Those who defy a prohibition ought not to be able to claim the fruits of their defiance."

Defiance was the operative word where Scargill was concerned. With his customary disdain for 'class justice' the NUM President airily dismissed Megarry's ruling. "The NUM amendment to rule was passed in accordance with the rules and constitution of the Union. That decision stands. It has the authority of the membership of the NUM, and will be operated and applied if and when circumstances warrant." Even the intransigent Scargill, though, could not prevent the Nottinghamshire Area Council from extracting its revenge on their stubbornly persistent pro-strike officials.

On 23rd July the newly elected Area Council held its first meeting since the Branch and Area elections of June and early July. Having been prevented from meeting by the occupation of Berry Hill, the new Council wasted little time in attempting to bring Richardson and Chadburn to heel. Electing the Area Executive from its numbers, the strike-breakers created what they felt was an unassailable position for themselves with all twelve of the Executive places going to working miners.

The meeting was acrimonious and the atmosphere was described by Keith Stanley as "poisonous." Henry Richardson was first in the firing line. The Area General Secretary stubbornly reiterated his support for the strike and was howled down by the assembly. Bloodied but unbowed he continued to insist that he had been entirely correct in calling upon the County's miners to support the strike and claimed he was acting well within his rights as an official of the NUM in accordance with its rules and constitution.

It was then Chadburn's turn. The Area President, who had been a lay official and then full-time officer of the NUM for over twenty years, did little to hide his contempt for scabs and for those who, he believed, were incapable of leading a trade union with even a modicum of competency. The ill-tempered exchanges grew increasingly heated until the fuming Chadburn lost his temper, openly mocking his opponents and challenging the working miners to find one among them capable of taking his place on the NEC.

The stormy proceedings eventually came to a close, after an astonishing six-hour span, with the Area Council declaring the strike in the County unofficial and unconstitutional. No striking miner anywhere in Nottinghamshire would be supported by the Area NUM nor would they be entitled to any funds for prosecuting and/or sustaining the strike. To hammer home the message, Richardson and Chadburn were expressly forbidden from making any further statements, either written or verbally, in support of the strike. This was an instruction both men would ignore, ultimately at the cost of Richardson's position as Area General Secretary.

For a brief, tantalising moment, it looked as though the miners were set to see a second front opening up in their struggle. On the 9th July a national dock strike was called in protest at scab labour employed by British Steel, used at Immingham to unload iron ore. But yet again, the much-vaunted support and solidarity action promised to the miners amounted to considerably less than the sum of its parts. The strike was called off just two weeks later, on the 24th.

In the same month, talks between the NUM and the NCB were dashed upon the rock of just one word: 'beneficial'. The NUM argued that a precise definition of 'beneficial' must be settled before agreement could be reached. If pits were to close because they couldn't be 'beneficially' developed, did that mean because they had exhausted their reserves or were unsafe? Or did it mean that the Board couldn't 'beneficially', i.e. economically, develop pits according to the rigged strictures of profit and loss as determined by them and the Government? The NCB refused to be pinned down and the latest round of negotiations fell apart.

Dave Douglass makes some interesting observations regarding the July talks.

"This was probably the closest we came to a virtual victory: the agreement would have withdrawn *all* pit closures and redundancies. It would have granted amnesty to all sacked or arrested miners. It would have put in place a joint conciliation board to review closure plans and no pit would be closed in which the coal could be beneficially developed.

146

"Had we agreed to this, it would have been a tremendous victory, the other side would certainly have been given a God Almighty bloody nose. Time could be bought to build on the position, especially in Nottingham, were we could demonstrate that action and solidarity gained results. We could have started to sort out the infrastructure and do a campaign of education and coordinated propaganda at pits.

"Would the other side come back with closures? It's hard to see how they could come back and argue that twenty-five or thirty pits couldn't be 'beneficially developed' though they might have tried a more gradual approach, pit-by-pit. If we had nailed to the floor that there would be no loss of wages during the period of review and nobody lost anything by going to the wire with every pit threatened with review, they could never expect to close more than one a year, even less maybe. Meantime remember what the strike was about. From Thatcher's point of view she would have *lost*, the NUM would *not* have been destroyed. In fact it would be immensely strengthened. The wind would have been in our hair.

"That's certainly one way of looking at it. Arthur, though, was fearful of the body-swerve which they gave us in 1981 when they backed off from the closure plan in response to mass strike wave then. He wanted a copper-bottomed agreement. But did we actually need one at the risk losing all the concessions gained? Would they *really* have come back a third time, and would it *really* have been so impossible to mobilize everyone again having demonstrated twice in three years we could force them to back down? How close we came at that time, cannot be underestimated."

On the 19th July, Thatcher made her now-infamous speech to the Tory backbench 1922 Committee where the miners were dubbed 'the enemy within', and on the 22nd the founding conference of Women Against Pit Closures took place.

July drew to a close with the focus shifting to South Wales. The Welsh miners were fined £50,000 for contempt of court. What, many wondered, would be the response of the South Wales NUM? No one had to wonder for long as their President, Emlyn Williams, gave Scargill some competition in the defiance stakes. The South Wales men refused to pay the fine and dared the enemy to do its worst. It did, and the entire assets of the South Wales Area NUM were sequestrated.

147

By August, the sixth month of the strike, militant miners had developed a number of illegal tactics to push the dispute forward. While most felt that violence did little to serve their cause, others deployed tactics including sabotage, terrorising of individual strike-breakers and the destruction of NCB and personal property. For these men, many of whom had drawn revolutionary conclusions during the preceding months, insurrectionary and guerrilla warfare was seen as a legitimate response to the violence and oppression of the state and its institutions. As one anonymous, now elderly, retired miner, who claimed to have been a member of the 'South Notts Hit Squad', explained, "They hit us and we hit 'em back twice as hard. We were only doing to them exactly what they were doing to us. That's fair. The only difference is that they were allowed to break the laws they said we had to obey while they tried to beat us. Well, they could piss off with that plan as far as we were concerned."

Referring to the assault of Sid Richmond, a seventy-year old retired miner who had seen his car window smashed by police, who then proceeded to drag him through the driver's side-window, before punching and kicking him and taking him away to the cells, the former South Notts Hit Squad member went on to explain, "It were war. Plain and simple. They did that to Sid and worse to other lads. They smashed up our cars and told lies about us in Court. Our families were intimidated, harassed and beaten-up. The coppers, scabs, media, Government and the Coal Board thought it was OK to steal our funds, stop benefits to starve us back to work. So why shouldn't we fight fire with fire?"

On the 6th August the *Nottingham Evening Post* treated its readers to their first glimpse of the Hit Squad. The paper claimed the Squad consisted of over a hundred strikers. My source merely smiled, winked and tapped the side of his nose when asked to confirm or deny that figure.

Described as a "commando-style raid on the National Coal Board Depot at South Normanton," the *Post* reported an anonymous spokesman for the South Notts Hit Squad claiming responsibility for the operation, which had caused "thousands of pounds of damage to sixteen vehicles."

Apparently, the readers learned, the Squad had a "hit-list" of working miners' leaders and intended to "inflict physical and personal damage." The spokesman went on to pledge that further attacks and acts of sabotage on NCB property and the homes of strike-breakers were planned.

Remaining cautious, my source would only speak in the general. "We carried out quite a few 'hit-and-run ops' as we called 'em. Mainly at night and everything was meant to hinder the enemy and cause 'em as many headaches as possible." Examples? "Oh, things like sneaking into pit-yards and cutting the power into the pits, wrecking cars and lorries and that, that were used to get scabs into work. Other things like retaliation. So if one of our lads was, say, grassed up by a scab for something he didn't do, we'd put the scab's windows in at his house. You need to remember that if a striker got in a fight with a scab, the striker would get sacked and that happened to loads of lads. Nowt ever happened to the scabs, though, see? So we had to terrorise 'em and learn 'em that their actions had consequences."

The Squad eventually just faded away. "It all got too much, what with all the other stuff going on. By autumn, most of us were too busy just finding enough snap to feed the kids. Plus we were picketing all over the place, raising money and that. We only had so many hours in the day."

Nearly thirty years later, our retired Squad member has no regrets. "I'd do it all over again tomorrow, kid. If me knees would let me! Like I say, it were war and all's fair in war, so they say. If we'd done them things in Nazi Germany, they'd have put up statues of us and give us medals. Thatcher wanted us wiped out so we just fought back. I'll never think that was wrong."

Meanwhile, the rest of August saw the majority of Nottinghamshire's strikers pursuing more conventional and traditional methods of resistance. On 10th August, the miners' Delegates again convened in Sheffield to hear an update from the NEC on the latest round of failed talks. Among the other items on the agenda was a resolution reaffirming the amendment to Rule 51, passed at the previous Conference: it was carried overwhelmingly.

Of greater controversy was the decision of the Nottinghamshire Delegation to boycott the gathering. A last-minute meeting on the eve of the Conference saw the working miners vote by twenty-seven votes to three not to attend. They stated that by attending they might find themselves in breach of the very injunction they themselves had brought against the Area and National Leadership. Chadburn publicly stated, "Personally, I think they should go to represent the Area's views." In reality, the Nottinghamshire President was baiting his strike-breaking members and daring them to back up, at Conference, all they were only too willing to say when safely ensconced in their home county. "Definitely," agrees Chadburn, readily. "They were always finding reasons and excuses not to attend Special Delegates' Conferences, from the strike right through until the breakaway. They knew the reaction they would get!"

Chadburn's assessment was shared by the recently-deposed Cresswell Delegate, Alan Fidler. "An out-and-out disgrace," he declared of the decision to stay away. "They are using the pretext of legal action not to attend. The real reason is that they are frightened men, quite prepared to go on television but afraid to come to a Conference like this."[44]

The following week, NCB Deputy Chairman, James Cowan, made a plea to Nottinghamshire miners. He spoke of the "unlimited reserves" there to be mined in a coalfield with a glittering future and professed his deep admiration for the County's working majority. "I have lived with miners all my life and grieve for the suffering being caused when I consider it unnecessary." He promised "... we will look after them when they come back. Because we are compassionate people ..." His intervention was greeted with much sneering in loyalist strongholds throughout the County.

Cowan was soon forgotten as the trial of Yorkshire Main picket-leader, Terry Dunn, drew to a close at Mansfield Magistrates' Court. Dunn had been beaten, assaulted and arrested by police during the 'Siege of Blidworth'. His crime was to be a Yorkshire picket staying with striking miners in Blidworth. There, McLachlan's officers had demonstrated admirable versatility: not only by breaking the law they were obligated to uphold, but by making up new ones on the spot. Dunn's hosts had also been arrested for the 'crime' of 'harbouring Yorkshire pickets.'

In yet another demonstration of corrupt practice, all the police claims of 'intimidation' and 'violence' collapsed amid a welter of contradictions, counter-claims and non-existent witnesses. Nevertheless the unfortunate Yorkshireman was found guilty of 'threatening behaviour and abuse'. The fact that said behaviour only occurred *after* he was falsely arrested and assaulted by the police seemed to count for naught. Dunn was found guilty and conditionally discharged for six months.

Summer was now over and striking miners all over the UK prayed for a long drawn-out and freezing winter. With Nottinghamshire's working miners now in a position of incontrovertible strength, the Government and NCB were slowly but surely reducing the number of cards the NUM had to play. The legal actions were mounting, meaningful support from the TUC had not materialised and still the dispute was only half-way through.

Chapter 9:
Wrapped Around
Your Finger

*"It isn't the rebels who cause the troubles of
the world; it's the troubles that cause the rebels."*
CARL OGLESBY

Despite the Government's and NCB's claims of miners flooding
back to work, the vast majority of NUM members were still
holding the line when September arrived. The NCB's 'back to
work' campaign, despite the herculean assistance afforded it by
the Notts Working Miners' Committee, had largely flopped.
Tactics then switched to placing a working miner in every pit.
Says Dave Douglass, "In September what happened to the mass
roving picket is two-fold: the more rank-and-file orientated
Strike Committees, based particularly in the four Yorkshire
regions, which had been given their heads to wild guerrilla
actions, had been rounded up into the more controlled
Central Area Committee, which reflected a more moderate
complexion.

"Secondly, the state had then gone onto the offensive
against the pickets with their own second-front strategy of
placing a scab in every pit in the country [England only]
which drew the flyers back into their own back yards and

drew the mass ranks of police occupation and war on the striking villages with them. This was even more so after the courts ruled that pickets could only picket their own pits, and after that they couldn't picket *any* pits, at which point the women took over the picket lines."

Any society based upon property relations produces inevitable class antagonisms, as two sets of conflicting interests — labour and capital — grind against each other. In times of relative prosperity and civil calm, the true purpose of the police and the machinery of the state are masked. The miners' strike ripped that mask away and laid bare its *real* purpose: to preserve the existing economic and social order *by any means necessary*.

The boundaries that normally exist between the separate and distinct agencies of the state became blurred and overlapped during the strike. The NCB, the employer, encroached far beyond its usual 'peacetime' remit and intruded into every aspect of people's lives. It took on some of the functions of a police force in its social policing of the coalfield communities. A fight between a working miner and striker, outside NCB property and outside working hours, would inevitably result in the striker's dismissal, usually deemed 'gross industrial misconduct.' Altercations in pubs and clubs saw the striking party summoned to the pit manager's office and the 'offender' disciplined. Hearsay 'evidence' and the uncorroborated word of the working miner were usually sufficient.

Kevin Parkin's experiences were typical of hundreds of striking miners. From mid-February through to the first couple of weeks of the strike, Parkin had been 'on the sick', waiting for a minor surgical procedure. For those first few weeks, he'd watched the build-up and followed the news closely.

He says, "I decided to get meself down to the picket line and talk to the lads; see what were going off and get the news." Quickly, Parkin decided to come out on strike. "But I were still on't sick, like, so I told the doctor I wanted off the sick and he said, 'but you're not fit for work; you could be signed off for another three months, easily.' I told him I wasn't going back to work, I was going on strike. I felt I should be with me mates and it weren't right me getting paid while they were getting nowt, I couldn't have that on me conscience, so I came off the sick and went straight on strike."

For the next few months, Parkin became heavily involved in picketing and all the other activities typical of pro-strike NUM activists. He was twenty-seven at the time and the young miner from Linby colliery quickly established a reputation as a committed and militant loyalist. Described by a colleague as, "A bloody good lad, Kev; solid, principled and gutsy, but a bit lively, if you know what I mean."

At the end of September, he became embroiled in an altercation with a working miner following a Friday night out at his local Miners' Welfare.

Says Parkin, "It were just after chucking-out time and this lad, Tony Fish his name were, from Hucknall pit, came up to me with his missus. We'd been mates, used to play pool and darts and that. Anyway, he were shouting, 'We're the men, here! Working men, not like you wankers!' He'd been working from the start, like. So I followed him round to the car park and said, 'What you saying that for? We're supposed to be mates and we're fighting to keep your jobs.' Well, he went for me, then. He leaned around his missus to get at me so I just decided to get the first one in, like; left-hook, decked him and down he went. Anyway, I picked him up and said, 'Look, mate; just get in your car and get off. Just leave it.'

"Two of my mates were there: Bill Bailey — Big Bad Bill from Butler's Hill — and Andy 'Archie' Newbold. They come round to the car park to see what were going off and this other youth just came flying out of nowhere. He just dived straight in at Bill. He were like a rabid dog! He were tussling wi' Bill; had him pinned up against the car. Bill hadn't hit him yet, they were just wrestling, like.

"Anyway, he broke away from Bill and put Archie on the floor. Anthony Sissons, his name were. We found out later he'd been in the army and he were just going mental! He ended up with a boot print on his chest from when he'd got Archie on't floor. Archie just lunged up wi' his foot; to keep the youth off him, defensive, like. Course, it all got swung around in court, later on: just lies from him, the prosecution and everybody.

"So I dived in 'cause Bill would've killed him. He were twenty-six stone, were Bill. I'm trying to pull 'em apart and as I grabbed him [Sissons], he grabbed me hand and bit it. He locked on and I couldn't get him off. Like I say, he just came from nowhere: he were a rabid dog! He took a chunk clean off.

He wouldn't let go, I had to physically batter him to get him off.

"I thought no more of it, at the time, it were just a Friday night. Anyway, Tony Fish's dad worked at Hucknall pit as well so first thing Monday morning he goes to the pit and reports the incident and it just went from there."

Parkin then received a letter summoning him to the manager's office but, in keeping with the NUM's usual practice at the time, he was advised not to attend and, instead, send his union representative to deal with the matter. "Henry [Richardson] said, 'No problem,' and he went to sort it out."

By this time, the police had been informed and charges were quickly levelled against the three striking miners: Parkin, Bailey and Newbold. The working miners, Fish and Sissons, were not charged with any offence.

Parkin continues, "So it just went from there. I got my letter on 10th October 1984, telling me I'd been sacked. The case hadn't even gone to court, at this time! It wasn't until April '85, after the lads had all gone back, that the case came to court. I were charged with affray and GBH and Archie and Bill, I think, got the same. They then reduced it to just GBH. I got found 'not guilty' but I were still sacked! Never got me job back and that were that."

Neither Fish nor Sissons lost their jobs or faced disciplinary action of any kind.

Similarly, the police intruded far beyond its usual remit and took on some of the functions of management: occupying pit offices and producing photographs and evidence of alleged offences to management to facilitate the sacking and disciplining of militants. As author and miners' advocate, Martin Walker observed, "What miners across the country [UK] experienced was a cooperative moral and political assault upon their behaviour within the community by the police and the NCB. While management extended its power within the social relations deeper into the community, the police extended their influence into employment practices and management."[45]

Those who decry such analysis as anti-police and the spoiling of a fine institution by a few bad apples fundamentally miss the point regarding the role and purpose of the police, and the state in general. Undoubtedly there were, and are, 'good' police men and women. Indeed Les Dennis remarked on the generally kind and thoughtful behaviour of police from Liverpool and South

Wales, for example. Officers from these constabularies fetched pickets fresh fruit and drinks and treated striking miners with friendliness and courtesy *but they were still policing an industrial dispute*: a civil matter that should not have concerned them. But as an *institution* the primary role of the police was, and always is, to *protect, uphold and further the interests of capital.* In the particular case of the miners' strike, this was even more pronounced. Thatcher had courted the Met, approved substantial wage increases and greater funding and ensured that, even on an individual level, the majority of officers consciously identified with her credo and willingly and enthusiastically carried out their historically allotted tasks.

It's common to dismiss claims of this nature as little more than left-wing paranoia. For those so inclined two very different publications make for informative reading. The first, *Police*, the official journal of the Police Federation, in its March 2009 issue, devoted to the miners' strike on its 25th anniversary, contained an article by Michael Downes, the then Vice-Chair of the West Yorkshire Police Federation. Downes wrote, "The police became the enemy having been used as political tools of the government to suppress the working man and policing by consent ceased to exist; policing was opposed and despised by local people who had previously been proud of their local police service, prior to the miner's dispute."

The former police officer, of mining stock himself, wrote of "despicable behaviour" and his disgust with "officers who boasted of burning £20 notes in front of the pickets; of new cars, caravans and house extensions they had paid for by endless overtime made available from central government, while I saw decent, proud and hard-working men and women lose their life savings, homes and self-worth. Some individuals had shamed themselves, the uniform but moreover the communities they were meant to serve."

The second publication, *The Guardian* on 12th October 2013, revealed that: "Police colluded in secret plan to blacklist 3,200 building workers." Reporter Daniel Boffey went on to write that: "Police officers across the country supplied information on workers to a blacklist operation run by Britain's biggest construction companies, the police watchdog has told lawyers representing victims. The Independent Police Complaints Commission has informed those affected that a Scotland Yard inquiry into police collusion has identified that it is 'likely that all special branches were involved in providing information' that kept certain individuals out of work."

In *The Origin of the Family, Private Property and the State,* Engels reasoned that: "Because the state arose from the need to hold class antagonisms in check, but because it arose, at the same time, in the midst of the conflict of these classes, it is, as a rule, the state of the most powerful economically dominant class, which, through the medium of the state, becomes also the politically dominant class, and thus acquires new means of holding down and exploiting the oppressed class..."

Thus, during the strike, hitherto unrelated arms of the state coalesced and united in the urgent task of breaking the strike and the serious threat that it represented; communicating to wider society that security, prosperity and continuing employment are only ever temporary, as the right of business to make profit must be absolute. Miners and their families asked why should *their* livelihoods and the future prospects of *their* children be sacrificed on the altar of profit? Why should working people unthinkingly accept a life on the dole, penury and fear so an artificial balance-sheet can show a net gain in a column on a spreadsheet? Shouldn't any system of economic organisation serve the majority of the people? In reality, the miners learned, quite the reverse was the case: they were disposable, dispensable units in a process that enriched the few at the expense of the many; and so the greater the violence of the state in its attempt to break the strike, so the resistance of mining communities became ever more intense in response.

From September on, the violence escalated as entire villages took on the appearance of occupied territories with an invading army prepared to go to any lengths to enforce the Government's will. The use of burning cars, barricades, battering-rams and missiles all increased dramatically as the "insurrectionary insubordination" of the strikers — for which MacGregor promised vengeance when the war was over — spread across the coalfields.

After six months on strike, and some frustrating near-misses at the negotiating table, a settlement now looked as far away as it had ever been and the Government continued to hammer away relentlessly at the absence of a national ballot. This was the issue that just would not die. Inside the NUM there were some growing uneasy and restless with the perceived lack of progress. Here, too, many committed loyalists were starting to regret not holding a ballot earlier in the summer. Or even earlier, in May.

"Looking back, I think it was a mistake not hold a national ballot," agrees Eric Eaton. "We'd have won it easily and it would have taken away the scabs' excuses." Indeed, Gallup and MORI polls taken on three separate occasions during the first four months of the strike showed a clear majority of miners in favour of strike action. Dave Douglass takes a similar view to Eaton's. "Tactically, we probably should have had a ballot, yes. Earlier on, while the mood was solid and the pickets were flying. But would it have stopped Notts scabbing? Some of them obviously, but the majority? No, I don't think so. What it would have done, though, was remove one of the sticks that Thatcher and Kinnock used to beat us with." Douglass, a consistent and longstanding advocate of the NUM rank-and-file, goes on to say, "But what could we have done, really? The *men themselves,* remember, voted not to have a ballot. For good or ill, it was the democratic decision of the rank-and-file."

Despite these facts, the absence of a ballot was the gallows upon which Scargill's critics continued to hang him. Scargill points out that, in stark contrast to the avalanche of disinformation and outright untruths that have prevailed for nearly thirty years, "McGahey, Heathfield and I were aware from feedback that a slight majority of areas favoured the demand for a national strike ballot; therefore, we were expecting and had prepared for that course of action with posters, ballot-papers and leaflets. A major campaign was ready to go for a 'Yes' vote in a national strike ballot. McGahey, Heathfield and I had done the arithmetic beforehand, and were truly surprised that when the vote was taken [Special Delegates' Conference, 19th April 1984] delegates rejected calls for a national strike ballot and decided instead to call on all miners to refuse to cross picket lines — and join the 140,000 already on strike."[46]

It still hurt the cause, though. Nottinghamshire had had no intention of joining the strike and the absence of a national ballot was all the excuse the Area needed. In turn, this fed the excuses of leaders of other unions who, in response to accusations of scabbing, simply pointed out that while NUM members were breaching their own picket lines, how could the miners expect others to respect their sanctity?

One of the problems was that the ballot question had quickly turned into a litmus-test of class machismo. As early as the April NEC meeting, the course had been set by those like the South Wales Area President, Emlyn Williams, who told his fellow Executive members, "To hide behind a ballot is an act of cowardice. I tell you this now: decide what you like about a ballot but our coalfield will be on strike and will stay on strike." A week later, at the Special Delegates' Conference, the General Secretary, Peter Heathfield, in his opening remarks, told the miners, "I hope that we are sincere and honest enough to recognise that a ballot should not be used and exercised as a veto to prevent people in other areas defending their jobs."

The ballot, then, had quickly become the dividing line. Even among committed strikers, to even raise the question was to invite accusations of 'going soft' or 'wobbling' and was seen as tantamount to treachery. Williams and Heathfield were correct but they, and the rest of the strikers, had allowed the ballot to become a matter of unbreakable principle and not the purely tactical consideration it should have been.

Picketing, too, was starting to be seen as an ineffective tactic in the new modern era of virtually unlimited police powers. In reality, picketing in and of itself was as legitimate and potentially effective as it had always been. The problem was in its application. Clearly, the huge set-piece picket line confrontations and mass blockades, à la Saltley Gate, when faced with formidable police numbers with the equipment, training and lessons of Northern Ireland behind them, and unlimited governmental license, were inadequate. Although, later, the Chief Constable of Yorkshire, Anthony Clement, revealed just how close the miners had come to shutting down Orgreave, conceding that " if mass picketing had continued after 18th June, the police would have had difficulty in keeping the plant open."[47]

Dave Douglass comments, "That was doubtless true but, like the Tet Offensive in Vietnam, neither could we [continue]! The only difference is the Yanks didn't know that whereas I think Clement did. We had no more bloody bones and liberties to throw back onto the line in the numbers of the 18th, especially since it had meant the total haemorrhaging of pickets from docks and wharfs and Notts and Leicester etc."

159

The hit-and-run picket, though, the lightning strikes of well-organised bands of men moving quickly from pit to pit, catching police unaware and stretching their resources, had proved impressively effective. By September, post-Orgreave, however, without the huge numbers of sympathetic trade unionists swelling the pickets' ranks, as seen at Saltley Gate, in many cases the miners were merely reacting to events, with the initiative having passed largely to the police as they pressed the strikers back into their own villages and communities.

Despite all this, the strikers were still, for the most part, in buoyant mood. For all the frustrations stemming from picketing failing to bring Nottinghamshire out, overall, picketing had still done its job: the increasingly exaggerated claims of the NCB of miners 'flooding' back to work were simply not true. The numbers of miners returning to work were still merely handfuls.

Nottinghamshire loyalists took consolation from the fact that elsewhere commitment to the cause remained unbroken. Mardy pit, for example, the Rhondda Valley's last remaining mine, was not alone in its proud boast that not one single miner had worked for even a single shift for the entire duration of the dispute. At the start of the strike, one-man picket lines were all that had been required to turn away dozens of vehicles by merely displaying placards bearing the inscription 'Official NUM Picket'. At several Welsh pits, as in Yorkshire, no picketing at all was undertaken: it wasn't necessary. The Nottinghamshire strikers envied such unswerving loyalty and could only imagine how it must be to strike with 100 percent backing from one's comrades and the wider community.

By contrast, Nottinghamshire miners had ensured their county had given Britain the phenomenon of the 'Tory miner'. In the General Election of 1983, barely eight months before the strike started, the newly-created constituency of Sherwood was won for the Conservatives by former Nottinghamshire County Councillor, Andy Stewart. What was remarkable about Stewart's victory, albeit by a majority of just 637, was that it occurred in a constituency containing ten working pits and the highest concentration of miners, per head of the population, of any constituency in the UK. The Labour Party was stunned and its candidate, the public school-educated, Oxford graduate, Willie Bach, denied a parliamentary career, eventually went on to join the Lords as a Peer in 1998 (interestingly, Bach is the great-nephew of none other than Emily Pankhurst).

The facts were indisputable: thousands of Nottinghamshire miners had voted Conservative. The newly-elected Stewart rubbed it in, crowing that he might even end up becoming the first NUM-sponsored Tory MP. Not quite as ridiculous as it might have sounded, Stewart proved the result was no fluke. In the first post-strike General Election, he went on to *increase* the Tory majority to 4,495 in 1987.

The warning signs had been there for some time. In a by-election in 1977, in neighbouring Ashfield, the hitherto rock-solid Labour seat fell to the Conservatives. Admittedly, the Labour candidate, Michael Cowan, did neither himself nor his Party any favours. Cowan was an unpopular and divisive figure in the local labour movement. Described by one Nottinghamshire labour movement insider as: "... he could be one of the best speakers there was and [he] had a brilliant mind. But he did little work in the seat, leaving a very bad impression."

The scale of the loss was staggering. A previous Labour majority of 22,915 was obliterated by the Conservatives' Tim Smith to take the seat by just 264 votes.

Cowan ended up a Nottingham City Councillor, eventually crossing the floor to join the Tories. No matter how bad the impression he created, however, it's difficult to imagine just one man being responsible for throwing away one of the safest Labour seats in the country. Again, the votes of Nottinghamshire's 'Tory miners' were decisive, with most commentators in agreement that this was also a protest by highly-paid Nottinghamshire miners at Labour's Social Contract depriving them of still higher earnings.

Mansfield constituency also reflected the rejection of traditional class loyalties by significant numbers of Nottinghamshire miners. The seat, which contained the NUM's Nottinghamshire Area HQ, saw Labour's previously considered impregnable majority hacked to just over 2,000 in 1983. Again, proving that Stewart's win had been a conscious political decision on the part of Nottinghamshire's miners, when the election of 1987 rolled around, Alan Meale barely managed to hold Mansfield for Labour in the face of an evaporated majority: the smallest majority in the UK at that time, just fifty-six votes kept the Tories out.

For any thrusting, ambitious, newly-minted Tory MP, a constituency in the heart of the Nottinghamshire coalfield during the miners' strike was a dream come true. The opportunities for raising one's personal profile and the priceless publicity were virtually endless. The rest of the new Tory intake must have envied Stewart his place right at the centre of the action. Not only that, but the strategic importance of Nottinghamshire to the Government and NCB war-effort meant Stewart enjoyed unprecedented access to the seat of power, his audiences with the Iron Lady herself unheard of for a mere backbench grunt. Stewart took full advantage and quickly inserted himself into the latest skirmish in the Nottinghamshire civil war.

At the tail end of the previous month, the NCB had sought to weaken the NUM still further by bribing the Nottinghamshire Area to call off the overtime ban in return for a lump-sum backdated settlement of the previous autumn's unresolved pay-claim. The final offer had been 5.2 percent, and if the overtime ban could be broken in the County, the propaganda value alone, never mind the significant increase in output, would be incalculable. Henry Richardson was contemptuous and described the offer as, "a bribe and an act of sheer desperation." For a while, the strikers were distraught: there was little doubt in anyone's mind that the working majority would seize the opportunity to inflict yet another damaging blow to 'Scargillism' and at the same time line their pockets still further.

For once, the working miners responded cannily and considered the implications of taking the cash. Their leaders were now being advised by a shadowy cabal of right-wing lawyers, Tory businessmen and spin-doctors. The move could well backfire and, horror of horrors, actually end up bringing more men out on strike. Those already deeply concerned about the strike-breaking leaders' links with the natural enemies of the trade union movement, might see the acceptance of the bribe as one betrayal too far.

Liptrott asserted there was little chance of his Sherwood members voting to end the ban although he conceded there was a sizeable minority in favour, as the overtime ban was costing them a great deal in lost earnings. He was quite happy to take the NCB's cash, he said, but not in return for ending the overtime ban. Enter stage-right, Andrew Stewart MP, the Honourable Member for Sherwood.

Stewart issued a statement calling on the Government to give the Nottinghamshire working miners the cash anyway, with no strings attached. "It would be no more than the action of a good employer," said the MP. If the Board moved first and made the award as a "gesture of good will" it would open the way for the men themselves to vote in their respective Branches to end the overtime ban. "It must be seen to be democratic, just as they democratically voted to continue working in the first place," he stated.

In a move that no one thought coincidental, the day following Stewart's statement, 30th August, saw Ian MacGregor himself visiting Nottinghamshire for the first time. The whistle-stop tour, which took in visits to Hucknall and Bentinck pits and Bestwood Workshop, gave the NCB chief ample opportunity to lavish praise on the working miners, thank them for their efforts and condemn the mob rule of the violent strikers. All predictable stuff and nothing that hadn't been said many times previously. The fact that it was being said, in person, in the Nottinghamshire battleground was perceived by the Left as an attempt to sweeten the bribe. It was seen in the same light by the working miners, too.

Ultimately, the proposal was rejected. Clarke, Liptrott and company had learned quickly and knew that such a move had potential to blow up in their faces and, possibly, push some working miners out of the pits and back onto the picket lines. Their efforts to break the strike and the NUM on behalf of the Government and NCB could not be jeopardised.

All the way through the dispute and even up to the break-away to form the UDM, the working miners reacted indignantly to any suggestions that they were doing tho Gov ernment's dirty work for them. All they were concerned with, they continued to insist, was 'restoring democracy' to the NUM and fighting for their right to work in the absence of a national ballot. They refused to accept that their actions were designed to break the NUM. Yet such claims couldn't withstand even a moment's objective scrutiny.

By September, the Nottinghamshire majority had won a landslide victory in the March Area ballot, in June they'd swept striking Branch officials from office and in July they'd completed the rout by taking twenty-nine of the Area Council's thirty-one seats and all of the Executive's twelve seats. They'd been working consistently for seven months and had absolute control of the Area machinery. One might imagine that such a slew of victories would easily slate their thirst for 'democracy'. And yet they continued to hammer their Union with legal actions, injunctions and prohibitions, all of which were damaging and costly to the NUM. They even tried to have striking miners thrown out of the NUM for being in financial arrears with their membership subscriptions. John Liptrott had written to his striking Sherwood members advising that they were no longer members of the NUM as they had run up subscriptions arrears. He went on to claim that the Area rule book automatically excluded those who were in financial arrears. Henry Richardson then wrote to Peter Heathfield asking for clarification. The ruling was clear: all strikers were, and would continue to be, members of the NUM. Furthermore, Liptrott was instructed to write to all his members retracting his previous statement or face disciplinary action.

Things had gone way beyond the stated aims of simply regaining control of the Area and ensuring Nottinghamshire's 'democratic' voice was heard. This was now a conscious and active campaign to break the NUM, destroy the strike and witch-hunt its supporters. With the full might of the state, and all its constituent parts, determinedly prosecuting the Conservative Party's political offensive, what on earth did the working miners think their efforts would achieve, asked the strikers, if not to decisively aid those very objectives?

Disingenuous claims of intending no damage to the NUM and the constant rejections of the accusations of aiding Thatcher were not credible. These were not stupid men and they were being advised by seasoned and skilled legal experts, sympathetic to the Government's cause. No Nottinghamshire working miner could claim not to be aiding the Government and the NCB. Many found it impossible to believe the working miners didn't know exactly what they were doing and what the implications were for the NUM and the strike in general. Henry Richardson sees things a little differently. "That was true for the ringleaders but not necessarily for the majority. Most of 'em were led by the nose and didn't think further than their next wage; as long as they could keep on earning, they didn't really

164

bother, even though they were helping the Tories, whether they knew it or not."

To the humiliation of the working miners' leaders, and in strong support of the strikers' accusations regarding their strike-breaking colleagues, Stewart had pulled off what he thought would be a powerful PR coup for the working miners. Understanding little of Nottinghamshire politics, he ended up making matters worse for his collaborationist charges when he asked Margaret Thatcher to send a personal letter of thanks to the Nottinghamshire majority.

Copies of the handwritten note were sent to all thirty-one of the Area's Branch premises and polarised opinions still further. Written on official Downing Street notepaper, dated 15th September 1984, it read, "A Personal Message to the Nottinghamshire Miners: Andy has been to see me today and let me know your views. May I say how greatly I and most other people appreciate what you're doing. You are an example to us all, Margaret Thatcher."

The uproar was immediate. All over the County strikers howled their fury and waved copies of the note on picket lines as cringing miners went into work. Others, with grim satisfaction, welcomed the note as proof positive of their assertions and wasted no time in confronting strike-breakers to say, 'I told you so.' "She had 'em wrapped around her finger," says Ray Chadburn.

Either defiantly or with an incomprehensible lack of tactical nous, some working miners responded favourably to the Prime Minister's words of praise. At Ollerton, the recently-elected working Branch Secretary, Jonah Porter, who had replaced Jimmy Hood, said, "The letter is a show of gratitude and the men will be cock-a-hoop after this. They need all the support they can get because it has been very tough on them." While many of his fellow strike breakers winced at Porter's servile response, likened by one militant to that of a slavish attack-dog receiving a condescending pat on the head from its mistress, others were equally grateful, with the Branch Secretary's namesake, Geoff Porter, adding, "This is very welcome. The working men need all the praise they can get. This will help them to keep going, knowing that their work is appreciated." In a statement one could be forgiven for assuming was deliberately crafted to incite anger and demonstrate political

165

ignorance, Porter went on to claim, "But this does not mean we are taking sides in a political battle."

The strike-breakers' ringleaders, however, were furious. This was most assuredly *not* the sort of support they wished to be made public. They'd gone to great lengths to try and keep under wraps the links they'd forged with right-wing anti-trade union interests and sympathetic Tories, all the while denying their activities were political or designed to help the Government. At a stroke, Stewart and Thatcher's clumsy intervention had handed the strikers a significant moral victory and a PR triumph.

Liptrott was aghast and stiffly responded, "The letter is not what we want at the present time. She should have sent it to the press or to the public in general."

Stewart defended his and the Prime Minister's actions. "As far as I'm concerned, it is no more than ninety-five percent of the population of this country would expect the Prime Minister to do." In that, he was correct: no one, either left or right, held any illusions that the Conservative leader didn't appreciate the working miners' efforts to derail the NUM on her behalf. The damage was irreparable: the working majority had gone way beyond the conventional definition of scabbing and had ended up in the camp of their own union's ideological enemies. All of which made Clarke's and Liptrott's frequent protestations that no breakaway was being planned sound dubious, if not derisory. And even if the duo were granted the benefit of the doubt, Roy Lynk was certainly aiming for exactly such an outcome. The ground was being prepared. With every passing day, with every additional attempt to strangle their Union in the courts, with every calculated move not just to keep on working but to prevent the strikers from exercising *their* right *not* to work, Lynk, Prendergast and their agents in the Notts Working Miners' Committee were on an inevitable trajectory to reconstruct a Spencerist trade union in Nottinghamshire. And they knew it.

September was a month of high drama. Talks between the NUM and NCB had restarted positively on 9th September, only to collapse again on the 15th, with MacGregor still unyielding on the central question of closures.

On 28th September, the NUM's hopes for solidarity action or a second front opening up were yet again raised and then dashed as the second national dock strike ended and on the same day the High Court handed down yet another anti-strike ruling: the strikes in Derbyshire and Yorkshire were now officially illegal.

The TUC Conference came and went with many meaningless resolutions and proposals of support for the miners sailing through by hundreds of thousands of votes. Meaningless because the General Council had no intention whatsoever of implementing any of them. As John Edmonds observed, "The TUC wrote the miners a blank cheque and forgot to sign it."

And yet the month ended with a historic triumph for the NUM within touching distance. After voting to accept their earlier pay-claim and not strike, NACODS, the pit deputies' union, had balloted its members on taking strike action in opposition to MacGregor's treatment of its members, among other issues. Dave Douglass, in typically dry fashion, observes, "We wondered what took 'em so long. After all, the pits were their pits and the jobs were their jobs as well."

There were several issues that had prodded the pit Deputies into balloting again, the central complaint being the decision of the NCB to dock pay from Deputies who, the Board felt, had made insufficient efforts to cross picket lines and get into work. In a show of passive-aggressive resistance, many Deputies, sympathetic to the NUM's cause, had seized on the excuse of the risk of violent retribution and had refused to cross picket lines. That they were now being ordered, with no consultation, on pain of docked wages, to cross NUM picket lines, even in reinforced 'scab buses' with working miners, if necessary, was, they protested, an insult and an affront to their dignity.

NACODS members were responsible for health and safety in the pits and their presence when production was taking place was a legal requirement. No NACODS presence at working mines meant no working mines. At *all*. The implication of a strike by the pit Deputies was game-changing. Every single pit in the UK, including all twenty-seven pits in Nottinghamshire, would cease production instantly and would be compelled to stay idle until NACODS members returned to work.

On the 28th September, the result of the ballot was announced. NACODS members had voted by 82.5 percent to strike and support the NUM. The result sent shock-waves rolling around Whitehall and saw impromptu parties and celebrations breaking out in mining communities all over the UK.

After seven months of the most determined Government offensive, the Conservative Party's worst nightmare appeared to be coming true. The miners were now poised on the brink of the greatest victory ever won by a trade union in British history.

Chapter 10:
Almost Paradise

"Moments, when lost, can't be found again.
They're just gone."
JENNY HAN

The National Association of Colliery Overmen, Deputies and Shotfirers was and is a curious organisation; neither fish-nor-fowl, in the view of many miners. Brian Evangelista says, "It was always a strange situation with NACODS. You never really knew which way they were going to go: management or workforce side. It was a strange union because they weren't in the NUM nor were they in BACM (British Association of Colliery Managers), which they would have liked to have been in, I think. And therein lay the problem: they were in the middle. I suppose it's like people from the far north of England: they can't make up their minds if they're Scottish or English, sometimes."

Evangelista is well-placed to make such a judgment. A career mining professional, he started his apprenticeship with the NCB in 1964. In a twenty-nine year career, he had postings at Comrie and Cowdenbeath collieries in his native Scotland before moving south. A position at Manton colliery followed, before moving to Bestwood Workshop as Superintendant and then rising to Manager. His role at Moorgeen, during the strike, was next before moving to Fence in the South Yorkshire Area, returning as General Manager of Bestwood Workshop after the strike, where he saw out the remainder of his career, retiring from the industry in 1993 as the miners' Alamo got underway.

Originally known as the General Federation of Firemen, Examiners and Deputies Association, NACODS' forerunner was, like the MFGB, a highly-federated organisation: a loose grouping of autonomous Areas and bodies. Unlike the NUM, by 1910 the union had largely made the transition to a genuinely national body. In 1947, the organisation rebranded itself as NACODS, the better to reflect the new nationalised industry in which it then found itself. In 1984 it had around 16,000 members nationally, and wielded a great deal of power for such a small union: a power it had never hitherto exercised.

The organisation's accidental arrival as the key to the entire dispute was as much a shock to its members as it was to Margaret Thatcher. Not by any stretch of the imagination a militant union, or anything even resembling one, NACODS members had found MacGregor to be insufferable. Both their leaders and the wider membership felt he treated them with a marked lack of respect.

It had taken some doing to push the historically conciliatory trade union into balloting its members for action: in its 100-year history it had never once been on strike. The strength of its members' offence at their treatment was reflected in the 82.5 percent majority they returned in support of action.

At Downing Street, Thatcher was horrified. Not only was the Government on the brink of defeat, with the hated miners set to complete a hat-trick of wins in their historic war with the Tories, her position as Party leader and, therefore, as Prime Minister was in serious jeopardy. Should NACODS win the dispute for the NUM, her position would have proved untenable. Resignation would surely have been the only possible outcome.

The clumsy and blundering MacGregor was summoned to Downing Street for a personal audience with the Prime Minister. He was told that the very survival of the Government rested on his shoulders. He must settle with NACODS at all costs and save Thatcher's skin and the Government's political future. The resulting drama would play out against the backdrop of the entire month of October as both strikers and strike-breakers, supporters and enemies, endured an agonising period of tension and uncertainty; waiting to see on whose side of the table the cards would fall.

Meanwhile, Labour's seventy-seventh annual Party conference kicked-off on 1st October with the strike dominating proceedings. Left and Right faced off against each other and, in the pre-Blair era, it was one of those typically emotive Labour Conferences: full of drama, passion and blood on the Conference floor.

Mansfield MP Don Concannon caused a near-riot with a speech berating Scargill, striking miners and the "violence of the mob," while extolling the virtues and democratic credentials of the Nottinghamshire strike-breakers.

Concannon had been a miner himself and quickly assumed pariah status among the NUM majority and their supporters for his perceived treachery and his support of Lynk, Prendergast and the NWMC. A hardline right-winger, as Defence Spokesman he had been booed off the Conference platform in 1982 for defending the use of plastic bullets in Northern Ireland and equating the election of IRA hunger-striker Bobby Sands as Sinn Féin MP with "approval for the perpetrators of the Mountbatten and Warrenpoint murders."

His 1984 speech was even more incendiary, so much so that the Conference Chair was forced to cut him off lest fighting break out among the Delegates.

Kinnock tried to block resolutions condemning police violence and was soundly cuffed as the Delegates confirmed their support for the NUM, and the various resolutions sailed through with pulverising majorities. Scargill was in his natural element and wowed the delegates with a typically rabble-rousing call to arms while Kinnock and the Party's high-command looked glumly on.

Nottinghamshire strikers were well represented as delegates from their local constituency Labour parties. For the working miners, it was not a happy Conference. They'd travelled to Blackpool, determined to enlist support from Kinnock and the Party of which many were still members. They had prepared a twenty-five page dossier highlighting the instances of violence, attacks, threats, arson, malicious damage and intimidation to which they claimed to have been subjected by 'Scargill's mob,' i.e. striking miners.

At first glance a pretty blood-curdling catalogue of outrageous brutality, the document, on further examination, revealed itself to be little more than a rehashing of articles previously published by such impartial journals as the *Daily Mail, Daily Telegraph* and *Daily Express.* While no reasonable observer could deny working miners had been subjected to some intimidation and violence, as had the Nottinghamshire strikers, the document's credibility was undermined by its lack of evidence in support of the newspaper reports that comprised the bulk of its contents.

It also made no mention of, for example, the Nottinghamshire striker being attacked in his home by a working miner with a chainsaw; an incident that had left the striker requiring over a hundred stitches and the attacker keeping his job. The report further omitted the case of Darrel Mathews, a working miner from Cotgrave, who had been convicted of stabbing a young student in the city centre for the crime of wearing pro-strike badges.

Conference 1984 was a bitter disappointment for Clarke, Liptrott and their strike-breakers. The resolutions they had wanted to see, condemnations of pickets and their violence towards working miners, had little chance of making it past a gathering overwhelmingly committed to the NUM's cause, whatever the feelings of the leadership. Furthermore, they soon discovered that not only were they most unwelcome at an official Labour Party Conference, the rank-and-file Party members felt no obligation to observe the polite formalities and social graces of the labour movement when in the presence of scabs.

Liptrott was thrown out onto the streets, having been leafletting in the hotel's foyer in support of the working Nottinghamshire miners, Inside, Scargill was establishing himself as the Conference's darling and the NUM Delegation couldn't drink all the free pints that came their way from admiring Party members, Liptrott suffered the indignity of scrabbling around on the pavement, trying to retrieve his leaflets in the blustery October wind.

To his credit, Liptrott wasn't short of guts. He could surely have been under no illusion regarding his likely reception. Undaunted, he continued to press upon Conference attendees his leaflets, which read, "The National Union of Mineworkers has always been proud of its democracy. But the present leadership has ignored local votes to work and has refused to

172

call a national ballot. Don't let Scargill tear the union movement apart."

Liptrott soon found himself at the centre of an outraged circle of Labour Party members. Reporting his ordeal to the *Nottingham Evening Post*, on 8th October, he said, "I told them I was a member of the Labour Party, but they said I had no authority to give out leaflets. I and three colleagues were harassed by up to 300 people. An NUM official then accused us of intimidating *them!* Seven policemen were helping us to do it [the leafleting].

"The Union official then turned to Colin Clarke and said, 'what are you doing scabbing here, Clarkey?' I said we were doing exactly the same as we were doing in Nottinghamshire — fighting for democracy.

"Another official then said, 'Get out of town. You have no right to be here.' I firmly believe I have every right to come and go in this country. We had a justifiable message — a message of democracy. But after what happened last week, I have now got to think about my position in the Labour Party. Even if it didn't agree with what we had to say, the Labour movement always democratically defended your right to say it." With suitable piety, he concluded, "Now I realise they don't want their doctrines polluted by truth."

Liptrott's loyalty to his beloved Labour Party had consistently expressed itself in an unusual manner. From writing to local Conservative Associations seeking support, up to the 1984 Conference when he and Clarke attended a fringe meeting organised by former right-wing Labour renegades, the Social Democratic Party. This was something the *Post* omitted to mention.

Undaunted, the working miners fired off a stern admonishment to Neil Kinnock:

May we, the National Working Miners' Committee, take this opportunity to point out to you that as from Friday, September 28th 1984, the current industrial action illegally initiated at Area level and endorsed by Mr. Scargill and the NUM Executive has been ruled unofficial in law through 69.5 of the Areas in the British coalfield in terms of manpower.

It is of paramount importance to the maintenance of the criminal and civil laws of our country that, where no legal strike exists, every worker is allowed to attend his workplace freely and without hindrance. Yet, at your Conference this week, the British public has been subjected to delegate after delegate decrying the fact that 60,000 working miners are, at this time, being given the full protection of the authorities to allow their right to work.

It appears to the majority of the electorate of this country that you yourself should have appreciated these facts from the outset of the dispute and the explanation which immediately springs to mind of this lack of understanding on your part can only be that your involvement in the dispute has only been from the side of Mr. Scargill, with no attempt to appreciate the views of the working miners and of their fight for the democratic rights that their rules and constitution demand.

It becomes increasingly more obvious that the leaders of the Socialist movement are being politically out-manoeuvred by the NUM leadership.

Violence in this dispute was not instigated by the police. There was no police involvement on the evening of March 13th, 1984 when the Yorkshire Area of the NUM sent into the Nottinghamshire Area thousands of their members to prevent Notts miners working. Thousands of pounds of damage was done and many men turned back from the colliery gates under the threat of violence.

There can be no doubt that if our democratic values are sacrificed now, then any form of proper government in the future will prove to be impossible.

The suggestion that Kinnock was sympathetic to Scargill's position required an imagination of prodigious dimensions. The working miners had adopted the Tories' strategy of baiting the Labour leader in an attempt to force him into a public declaration of support for them. In private, Kinnock was certainly far more sympathetic to them than the strikers, but such public avowals were out of the question. Lest he split the Party and cause further damage, Kinnock chose to walk a fraught middle-course: making formal noises of support for the strikers' plight while consistently attacking their 'violence' on the picket lines. During his speech, the Party leader's declaration that "... I abhor *all* violence" was seen as an attack on striking miners and was roundly booed.

One wonders if he ever reflected bitterly on the words of one of his heroes, fellow-Welshman and Labour movement icon, Nye Bevin, who once said, "We know what happens to people who stay in the middle of the road. They get run down." Certainly Kinnock was now consistently attacked by both the Left, who saw him as a traitor or, at best, a coward, and by the Right who insisted he was soft on Scargill.

Liptrott, Clarke and company had to content themselves with the consolation prize of seeing Scargill and the NUM leadership issued with a writ on the Conference floor. Posing as a journalist and conning his way into the Conference arena, David Hart had the writ-server deliver it personally to the NUM President. The writs had originated on the Friday before the Conference, with Mr Justice Nicholls's ruling that the strike was unofficial and that Scargill and the miners' leaders must stop saying otherwise. Scargill immediately went on TV to rubbish the judgement and state that, whatever Nicholls might think, the strike most certainly *was* official.

The writ gave the NUM leaders forty-eight hours to appear before the judge and explain themselves. Not that that was ever going to happen.

Speaking at a Conference fringe meeting, Scargill, playing to his adoring gallery, induced cheering and stamping of feet, fit to bring down the roof, when he said, "I want to make it clear that if the offence I have committed is contempt, I plead 'guilty'. Because the only crime I have committed is to fight for my class and my members."

Little over a week later, the NUM President was personally fined £1,000 and the NUM £200,000 pounds for contempt of court. Both parties refused to pay either fine. An anonymous donor, widely rumoured to be Robert Maxwell, paid Scargill's fine against his wishes. (Why might Maxwell have paid the NUM President's fine? Some believed the press baron was terrified of Scargill ending up in jail and becoming a martyr for the cause, which might finally trigger much-needed secondary action. Others believe that, despite Maxwell's personal dislike of Scargill, the *Mirror* boss had a soft-spot for the miners and wanted the glory of resolving the dispute himself.)

Increasingly, the working miners made some strange and counterproductive moves. Possibly the most astonishing was a letter they sent to the bereaved parents of David Jones, the strike's first casualty at Ollerton, back in March. Nearly six months after the young picket's death, Colin Clarke, on 1st October, on behalf of the National Working Miners' Committee (to all intents and purposes, the *Notts Working Miners' Committee*), sent what was felt to be an extraordinarily insensitive missive to Jones's mother. It was accompanied by a cheque for the sum of £250. The letter read,

"Dear Mrs. Jones, may we, the National Working Miners' Committee, pas [sic] on to you our deepest sympathy with regards to your resent [sic] tragic loss.

"We earnestly hope the enclosed cheque may be of some use to you at this present time."

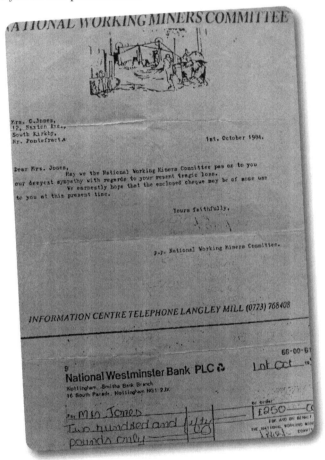

The letter appalled and puzzled friends of the Jones family and their supporters. Why wait nearly six months to send such a letter? Why send such a letter at *all* to a family who had fully supported both their sons' decision to strike? Since their son's death, the Jones family's support for the strike had only hardened and this was widely known. The NWMC must have known the response their letter would receive. Clarke, now dead, cannot answer the question. Neither can Liptrott, who is also deceased, and several efforts to secure an explanation from other former working miners have been ignored. Former strikers surmise that the letter was a cynical attempt to generate favourable publicity for the strike-breakers.

Jones's father spent some time considering his response, his answering letter not penned until 19th October. When it did arrive, however, it left no room for ambiguity. Addressed to Clarke, the painfully proud and dignified response read,

"Dear Sir, I received your letter dated 1st October, 1984, along with a cheque. I want to record my disgust at receiving both the letter and the cheque which I regard as an insult to my son who died on the picket line at Ollerton and to the miners who are still on strike and who would not sell their self-respect or their integrity for any amount of money.

19th October, 1984

Mr. Colin Clarke,
National Working Miners Committee,
Langley Mill
NOTTS

Dear Sir,

I received your letter dated 1st October, 1984, along with a cheque. I want to record my disgust at receiving both the letter and the cheque which I regard as an insult to my son who died on the picket line at Ollerton, and to the miners who are still on strike and who would not sell their self-respect or their integrity for any amount of money.

I neither want correspondence nor "tainted money" from you or your organisation which is backed by the Conservative Party and by those who support the enemies of the NUM.

My son died fighting for his Union, his job, his pit and the communities of which he was proud. I would not taint my son's name with even handling this money. Send it back to the Conservative supporters who presumably gave it to you.

Mr. & Mrs. Mark Jones

"I neither want correspondence or 'tainted money' from you or your organisation which is backed by the Conservative Party and by those who support the enemies of the N.U.M.

"My son died fighting for his Union, his job, his pit and the communities of which he was proud. I would not taint my son's name with even handling this money. Send it back to the Conservative supporters who presumably gave it to you."

Whatever Clarke's detractors might have said about him, he couldn't ever have been accused of laziness. The man just kept bouncing back with one scheme after another. Of the potential NACODS strike, he announced that: "There might be difficulty but it could be overcome."[48]

His reasoning was that there might be sufficiently qualified managers and working miners who, between them, could meet the legal requirements, stipulated by the Mines and Quarries Act 1954 that normally fell to NACODS, and keep production continuing in the Nottinghamshire pits. This was something the BACM quickly refuted, stating that none of their members would handle NACODS' duties.

Regarding the position of his working miners, Clarke and company had already attended meetings with the NCB's local Industrial Relations team. On behalf of the Nottinghamshire Area NUM, Clarke had made it clear that his men would cross NACODS picket lines. "No surprises there," observed Gordon Skinner. "They've had six months practice at crossing picket lines. They must be brilliant at it. In fact, if scabbing was an Olympic sport, no one would touch them: they'd scoop gold every time." Clarke went on to inform the Nottinghamshire Area NCB that if his men were prevented from working by NACODS pickets, they'd still require paying.

This did little to endear the Nottinghamshire Area NUM to Midlands Area NACODS (comprising Nottinghamshire, Derby-shire and Warwickshire), with the Deputies there recording a surprising 75.8 percent vote for the proposed strike action.

Its leaders responded angrily to Clarke's statement that Nottinghamshire miners would cross NACODS picket lines. Ray Hilton, the Nottinghamshire NACODS Treasurer, described the working miners' attitude as "diabolical". Throughout the overtime ban and then the strike itself, NACODS members had refused to carry out NUM members' duties yet "... as soon as we mentioned

178

our difficulties last August, they were talking about doing our work."[49]

Hilton continued to explain that while NACODS enjoyed good relations with the Board generally and certainly in their own Midlands Area, things had broken down under MacGregor's stewardship. Sammy Tucker, NACODS Branch Secretary at Shirebrook colliery added, "The biggest problem is Mr. MacGregor. If he can't negotiate with our Executive, who are fair people, he can't negotiate with anybody."[50]

Midlands Area Secretary, Eddie Lane, was of a similar mind. "His style of management is at fault. He might be a good businessman, but he doesn't know anything about human beings. He treats you with contempt."[51]

Reflecting the odd, piggy-in-the-middle position of the Union, some NACODS members were happy to use their strike mandate as an opportunity to back the NUM and settle the dispute in their favour, while others were appalled at such a suggestion. Hilton declared, "I would expect our members to honour the mandate they have given us if necessary but not to use it to help other people solve their problems."[52]

Tucker went further. "This dispute is for our own Union and its dignity. It's got nothing to do with the NUM."[53]

The working miners certainly saw the NACODS ballot as nothing more than an excuse by the Deputies to win the strike for the NUM. Clarke said, "Our lads cannot see any reason why NACODS should threaten to take action at this time."[54]

Regarding keeping the pits working, he added, "It all depends on how many BACM members there are and how many people in the NUM have the qualifications."[55]

Given that NACODS had properly voted to strike, in accordance with its rules, constitution and the law, in a national ballot, and given Clarke's trenchant commitment to 'democracy' and his insistence that a national ballot was the unassailable reflection of that democracy, some may have found his interference in the affairs of another trade union, and his support for the NCB in its efforts to thwart the looming NACODS strike, as somewhat contradictory. Roy Lynk expressed his support for Clarke's stance, stating that the official position of the Nottinghamshire Area NUM was to advise its members to cross NACODS picket lines and attempt to work as normal. Solidarity with other trade unionists in dispute, despite them having arrived there by the correct and proper mechanism of a national ballot, was, oddly, not something Nottinghamshire's self-declared champions of democracy felt they should respect. Lynk was not at all happy with NACODS. "In 1972 and 1974, they told us NACODS couldn't strike; now they find they can. The majority of us feel a bit let down."[56]

In the event, Lynk need not have worried. The NACODS negotiating team, led by its General Secretary, Peter McNestry, and the Union's President, Ken Sampey, had been in and out of talks all month, eventually requesting the intervention of ACAS. For all the miners' jubilation at the end of September, NACODS accepted a worthless fudge from the NCB in the form of the 'Modified Colliery Review Procedure' (MCRP). While giving 'full weight' to any pit submitted under its auspices for consideration for exemption from closure, it was not binding on the Board or Government. The final decision was to be made by a judge after having studied the representations from both the unions and the NCB, but with nothing at all to make any judgment legally stick.

The NUM was unimpressed. They felt the MCRP was transparently meaningless and had rejected it in the form that it had been presented. With its recommendations not binding on any party, it was even worse than previous proposals the NUM had consistently rejected throughout the preceding months. The striking miners were almost demented with rage and disbelief. NACODS had been conned and the NUM, so close to success at the end of September, was now, after seven months of struggle, back where it had started. Henry Richardson recalls, "The only thing that stopped a settlement being reached was the fact that the Review Procedure wasn't binding on anyone. Arthur said that if it was binding on both parties; if we lost one, we'd accept it and if they lost one, they'd have to accept it. If it was agreed like that, that it was binding on both parties, we'd have recommended to the members that we'd be prepared to sign.

"Willis came back and told us they wouldn't agree to it being binding. So what bloody good was it? It was useless and the Deputies couldn't see it! Sampey, though, was gloating. 'Look,' he said, 'we've won it for you! They wouldn't *dare* shut a pit now if the judges came down on our side and said a pit should stay open.' Arthur said, 'Don't bloody kid yourself.'

"It was as near to an agreement as you could get. If only they'd made it legally binding. Next thing we knew, they'd [Sampey and McNestry] gone back to their Executive behind our backs and said, 'this is good enough for us. No need to strike.'

"They betrayed us.

"At the end of the day, when the strike was over, they imposed this agreement on us and Manvers Main won their case to stay open under the Modified Colliery Review Procedure. The independent judge ruled it should stay open. And what happened? They ignored it and shut the bloody pit anyway. So we were right to take the stance we took."

The worth of Richardson's assertions have been shown in the twenty-nine years since the inception of the Modified Colliery Review Procedure: not one single pit has ever been reprieved under its provisions.

Others refused to believe seasoned negotiators like McNestry and Sampey could have been so gullible: they'd been 'got at', insisted some.

"No one could understand what happened there," says Dave Douglass. "Had they been bought off? Who knows? Possibly, but we'll probably never find out. It stank, though: something wasn't right."

The resolution of the NACODS dispute also gave Scargill's critics more ammunition to fire at the NUM President. He should've settled, they said, and lived to fight another day.

What they couldn't, or wouldn't, see was that there was no second chance. This was a fight to the death: either Thatcher would win and destroy the NUM and the industry or she'd lose and she wouldn't. It really was that simple, but such was the hatred of Scargill that the latest failed talks were seized on to denigrate the miners' leader still further. Even twenty five years after the dispute, the myths and falsehoods lived on. In Beckett and Hencke's *Marching to the Fault Line*, published in 2009 on the twenty-fifth anniversary of the strike, there is a telling revelation on page 152. Referring to the NACODS deal, the authors write, "This was one of many moments during the strike when Scargill, if he had acknowledged the reality of the situation, might have grabbed a settlement. *Of course, it would not have been a victory — the review body was established but it never saved a single pit the Board wanted to close — but it could*

181

have been dressed up as a partial victory ..." (emphasis by the author).

It is well worth considering this statement in some depth. The "reality of the situation," as the authors concede, was that the MCRP "...never saved a single pit the Board wanted to close." Yet Scargill is castigated for not ignoring this truth and is further derided as an incompetent negotiator for not lying to his members, selling them out and conning them that a proposal he knew to be utterly worthless, was a "partial victory".

NACODS settling was the strike's turning point. Although the miners struggled on for another five months, they'd never come as close to victory again.

On October 12th, the IRA bombed the Grand Hotel at Brighton where senior Tories were billeted for their annual conference. Five were killed and over thirty injured, with Thatcher herself escaping by the narrowest of margins. Many miners were torn in their reaction to the news. Whilst many had a hatred of the IRA, there was frustration among some that they'd missed taking out the despised Prime Minister. Said one striker from Cotgrave, "Fucking Paddies! Couldn't rely on 'em to do anything right. The one time they'd have had massive support from the British, they bodged it."

October had been a bad month for the NUM. With NACODS fleeing the battleground and taking their settlement with them, the strikers didn't need any more bad news. They got it, though. On 25th October, the High Court ordered the seizure of NUM assets, nearly £11 million, after the Union had refused to purge its contempt of court and pay the £200,000 fine. The writs and fines were now amassing at NUM HQ. Scargill joked that he used them for papering his office walls at Sheffield, but it was no laughing matter.

Eric Hammond, leader of the electrical and plumbing union, the EETPU, expelled from the TUC after the strike, along with his 225,000 members, for breaching the Bridlington Agreement (which governed the transfer of members among TUC-affiliated unions) twisted the knife a little further. He announced that as a result of an eighty-four percent majority in their recent ballot, his members would not be supporting the miners and would cross picket lines, move coal and generally behave as though there was no dispute taking place at all. In truth, Hammond's men had acted thus all along but now it was official. The TUC offered no comment and took no action against one of its affiliates scabbing on another.

There was more to come. At the close of the month, the *Sunday Times* ran an explosive front page story, detailing how NUM Chief Executive, Roger Windsor, had made a covert visit to Libya to seek support and financial aid from Colonel Gaddafi.

Our anonymous former striker from Cotgrave reflects: "I'll never forget October '84. I knew then, deep in me guts, that we'd lost. That it were all over. It were like you get at high-stakes matches at the football. I'd seen it loads: the underdogs, holding out, soaking up the pressure and the big team getting all frustrated because they can't quite get the upper hand. That were us and the Government. Even with all the police, dragging our lads to court and hauling 'em off to jail, the scabs and the violence and other unions letting us down, the hardship and everything else, Thatcher still couldn't quite get a grip on us. We were holding out brilliantly. October were like the big team finally sneaking a goal in the 80th minute. Something changes then. The run of the pitch goes their way and they get the critical luck-factor and go on to bang in another three or four before the final whistle.

"And we were so bloody close! So close. Can you imagine if NACODS had struck and the Paddies had got the Iron Lady? It makes me giddy to think about it. We'd have romped home. Instead, we got the Gaddafi mess. That was when it all started going wrong.

"I remember me youngest lass were daft on that film 'Footloose' at the time. She played the LP to bloody death. You know the thing: with all the songs from the film on it. Like *Grease* and that. Anyway, there were this one song she used to play over and over again. Drove me bloody mental, it did. 'Almost Paradise' it were called. And that were us in October '84. 'Almost Paradise.'

"If I ever hear that song it takes me straight back to October '84 and how close we came. I could cry thinking about it. In fact I have done, a few times, over the years since.

"Yup. 'Almost Paradise.' October 1984. You've got to laugh, really. What else can you do?"

Chapter 11:
Hammer to Fall

"It is not those who can inflict
the most, but those who can endure
the most who will conquer."
TERENCE MacSWINEY

November opened with the national newspapers scenting the blood of the NUM. The decision to send Roger Windsor to Tripoli to seek aid from 'Mad Dog' Gaddafi had conjured a storm of condemnation.

Back in April, with the dispute barely a month old, WPC Yvonne Fletcher was shot outside the Libyan Embassy in St. James's Square. The Embassy was the site of a noisy protest by anti-Gaddafi activists when, at around 10.15am, bullets were fired, reportedly from inside the Embassy. Eleven people were hit with Fletcher dying shortly afterwards from the round she'd taken in the stomach. Revulsion was widespread, but with the alleged shooter enjoying diplomatic immunity, no one was ever charged with the constable's murder.

Windsor claimed his visit was authorised by Scargill. Scargill said that he himself had refused to go, when the idea was first mooted. In *Marching To the Fault Line*, Beckett and Hencke report Scargill saying that his response was that Libya should stop supplying strike-breaking oil if they were really serious about helping the NUM.[57]

It was an unmitigated public relations disaster for the miners. With the dust from the IRA's Brighton bomb still swirling around the site of the Grand Hotel, and Thatcher's provocative description of the miners as "The Enemy Within" still ringing in the public's ears, here was yet another link in the chain. General Galtieri, the NUM, the IRA and now Colonel Gaddafi: an unholy assortment of terrorists, communists and murderers, all intent on bringing down good old British democracy and the superior British way of life.

There was a great deal more to the affair, not least strong evidence that Windsor was an MI5 agent. This allegation gained further traction when, in 2001, Dame Stella Rimmington, former Head of MI5, during the strike heavily involved in its counter-subversion section working against the NUM, said, in a strangely-worded statement, that Windsor was "... never an agent in any sense of the word that you can possibly imagine." Tam Dalyell then named Windsor as a security services spy from the floor of the Commons.

It wouldn't be until ten years later, in 1994, when Milne's forensic account, *The Enemy Within: the Secret War Against the Miners,* was published that the truth about the Libyan affair and the extent of the dirty tricks campaign against Scargill and the NUM would finally surface.

All that was ten years and more away, though. In November 1984, strikers remarked on a shift in public attitudes, in certain parts of the country. Fundraisers reported a hostile response from members of the public. A striker from Moorgreen colliery recalled being harangued in the streets as he collected in Letchworth. "It were funny, really. This angry bloke shouting, 'fuck off back to Libya.' I thought we were all supposed to go back to Russia?

"It were a bit of a nine-day wonder. We got stick at the time but it also made us and our supporters more determined to carry on. Any road, we'd had that much shit by then, us and Arthur, that we were past caring or being surprised, really. If *The Sun* had printed that Scargill was the Yorkshire Ripper, we'd have just laughed. They were pathetic the way they picked at everything we did. And if they couldn't find anything, they'd make it up. So we couldn't win either way.

"As for the Libyan thing, so what? We were on our arses by November, Christmas was coming and we'd have taken money from Satan himself if it had meant we could have held out a bit longer.

"I mean I were sorry about that young lass. No one wants to see things like that but a lot of the lads had a different view, like. All them folks pointing the finger at us, they hadn't seen the Met like we had. They didn't know what they were really like. Some of the lads said the only thing that was a shame about the copper being shot was that they'd only managed to shoot one: it were a shame they hadn't shot all of the bloody Met."

Meanwhile, in Nottinghamshire, conflict was brewing again among Labour Party activists, local councillors and the Party's East Midlands regional command.

Labour left-wingers, some of whom were striking miners themselves, put together a controversial initiative that sought to ban working miners from standing as Labour candidates in the local elections, which were due the following May.

The striking miners, with whom the proposal had originated, enjoyed the support of Party members throughout the County, who enthusiastically backed the move.

For the Left, this was nothing more than common sense and a reasonable course to take in order to preserve the Party's historic role as the organised voice of the trade union movement. The trade unions formed the Labour Party, they argued, the trade unions funded the Labour Party and it was the duty of every Labour Party member to keep that fact at the forefront of their thinking and conduct and not to betray its fundamentals. In short, the Labour Party should be no place for scabs.

The move had been planned by striking miners from the Mansfield and Sherwood local Parties. The county organisation gave into pressure from the activists and soon a bandwagon was rolling in support of the proposal, which gave County Council leader Dennis Pettitt yet another headache. In reality, he had his hands full trying to cope with just Gordon Skinner, the brother of Dennis Skinner MP, who was waging a one-man war against the working miners on the county's Labour group. His widow, Helen, comments, "Gordon always prefaced every speech at County Hall with 'and you scabbing bastards', as he pointed them out. He was asked to leave the chamber for wearing a 'Coal Not Dole' T-shirt and he found out which councillors changed from claiming 'financial loss' to claiming 'expenses' whilst pleading poverty."

Throughout the course of the dispute, Pettitt had expended huge reserves of time, energy and no small amount of Machiavellian plotting, scheming and horse-trading, in a bid to hold together his fractured Labour Group. With both strikers and working miners among his ranks of Councillors, it was a tough job running Nottinghamshire County Council in 1984. The Tory opposition were at pains to exploit the situation, with Pettitt frequently taunted with suggestions that he express his support for his Labour Councillors who were crossing picket lines and condemn the 'left-wing thugs' who were preventing them from doing so. This new challenge threatened to tear apart the Labour movement in the County and with it Labour's authority on the County Council.

The strikers were uninterested in such concerns and said their proposal should have been perfectly acceptable in any organisation purporting to be socialist. The fact it had met with any controversy at all, they said, was an indication of how far Labour had strayed from its role as the representative of the working class and trade unions and was, in and of itself, scabbing on the miners. If you aren't with us, you are against us, was the only rule of thumb that counted in Nottinghamshire.

In a plea to Labour's Regional Executive to endorse the ban, a written explanation of the move was signed by a veritable who's who of the county's Labour Left: Deposed Ollerton Branch Secretary, Jimmy Hood, City Councillor Nigel Lee, Hood's exiled Branch counterpart at Bevercotes, Paul Whetton, District Party Chair Vernon Gapper and the 'Beast of Bolsover's' equally intransigent brother, Gordon Skinner, among others.

Their statement read: *"The Labour Party, through the financial and political support of its membership for the miners, has gained considerable credibility in the eyes of the NUM membership.*

"Hundreds of miners locally and many thousands nationally, are joining the Labour Party as a result. This work would be seriously undermined if the Labour Party were to now allow 'scabs' to go forward to secure positions of responsibility in the Party's name."

Unsurprisingly, the Party's Regional Executive quashed the move, citing it as unconstitutional and purely the business of local Party members to decide who they could and couldn't select as candidates for local elections.

The divide continued to widen and local Party branches became war-zones where supporters of the strike and strikers themselves slugged it out with the working miners and their supporters.

Increasingly, such moves were tinged with an air of desperation. While Nottinghamshire's loyalists remained undaunted, there were now few signs of any resolution to the crisis. Indeed, following the collapse of the October negotiations involving all three of the industry's unions, NUM, NACODS and BACM, the Government now had no desire to settle. It had always hoped for the complete vanquishing of the NUM. Now, it was determined to settle for nothing less. Between Nottinghamshire's working miners keeping up coal production and non-union (and even strike-breaking union), labour moving the stocks, it was now simply a case of waiting the miners out and starving them back to work.

The NUM's tragedy was that on the issue of coal stocks, once again, they'd been correct. As early as the Mansfield rally of 14th May, Scargill had said, "If no more coal from Nottinghamshire was to go in, the CEGB would be in a desperate situation within a matter of eight to nine weeks. The only thing that keeps them afloat is the supply they are getting, albeit limited, from the Notts coalfield."

In a series of documents leaked from the North Nottinghamshire NCB to strikers from Hucknall pit, a stunning picture emerged. Both the overtime ban and the strike had had a much greater impact on Nottinghamshire than anyone had suspected. The documents detailed a forecast loss of £18.9 million and a drop in output to 1,379,000 tonnes below budget. In August, output had fallen to 216,000 tonnes below budget and in the same month 11,000 man-shifts per week were worked less than budget. Total lost man-shifts up to that point totalled 45,000 which meant the stock position as of 1st September was only 602,000 tonnes. But even this figure had been reached *before* the preceding five weeks' stocks had been moved out, the document went on to say. The stock supplied mainly Cotham and West Burton power stations. In August a total of 207,000 tonnes had been shipped out by road which reduced the actual stock to 395,000 tonnes. At an average output of 41,400 tonnes per week, this meant North Nottinghamshire had just 9.54 weeks' worth of stocks left. Also, the figures had been based on August production — probably the single month of the year when demand was at its very lowest — *and* the figures only accounted for half the Nottinghamshire coalfield, the half, interestingly, that had seen the most miners returning to work. This showed just how close the strikers had come to putting out the lights. One would surely have expected such explosive data to have been splashed all over the pages of the *Nottingham Evening Post* and the national dailies. Mysteriously, not a hint of the real situation appeared anywhere, with the strikers reduced to reproducing the information in a special edition of *The Strike Bites,* one of the many grass roots bulletins and news-sheets produced by the Nottinghamshire loyalists.

Scargill had been more correct than even he knew.

His assertions regarding stocks, widely rubbished by not only the Government but also by many on the TUC, were further borne out when, many years later, it was revealed that on 24th July, Norman Tebbit had told the Prime Minister that stocks were now so low that they wouldn't last the winter and, therefore, the NUM *had* to be broken by the autumn at the latest.

By October, CEGB chiefs were, privately, panicking. Barely six weeks' worth of stocks remained and had the NACODS strike gone ahead the remaining reserves would have disappeared before Christmas. But it was not to be, the lights would stay on and the opportunity for an autumn victory by the miners would slip away.

Now, sensing the tide had turned, the NCB ramped up its propaganda. On 19th November, the Board reported that 2,190 new faces had returned to work, overtaking the 1,999 across the three shifts of the previous Monday. Its spokesman announced, "It proves what we have been saying — that the return to work is continuing to grow. And it is growing at an encouraging pace. We believe 7,000 people will return this week."

The Board went on to claim that there were now fifty-nine pits working normally. Of that total, Nottinghamshire accounted for twenty-seven of the working pits, leaving thirty-two. Thirty-two extra pits from a total of nearly 150 wasn't a particularly impressive figure. Especially after nine months and an astronomical amount of money spent on breaking the strike. Even if the statement was true, and figures hadn't been massaged, that meant there were still nearly ninety pits standing idle.

Scargill disputed the figures, naturally, and pointed out that, if true, it still meant 151,000 miners were holding fast. The Board could only count on 50,000, at most. NCB Spokesman Michael Eaton disagreed and said working miners were actually around 60,000. And so the dance continued. In any event, the overwhelming majority of the miners were still out, and now the objective was to hold out up to and throughout Christmas when, it was hoped, the New Year would, somehow, bring a new solution to the crisis.

Nottinghamshire's striking miners still had battles to fight before the dubious pleasure of an uncertain Christmas on the breadline could be enjoyed. The first of these was a campaign by the working majority to introduce a series of rule changes which would exempt the Area's members from any future disciplinary action by the NEC. The move included the complete deletion of Rule 30 which expressly rendered the Area subordinate to the NEC.

Seen by the strikers as yet another move by the dissidents towards a breakaway union, there was virtually no chance of its defeat. The Branches would vote in early December and, if a majority emerged, the changes would be endorsed by the Area Council when it convened on the 20th.

Lynk had enlisted a team of non-NUM lawyers to assist in the formulation of the new rules and claimed that their purpose was not to facilitate a breakaway but merely to ensure the maximum autonomy of the Area while remaining a constituent part of the NUM. No one placed too much weight on such a claim.

The proposal was Nottinghamshire's revenge for the adoption of Rule 51, seen by the working miners as a measure specifically tailored to punish them for their disloyalty. Admittedly, Rule 51 must have induced anxiety, if not outright terror, among the Nottinghamshire rebels. Widely known as the 'Star Chamber Rule', Rule 51, since its birth at the Special Delegates' Conference back in the summer, had assumed an almost talismanic power in the Nottinghamshire coalfield, with strikers making the most of their enemies' discomfort by wearing lapel badges that read 'Rule 51. Expel The Scabs'. The working miners were convinced that once the strike was over, they'd be hauled before the National Disciplinary Committee and punished under the Rule's provisions. Let's get our retaliation in first, was the consensus, and get out from under. All of which suited Roy Lynk just fine as a decisive step towards trade union UDI for Nottinghamshire would be taken with the abolition of Area Rule 30.

Despite denials that the series of amendments to rule were a precursor to the birth of a Spencer Union Mk.2, they barely paid even lip service to the NUM as a national body of which Nottinghamshire would still be an integral part. Where the NEC was concerned, the proposed changes were peppered with phrases like "take into consideration", "... will give full weight to..." and "will consider advice". In short, the NEC's overarching role as the supreme authority between Conferences was to be removed.

That wasn't the end of the matter, either. It was also proposed to add a sub-rule to Rule 24. This rule specified that changes to Area Rules could only take place once a year, in December. The proposed sub-rule read: "If it is resolved by a simple majority of the members of either the Executive Committee or the Council that particular alterations, amendments, rescissions of these rules or additional rules are immediately required, then such alteration, amendment or rescission specified in such resolution shall be made if approved by a two-thirds majority of members voting on a ballot of all members of the Union. In these circumstances the Executive Committee shall take all necessary steps as soon as practicable to hold such a ballot."

This was soon dubbed the 'scabs' get-out-of-jail-free' card. The implications were clear: if, at any time, the NEC or Conference introduced any rule or amendment to rule that was not to the liking of Nottinghamshire, the Area need only hold its own Area ballot to change their rule. Nottinghamshire could then ignore any rule in the national rule book, decision of Conference and/or the NEC by adopting this process.

Under such a Rule, coupled with the removal of Rule 30, it would be virtually impossible to get the Area out on strike, under any circumstances. For example, even if the activation of Rule 43 produced a majority for strike in a national ballot, all Nottinghamshire needed to do to exempt itself from the action would be to change its own rules to give its own Area strike ballot primacy.

This was serious. Even if the intentions of the working majority were not to break away, as they continued to insist, the rule changes would set the Area on a trajectory from which it was impossible to foresee any other outcome.

The strikers had little time to consider this latest move by the working majority before the next bone of contention arose. Happily for the loyalists, this time the events saw disagreements breaking out among the strike-breakers at Branch and Area level as, once again, the overtime ban rose to the top of the Nottinghamshire agenda.

By the 23rd November, petitions demanding the end of the overtime ban had sprung up all over the coalfield. First appearing at Babbington and Newstead pits, support for a return to fully normal working was gathering force. The demands for a scrapping of the ban had been given a second wind with the proposed Area rule changes and amendments. Members of the Notts Working Miners' Committee sensed that now would be the time to push for a full scrapping of the action. Although no one individual ever admitted responsibility for the petitions, they were widely assumed to be an initiative that had originated with the Committee. Certainly, those seen at pits passing around the petitions and speaking forcefully for its signing were prominent Notts Working Miners' Committee members. It presented Lynk, Prendergast and the Area and Branch officials with a problem, who described it as "ill-advised".

The more cautious members of the Area Council opposed the petition on the grounds that it challenged a legitimate decision by the NEC and would put Nottinghamshire firmly outside existing rules, as well as generating damaging publicity for the working miners' cause.

Ken Duckworth, the working Branch Secretary at Babbington, condemned the move, saying, "Such things as pay and overtime take place within the procedures laid down between the Board and the Union. Petitions are out of order."

By contrast, the NWMC leaders insisted they'd be unable to hold back any demands on pay and overtime once they'd accrued a head of steam. Some felt this was a particularly duplicitous position to take, given it was widely believed the petitions had started with the Committee in the first place, for the express purpose of generating just such a head of steam.

192

Dave Douglass comments, "Unbelievable. It wasn't enough for them to scab on the strike; they had to scab on the overtime ban as well. I suppose they just weren't earning enough."

The Board chipped in with a series of incentives designed to put pressure on strikers facing a bleak Christmas. Miners retuning to work before the end of November could expect to pocket around £1,300. Comprising four weeks' holiday pay, three weeks' incentive bonus, advanced wages before Christmas, annual holiday pay and annual service bonuses, the Board hoped to break miners, especially family men, wracked with guilt about depriving their children of a merry Christmas. To the surprise of many, the offer was taken up by none of the Newstead strikers, something Keith Stanley noted with pride. In truth, most of Newstead's striking miners had long since passed the pain barrier and were dug in deep, committed to striking until they physically dropped. What was seen as little more than a cheap bribe only produced the effect of bolstering weary spirits.

Sadly, the same situation wasn't replicated across the Area. "Christmas killed us," says Eric Eaton. "We lost a lot of good lads then. Solid lads who'd been out from the start." It wasn't easy. "It was brutal," says Jimmy MacDowall. "Terrible, terrible times. But good times as well, you know? I wouldn't have missed it for the world. It was hard to stay out all that while but I'm glad that I did. Really glad that I did."

MacDowall knew better than many just how hard the strike had become by the winter of 84/85. Just one week before the strike had started, his wife had left him and their three young daughters. All through the summer months he'd struggled to balance what he saw as his duty to his young family with his duty to his Union. "I were never in and that made me guilty, sometimes," he says. "I'd get in from a picket after 11.00pm and get a phone call to go to Harlow or Stevenage at seven the next morning to collect food parcels or toys for the kids. It was non-stop. But my main job was as a logger: I'd drive the van and chop down trees, anywhere I could find a tree to chop down, and then dish out logs, coal and coke to everybody."

He is firm in citing the generous support of other local trade unionists as key to keeping him and his comrades out. "We had very good friends in the railway unions who helped us out; we had help from the Fire Brigades' Unions. They gave us brand-new chainsaws and all-sorts."

Invaluable, too, was the help and aid from others entirely unconnected with the miners or even trade unions in general. "We even had help from people you'd never think would give to miners; people from down south. The stuff they sent up to us was out of this world. You couldn't imagine it."

As one of MacDowall's striking Linby comrades shrewdly observes, "Some of them folk from down south, rich compared to anything we'd ever been used to, but still working class, I suppose you'd call 'em, knew that it were never just about us, the miners. It were us first and then it'd be them. Some of 'em had never even seen a miner but they knew the strike was about every working class person in the country. Once you got your head around that, me duck, that and the support we got, that was what kept us going when it were really bad: winter, Christmas and that."

MacDowall says he was close to cracking on two or three occasions. "It was only my eldest getting a job that helped us out. That was the only thing that kept me going." It made it easier for him, he says, to show some compassion to those who'd given all they could but had reached the end of their endurance. He drew a sharp distinction between those who had deliberately broken the strike from the beginning and those who simply had no more left to give.

"I knew one lad, he'd been out on strike with us from the beginning, nine, maybe ten, months. Bills to pay and in debt up to his eyeballs, like we all were. He was heartbroken about going back. The lads went up to see him, spoke to him and told him we'd help him all we could but he was a proud lad and his daughter got pregnant. So he had that to deal with as well. That business with his daughter, that's what killed it. She was in a mess and he just couldn't manage anymore. So he went back, after all that while. He was heartbroken. It was just one of them things: he just had to go. I can understand it. I can sympathise with him."

There was little sympathy for the miner who attempted to return to work at Cortonwood on 9th November, though. The place where it had all started, the catalyst for over 160,000 men and their families risking everything they had, in support of the Cortonwood miners, had finally been weakened to the point where the unthinkable was now happening: a miner returning to work. Thousands poured into the area to prevent his return

194

and rob the Government of an early Christmas present.

Adding to the November drama, Price-Waterhouse, international accountancy giants, were instructed to seize NUM assets after the High Court ordered sequestration and on the 12th Margaret Thatcher likened pickets to the IRA.

Still the miners' chain held and the next day, 13th November, saw Welsh strikers demonstrate their contempt for TUC General Secretary, Norman Willis, when, at a rally in South Wales, he attacked violence by pickets. His infamous speech, featuring a scathing aside directed at those he saw as trying to further the dispute by use of "... the brick, the bolt and the petrol bomb", was greeted by roars of fury as Welsh miners lowered a hangman's noose over his head from the ceiling.

Upping the ante, on the 21st, the Government docked £1 from the benefits paid to striking miners. They'd already slashed £15 from benefits, earlier in the dispute, on the basis of miners' non-existent strike-pay. And yet November still had further punishment in store.

On the 30th November, David Williams, a working miner from Merthyr Vale pit, was travelling into work in a taxi driven by David Wilkie. The taxi was accompanied by a team of police cars and motorcycle outriders. The convoy turned onto the A465 at Rhymney Bridge roundabout when a concrete block was dropped from the bridge overhead. At a height of nearly thirty feet from the road, coupled with the weight of the block, over twenty kilos, the impact was devastating. Wilkie was killed instantly when the block landed on the roof of his taxi. His passenger was unhurt.

Fleet Street went into overdrive. Wilkie, it transpired, had had a pregnant fiancée who was also the mother of his two-year old daughter. Newspapers across the land wrung every ounce of pathos from the horrific incident. Less inclined towards sympathy for the family of the deceased taxi-driver, instead motivated by an overriding desire to use the death to finish off the strike once and for all, the backlash was catastrophic.

The two miners responsible, Dean Hancock and Russell Shankland, both just twenty-one, were convicted of murder and sentenced to life imprisonment, later reduced on appeal to manslaughter with the sentences shortened to eight years each.

The severity of the initial sentence caused outrage among the Welsh mining community. The verdicts weren't delivered until

May '85, after the strike had finished, but feelings were still sufficiently high to see 700 miners walk out of Merthyr Vale pit in protest.

Among striking miners, reactions to the death were mixed. Some were truly horrified and felt the strike had suffered a fatal blow. Others were unmoved and felt Wilkie's death was merely the inevitable outcome of scabbing and betraying one's own. Most, though, contrasted the reactions to his demise with that of David Jones at Ollerton. The differences couldn't have been more apparent.

Chapter 12:
Do They Know
It's Christmas?

> *"Jingle bells, jingle bells, jingle all the way*
> *I'd rather be a picket than a scab on Christmas Day"*
> Sung on Nottinghamshire picket lines,
> December 1984

Ray Chadburn was an unlikely maverick. In contrast to Henry Richardson, who was firmly of the NUM Left, Chadburn was regarded as a moderate or a right-winger. The Left viewed him with suspicion, as someone who couldn't always be relied upon to vote the right way. In reality, Chadburn was not really a right-winger at all and his voting record bears this out, voting as often against the Right, both at Area level and on the NEC, as he voted against the Left. What he was, in fact, was simply independent of both the Left and the Right.

"Yes, that's true," he says. "I *was* thought of as a moderate. Sometimes I think you shouldn't tar people with a particular brush. If there were left-wing policies that I supported, I supported them. If there were others policies I supported, I'd support them. What I believed to be right was the most important thing; not whether it was left, right or centre. That didn't matter to me. If I thought what Arthur Scargill was doing was right, I'd support him. If I thought what he was doing was

197

wrong for the vast majority of people I represented, I'd oppose him. That's how it was. I didn't think, 'Well, I'm a left-winger so I'm going to support this' or 'I'm a right-winger so I'm going to support that', so I was classed as a moderate.

"My grandfather was a member of the Communist Party, I was a socialist but I'd get the Left saying, 'Ray, you should've supported us on this issue' but I always took a position based on what I thought was right at the time. I never supported Arthur because he was of the Left and I never opposed him because I was thought of as being on the Right: I supported him many times because he was right on the particular issue at that time. Just as I sometimes opposed him because I thought he was wrong. When it came to pit closures, I was 110 percent behind him because he was 110 percent right."

Chadburn started with the NCB in 1952, joined the Labour Party and its Young Socialist section in 1955 and was elected to his Branch Committee at Welbeck colliery in 1964. It was during the 'October Revolution' of 1969, when he met a young Arthur Scargill, that Chadburn decided he wanted the Delegate's position, which he won a year later.

In 1970 he was part of the delegation that gave evidence to the Wilberforce Enquiry before ascending to the Nottinghamshire Area Executive Committee and then becoming a full-time NUM Official in 1976.

He became President of the Nottinghamshire Area in 1979, succeeding Len Clarke, a right-winger much disliked by the Left. Chadburn was perceived by some of the Left to have been Clarke's *protégé* and while some predicted that would lead to clashes with his left-wing General Secretary, Henry Richardson, the two worked reasonably well together, most of the time, and disagreements were few.

Nottinghamshire, despite its reputation as a right-wing coalfield, had a left-wing General Secretary, a left-wing Area Council and a left-dominated Area Executive. It also had something of an odd tradition of electing its two senior Officers from both the Left and the Right. Chadburn's predecessor had been Len Clarke and Richardson's had been Joe Whelan, an Irishman, Linby miner and Communist Party member who had been immortalised on the Linby banner.

Whelan stood very much in the Celtic Left tradition of the NUM, alongside the Scot, the much-loved and admired Lawrence

Daly, the former national General Secretary: cultured, self-educated men, much given to poetry, music and philosophy. And whisky.

Clarke, by contrast, was a 'realist' and an operator of the Gormley school. For him, politics really was all about the art of the possible.

Henry Richardson and Chadburn had, in Chadburn's words, "parallel careers" although Richardson, by the time of the strike, was inexperienced in comparison to Chadburn, who had been a full-time official for eight years.

Elected in December 1983, Richardson says, "I was a green-horn. Wet behind the ears. I'd only been in the job ten minutes before the strike. I was looking forward to easing into the job and finding me feet and then next thing I knew, I was in it up to my neck!"

His arrival as the dominant Left presence in the Area was as much a surprise to him as it was to his opponents. It had started with the death of Joe Whelan in August 1983. As one of the Area's two NEC delegates, Whelan's replacement needed to be elected as a matter of priority. As Richardson explains, "Normally, in the Notts Area, the NEC place would be taken by a full-time Official. Now, for the first time in our history it didn't: I won. This was a slap in the face for Lynk and he never forgave me." At the time, Lynk had been a full-time official for a few years and the Area's Finance Officer. He, understandably, expected to beat a rank-and-file miner from Cresswell pit. "Then in December I was elected full-time. And in the January we had the vote to see which official would be General Secretary, which was the job Lynk had always wanted. And we expected him to get it, actually." The Left had done their sums and predicted Lynk would win by one Branch. To everyone's surprise, Richardson ended up winning by one Branch. Moorgreen Workshop, considered a Lynk stronghold, had voted for Richardson instead. "That was it then," says Richardson. "Nothing but pure animosity from Lynk. He never, ever forgave me." From that point, the Area's officials cleaved into two mutually-hostile, irreconcilable camps.

As the strike wore on, Richardson's alienation from his working majority increased so that by the time December arrived, both he and Chadburn knew it was only a matter of time before one or both were forced from office. While both men had walked a tightrope since March, something had to give.

Carefully following the rule book to avoid handing excuses to Lynk and his supporters, while supporting at every opportunity the pro-strike line when it didn't involve breaking the Area mandates Scargill had been at pains to insist they both observe, December saw Richardson finally provide the excuse for his dismissal the Right had long sought.

The showdown had started at the end of November when, in defiance of the NEC and NUM policy, the Nottinghamshire Area decided to resume talks with the NCB in Area-level consultation meetings. Since the start of the strike, these had been boycotted by the NUM, and the move was seen as yet further scabbing by the rebels. They countered that the boycott left them unable to safeguard their members' interests, particularly those at the threatened pits.

Loyalists viewed the move as nothing more than a ploy by the Area to prod the NEC into further action against it. By now, the widespread view was that a breakaway was not only inevitable but was actively being pursued by Roy Lynk and Prendergast. However, Lynk wanted the breakaway on *his* terms: in circumstances that forced the NEC to expel the Area and leave him claiming martyr status as a victimised defender of local democracy.

Why, his opponents argued, if this wasn't the case, as Lynk continued to protest in public, resume talks now? The working miners had been in control of the Area since the summer and could have taken the decision then. Also, what 'threatened pits'? Hadn't the Right, the Notts Working Miners' Committee and indeed the overwhelming majority of Nottinghamshire miners argued, from even before the strike, that they were safe? That Nottinghamshire would be exempt from any mass closures? Weren't they even safer now that they had the personal gratitude of the Prime Minister? Wouldn't Margaret Thatcher reward them for their service?

Resuming Area-level talks was seen as a measure to raise the stakes prior to the vote on the rule changes later in the month. Provoking the NEC into further sanctions against Nottinghamshire, Lynk guessed, would only serve to push more miners into voting for the rule changes, and the breakaway union would be that much closer.

Interestingly, at the same time, the Area Council had pulled back, yet again, from overturning the overtime ban and accepting the 5.2 percent pay offer, on the basis that it had been constitutionally endorsed by a Special Delegates' Conference. Just like the decision not to hold a national ballot had been...

The Branch votes on the proposed rule changes over the two weekends of December and then the Area Council meeting of the 20th would settle matters once and for all.

The county's strikers soon found themselves with more than enough to deal with as the working miners' proposed rule changes triggered a counter-move by the NEC, and Henry Richardson finally gave the Lynk faction the excuse they needed to start the process of ousting him.

By 13th December, the NEC's next scheduled meeting, half of the Branches in the coalfield had voted on the rule changes and all had voted in favour. With straw polls indicating the same result for the remainder, the NEC had put Nottinghamshire at the top of its agenda. Speaking on the eve of the meeting, as he surveyed the Nottinghamshire coalfield finally splitting away from the NUM, Richardson tore into the working miners. "It will be discussed at the Executive tomorrow and I know they [NEC] envisage taking certain action to stop Nottinghamshire putting the necessary amendments into their rule book.

"They are living in cloud cuckoo land if they think they can take authority away from the National Executive. I have spelled that out to my coalfield Executive and to the Council but some people are trying to break away and are trying to do it via the back door."[58]

Following the first voting session, a handful of strikebreakers finally put the overtime ban out of its long drawn-out Nottinghamshire agony by breaking it. Although the official position of the Area Council was still to continue and uphold the ban, several miners worked overtime at four pits. In truth, the ban was only being observed as a formality by this time while the Branches voted on whether to officially abandon it or not. As half of them had already done so, along with voting in the rule changes, 'in for a penny, in for a pound' was the rather apposite thinking.

The next day the NEC convened and decided to take the Nottinghamshire Area to court to prevent the rule changes. Both Richardson and Chadburn had been mandated to vote against any such action. Chadburn, continuing to follow the letter of the Union's law, voted against the NEC, as his Area mandate instructed, but Richardson had had enough: he voted with the NEC majority to take legal action against his Area. For the first time in his short-lived term as Nottinghamshire General Secretary, he had defied his Area, broken his mandate and given Lynk exactly the opportunity he'd craved.

Retribution was not long in coming. First into action was David Prendergast who fumed, "He has decided to go through 360 degrees. He has voted for court action against his own men." Clearly, taking court action against one's own men was a privilege reserved exclusively for strike-breakers. He accused Richardson of being "two-faced", to which the General Secretary carefully responded, "I have consistently voiced my opinion inside Executive meetings that I construe the proposed changes could be deemed to be a breakaway and that some people would use it for that purpose. Members of the Area Executive have not agreed with my interpretation."

Neil Greatrex, then Bentinck Branch President, joined in condemning Richardson. "He deliberately ignored a mandate and for that he should go. Having decided to take his own men to court he should have the courage and the decency to resign." This was an interesting hypothesis. If every Nottinghamshire working miner who had "taken his own men to court", or supported such action, had resigned, the NUM membership in the County would have struggled to field a Welfare football team.

Richardson had had no qualms about finally breaking his mandate. As far as he was concerned, it was long overdue. The rule changes *were* the precursor to a breakaway, and what kind of principled trade union official could stand meekly by and see the ghost of George Spencer rising from its grave to split the Nottinghamshire coalfield once again?

By acting the way it did, the Nottinghamshire Area had squandered any moral authority it might have had and all bets were now off.

Richardson had had a hellish year. The least experienced official in the Area, he had been thrust into the national spotlight during the most turbulent industrial dispute in British history, all the while attempting to avoid the traps laid out for him by the strike-breakers. For the first few weeks, he'd been cruelly and mistakenly branded a scab and through it all he had remained loyal to his striking-members and the values and ethos of the trade union he loved. The pressure had been relentless and constant. Now he felt liberated and a strange feeling of relief washed over him. He had, he felt, done his duty to his members, his class and his union. No one could have expected more.

The vote also demonstrated the differences between Richardson and Chadburn. The General Secretary's resistance had always been more overtly class-based, albeit while seeking to observe the bureaucratic formalities that would not put him outside the rules. It was a difficult and torturous path to follow. Chadburn, on the other hand, perhaps reflecting his lack of a fixed and consistent ideology and also his greater immersion in the horse-trading and murky deals of the professional trade union leader, twisted and turned according to what might yield the greatest advantage. While he was as pro-strike as Richardson, his voting against the NEC was seen by many as capitulation to the strike-breakers, and earned him the scorn of some Nottingham-shire loyalists. Now was the time when breaking the mandate was necessary, they felt: to show, clearly, whose side one was on.

In the meantime, a curious spat broke out as both the Notts Working Miners' Committee and the National Working Miners' Committee suddenly found themselves under heavy fire from the Nottinghamshire Area.

David Prendergast attacked the idea that working miners might have need of "pseudo clandestine-type committees". Administering an unequivocal beating to Clarke and Liptrott, he said, "I want it reaffirmed that that we, as an Area, disasso-ciate ourselves from the National and Notts Working Miners' Committees. They do not represent the working miners and they have no sphere of influence." This wasn't true. The fact was that all the leading lights on the NWMC were also Branch officials and Area Council members and Area Executive members: the crossover between the NWMC and the official Area structure was considerable and in terms of intent, policy and politics, the two structures were indistinguishable.

Prendergast continued, "The elected members at Branches, through their Area Council, are in control of the Notts coalfield and we have no need of clandestine-type committees. What we do is above board for everyone to see."[59]

Along with votes on the rule changes and scrapping of the overtime ban, Nottinghamshire members had also voted on a motion calling on the Area to disassociate itself from the various working miners' committees, and Prendergast found himself receiving unexpected support from a most unusual quarter.

Robert Taylor and Ken Foulstone, from Manton colliery, had been among the first of the rank-and-file working miners into legal battle against their Union. It had been their action that had led to Scargill and the NEC receiving the fines for contempt of court following the Labour Party Conference.

In a bewildering broadside, with Taylor and Foulstone's pot calling Clarke and Liptrott's kettle black, Taylor told the *Observer*, on 16th December, that "...they are union bashers, not union builders. They have attempted to involve us but we have flatly refused. We think that the majority of working miners could be immensely damaged by their aims and tactics."

The source of his ire had been an advertisement by the National Working Miners' Committee which had appeared in the *Daily Express*, claiming to represent strike-breakers in Yorkshire and Lancashire. "They were that democratic they had not bothered to ask any working miner about it," said Taylor.

Justifying his legal assault against his Union's President and NEC, Taylor said, "The law is made to be obeyed in this country and just because you are Arthur Scargill does not mean that you can flout the law. We are going to bloody well show him that he cannot."[60]

One wonders if Taylor observed an equally firm application of these lofty principles, in respect of his partner in the legal action, when Foulstone was later convicted of burglary.

Liptrott responded angrily and untruthfully, claiming that David Hart had had no links with the Committee, only to be contradicted by his Shirebrook Committee colleague, Roland Taylor, who admitted Hart had indeed met the Committee. Undaunted, Liptrott continued to unravel. Apparently, even the overtime ban was illegal now because it had not been the subject of a ballot under Rule 43.

Rejecting charges that the Committee was designed to damage the NUM, Liptrott felt individual Areas should be free to negotiate bonus and incentive schemes with the Board and told the *Observer* on 17th December that he objected to "... all these insinuations. I have done nothing but fight for this

204

Union." What, some strikers wondered, would have been the outcome if Liptrott had fought *against* his Union, if this was him fighting *for* it?

Demonstrating a worryingly faulty memory he now denied taking aid from Conservatives and other enemies of the NUM, saying, "We had the chance of donations from the Conservatives and Liberals but we sent them back," before bizarrely concluding that because the NUM had accepted help from the Soviet Union, "so now we [Working Miners' Committees] have said we will take money from any source."

There were several reasons for the row. As noted previously, there is no doubt that many rank-and-file working miners were concerned about the Committees' sources of funds and support. There were others, too, who saw no need for them now the Area was under the control of the rebels. Of most significance, though, was that Lynk, who had very carefully and skilfully maintained a public distance from the Notts Working Miners' Committee, while indirectly and quietly encouraging it to further the breakaway, now saw that the time had arrived to cut it adrift. After all, in the new breakaway union there would be lucrative positions, jobs and other benefits to enjoy. Clarke and Liptrott represented the most obvious challengers to Lynk and Prendergast for these roles and the leadership of the new union.

Lynk, it is suggested by Henry Richardson and Ray Chadburn, had always been an ambitious man who had long nurtured resentment at what he perceived to be his demeaning and junior role in the Area's hierarchy.

Chadburn says of Lynk, "All Roy Lynk ever wanted was power. He was always out for number one, always wanted the top job. He was a rat: you couldn't trust him."

Richardson is equally scathing in his assessment. "He were a scoundrel, always been known as a scoundrel and had a repu tation as a scoundrel. When he was elected, he were Branch Secretary at Sutton. Now, he wasn't a bad Branch Secretary. He looked after his men, he were very popular with them. It was only a small pit, one of the smallest we'd got, only about 500 men, but he certainly looked after his men there. But, when he was elected, a bit of money went missing from the Welfare at Sutton and he was involved in it."

Chadburn agrees with Richardson's account and adds, "Joe [Whelan], I don't know why, could have had him then but he didn't." Richardson says, "Joe Whelan, of all people, who was the class enemy of somebody like Lynk, covered it up because he didn't want to bring anything bad on the name of the Union. He got Lynk off the hook and that were sort of bloke he [Lynk] were."

Chadburn says, "That's how dishonest he was, in his social activities. If it'd been me, I'd have shopped him. And he became Financial Secretary! That was pretty ominous, wasn't it? Nobody ever trusted him. All Lynk ever wanted was power.

"When you did press statements, it was always the President or General Secretary and Lynk used to say, 'Why don't you let me go on telly?' 'Well, you're not President or General Secretary' and he'd go, 'Oh, I'm only the rubbing-rag here, aren't I?' All he wanted was to be seen, to be big."

Chadburn explains that in the Area pecking order, it was always the 'junior' official who dealt with benevolent and financial concerns for the members but "Lynk didn't like that: 'I may as well be an insurance salesman', he said," so he changed his job title "… to make himself look more important. That was Roy Lynk."

Richardson also says Lynk was an "utter liar" and recounts the tale of 'Lynk's rock'. "I got in early one morning and the caretaker was sweeping up a load of glass. Someone had thrown a rock through the office window, during the night. Now we never knew who did it: we never knew if it was thrown by a striking miner aiming for Lynk's office or a working miner aiming for mine or Ray's. But Lynk had it mounted on his desk with a plaque that said 'From Arthur Scargill's Flying Pickets'. When you saw him on the telly, that rock was always there and he'd tell folk, 'It just missed my head.' What a bloody liar! He hadn't even been there when it happened! None of us had and no one knew who it had been meant for. That's Roy Lynk, though."

Richardson is convinced that Lynk's drive towards establishing a breakaway Union had little, if anything, to do with any sense, however distorted, of political principle or a desire for 'democracy'. Like his predecessor, George Spencer, "his big thing was keeping politics out of the union. That's what he was about." Lynk, it is alleged, was motivated by nothing more than a desire for personal advancement and enrichment. "Definitely," says Richardson. "Without a doubt. I never had any direct evidence that Lynk had been involved with what would become the Notts Working Miners' Committee, before the strike, but once that bandwagon was rolling, that was it: he was in. That was his chance."

Chadburn, though, suggests Lynk could have been involved in moves to form a breakaway as early as 1981. "When there were miners threatening to come out on strike, there was James Cowan, then the Industrial Relations Officer from Hobart House [the NCB HQ], and we used to have the Notts and District Miners' Pension scheme, which was from the old Spencer days. I was the chairman, and I can remember at this meeting, with Lynk and George Cheshire [former Area Official] and James Cowan comes to me and says, 'Can I have a word with you?' And I said, 'Well, if it's anything to do with the pension scheme, you've a right to raise it,' and he says, 'No. It's personal.' And then he says, 'I'm going to give you a proposition. You know we've got a possible strike looming in Wales: have you ever thought of leading Nottingham away? You've got the best productivity, you'd have the best wages, and you'd be looked after.' So you see a seed was being sown. This was 1981! They were going to take on the Welsh miners then they backed off and he's there trying to sow a seed in Nottingham. A lot of people don't know these sorts of things: the undercurrent was already there. I told him we're National Union of Mineworkers: don't talk to me about breakaways."

Following this exchange, there were several unconfirmed reports that Cowan then made the same advances to Lynk. Around the same time, Lynk was noted to be absent from his duties at Berry Hill, with no explanation, on several occasions, and on one of those occasions, was alleged to have been seen in the company of Cowan at the NCB offices in Edwinstowe. From this point on, former associates say Lynk became an outspoken advocate of policies favourable to the Board no matter how detrimental they might have been to miners, with Chadburn even stating that Lynk had been involved in discussions to form a breakaway involving Craftsmen from Hucknall and Calverton collieries.

"You could see the old Spencerism beneath the surface and you'd got people like Johnny Bonser of Annersley: these became big advocates of the breakaway. And Moorgreen: they were big advocates of the breakaway. This was before the strike. You could sense Spencerism. You'd only just got to scratch the surface and it was there again.

"Me and Scargill went to Calverton Miners' Welfare to address the Calverton men, to persuade them to come out on strike, and Lynk spoke against it. He'd got some people, a gang at Calverton, and they linked up with some at Linby and they linked up with some at Hucknall and you could see *then*, these were Craftsmen, they were getting ready to break away, as Craftsmen, away from the national union. Lynk had tried this once before with Craftsmen in Nottinghamshire: to break away, and Lynk, when he was Secretary at Sutton, was supporting the move. Anyway, it was defeated but you could see the old Spencerism beneath the surface again, in Nottinghamshire." What Chadburn and Richardson didn't know then, of course, was just how far Lynk was prepared to go.

On the eve of the Area Council meeting, it appeared the NUM might prevent the Area from pushing through the rule changes after all. The working miners QC, Igor Judge, demanded the NUM be prohibited from even bringing their case to the High Court at all, based on the persistent contempt of court shown by the leadership. "The NUM's contempt is not technical," implored Judge. "It is deliberate, persistent and flagrant. They have come to this Court without any attempt to purge their contempt, without the hint of apology."

To the NUM's surprise, Mr. Justice Warner rejected the argument. He judged that the contempt rulings were an entirely separate matter and should have no bearing on another, quite different issue. Was this that rarest of creatures in 1984? A High Court judge sympathetic to the miners' cause? Fortunately, the leadership were sufficiently well versed in the attitudes and views of judges towards striking miners: they declined to start the celebrations early. Which was wise. The case was lost, with Justice Warner finding in favour of the Nottinghamshire Area: it could change its rules if it so wished. He held out the slim hope that the NUM could return to court once the impact of the rules was clear, when there *might* be a case under breach of contract to quash the change. That couldn't be heard until February at the earliest, however. For now, it was a done deal.

The following day, 20th December, saw the Area Council endorse the main change, the deletion of Rule 30, on the basis of the mandate produced by the Branch vote. Twenty-nine Branches to two voted not to recognise the authority of their union's elected leadership.

Roy Lynk at last came clean. The next day he told journalists John Lloyd and Martin Adeney that he and his colleagues were quite prepared to run a 'wholly autonomous union'. Because "once you've started down a road, you have to be prepared to follow it through."[61]

What had changed from just twenty-four hours previously, when he had emphatically denied, as he had always done, that there was any intention of a breakaway, was not explained.

December 1984 offered the strikers only a small crumb of consolation. Chief Constable Charles McLachlan was savaged as the National Council for Civil Liberties released its report detailing its investigation into the dispute in the County.

The report infuriated McLachlan, highlighting dozens of specific criticisms of his force and its conduct throughout the dispute. All of which pointed toward one conclusion: the police had not been concerned with upholding the law but had, instead, been actively prosecuting a specific political agenda. To whit: the furthering of the Government's conscious plan to break the strike and the NUM. Among the more serious and controversial conclusions were:

— *We think it is reasonable to assume that Special Branch police officers have been active in this dispute, providing general and specific intelligence to assist police operations.*

— *One specific area of surveillance on which we have received a number of complaints is the tapping of telephones and interception of mail. In some instances, circumstantial evidence in support of the complaints has been very strong.*

— *One of the most disturbing aspects of the policing of the dispute is a small number of incidents in which witnesses described as rampaging groups of police officers have run through mining villages, bursting into houses in pursuit of pickets, causing extensive damage to property and assaulting residents. These incidents require the most thorough and urgent investigation.*

— *Intimidation of, or attacks on, striking miners and their families have received far less publicity and, as far as we can judge, less response from the police.*

McLachlan responded indignantly. The report paid only "lip service" to the role of the police. It was far more concerned with the rights of those who wished to stop others working than those who wished to work. He denied his force was a strike-breaking operation and insisted his officers did not "take sides". Regarding the allegations that dealt with police violence, these were isolated incidents or "myths" and "there almost seems to be a manufacturing house of rumours intent on discrediting the police." He concluded in robust form, stating, "I think members of the public must judge from the bias of this report whose civil liberties the NCCL are concerned about."

'Bias' was an interesting accusation to make, given the composition of the NCCL panel that had carried out the investigation and compiled the report. While Ian Martin, General Secretary of the Fabian Society, might reasonably have been considered a natural ally of striking miners, it would take a leap of considerable proportions to imagine the former Chief Constable of Devon and Cornwall, John Alderson, to be some sort of Scargillite stooge.

The panel was rounded out by Sarah McCabe of the Oxford University Centre for Criminological Research, Chris Mason, lecturer in International Relations at Glasgow University and Larry Gostin, the NCCL's Chair.

While the report was welcomed by the striking miners' leaders it was of little practical assistance to them at that juncture. Any action against the police would take months to resolve and would do nothing to push the strike forward in the here and now. Besides, there was Christmas to organise.

A strange mood existed in the pit villages of Nottinghamshire that December. While there was still a small hard core of strikers refusing to countenance anything other than total victory, most knew, even if they only admitted it to themselves, that it was all over. With winter coming on fast and a hostile world surrounding the few loyalist enclaves, Christmas 1984 was seen as something of a defiant last hurrah. Striking families drew closer together and to other striking families. This had been a strike by whole families and communities, not just

210

miners. They turned inwards towards each other, and the spirit that had given birth to instances almost of dual-power, and entire villages cleaving from the mainstream, in the loyalist strongholds of Yorkshire, South Wales and Kent, made itself felt in beleaguered Nottinghamshire. A spirit still not broken by ten months of imprisonment, beatings and deprivation, ensured that Nottinghamshire's strike children would still have a merry Christmas.

Celebrity popsters, Band Aid, had released a single, *Do They Know It's Christmas? (Feed the World)*, to raise funds for victims of famine in Africa, and the extensive publicity given to their fundraising endeavours had touched the conscience of millions. Nevertheless, the famine relief appeal had diverted funds from miners' support groups and so the miners' supporters had to redouble their efforts.

Activity in soup-kitchens, strike centres and committee rooms across the County ramped up still further as the generosity and kindness of hundreds of thousands of supporters around the UK saw toys, turkeys, hampers and gifts arriving, all of which required packaging and distributing. No striking miner's family would go without a Christmas dinner, and if many of them were eaten in freezing homes, with their residents wearing four layers of clothing, maybe pride lent an inner warmth.

At least the festive season had seen a slight lightening of the mood on picket lines. For months, picketing had been completely ineffective in Nottinghamshire, and it had only been maintained for reasons of sheer stubborn loyalty and to provide a conscience-pricking reminder to the working miners of the consequences of their actions.

The odd brave or foolhardy working miner would wave his bulging Christmas pay-packet when driven across the picket lines, only to be greeted by a defiant verse or two of *I'd rather be a picket than a scab on Christmas Day*, sung to the tune of Jingle Bells.

Many strikers speak of the Christmas of 1984 as one of the best they ever had, and that was a sentiment endorsed by many in Nottinghamshire. The generosity from supporters and sympathisers had been magnificent and the County rocked to the sounds of celebration. Children in Miners' Welfares met Santa Claus and huge communal lunches were served up to sittings of several hundred striking families. Older, wiser heads, who knew what the New Year would bring, kept their thoughts to themselves and watched the youngsters exorcise the past ten months of struggle.

Chapter 13:
Everybody Wants
To Rule the World

"There is a tide in the affairs of men. Which, taken at the
flood, leads on to fortune; omitted, all the voyage of their life
is bound in shallows and in miseries. On such a full sea are
we now afloat and we must take the current when it serves"

SHAKESPEARE

Despite the introduction of a battery of anti-trade union legislation, the Government had been careful not to invoke its
provisions in the fight against the NUM. Peter Walker, the key
Tory strategist during the dispute, had been at pains not to
force the TUC into the miners' camp by using any of the Acts
which, he felt, might have triggered mass solidarity action. His
caution, though prudent, was entirely unnecessary. Thanks to
the number of NUM members happy to take their own union to
court, the Government's job of using the law to obstruct the
strike was largely done for them.

In addition, the TUC had singularly failed to deliver any kind
of meaningful support to the miners. While individual unions had
loaned the NUM enormous sums of money to help it through the
year, Scargill was at pains to point out in December that, "We are
not asking for moral support or resolutions, we are asking now for

practical assistance and we have asked the General Council to be convened to mobilise industrial action in support of this union." His was no lone voice. At the Special Delegates' Conference before Christmas, a resolution to that effect had been passed by the attendees. "... that the General Council mobilise industrial action to stop this most vicious threat in our history to the freedom and independence of British trade unionism." Scargill added, "... we want the decisions of the TUC Conference in September put into practical effect."

Why, with the dispute nearly a year old, the miners were still begging and pleading for the assistance a trade union might have taken for granted, lay with the Employment Act 1982 and the Trade Union Act 1984.

In the case of the former, described by its architect, Norman Tebbit, as his greatest achievement, the Act set out wide-ranging edicts designed to seriously impair a trade union's ability to operate effectively. Among its elements were:

— Authority for the Government to pay compensation to employees who lost their jobs due to the closed-shop practices enshrined in previous Labour administrations' legislation.

— A substantial increase in compensation to those whose employment was terminated for refusing to join a union in a closed-shop workplace.

— The repeal of the previous immunity from civil action for trade unions.

— The banning of secondary action by a trade union.

— The right of employers, protected by law, to sack workers on strike.

In response, the 1982 TUC Conference voted to defy the Act. The General Council endorsed an eight-point plan around which the resistance would coalesce.

Scargill led the charge. "There is only one response that this movement can give, faced with this legislation. We should say, 'we will defy the law'." While there was nothing remarkable about the NUM President making such a declaration, SOGAT's Bill Keys must have looked back with some embarrassment at his conduct during the miners' strike, considering his remarks at the 1982 Conference: "I will say publicly anywhere, if it is a bad law that doesn't nurture good, that doesn't look after the interests of ordinary people in this nation I will oppose the law and I will influence other people to oppose the law... if that means breaking the law I will do it."

It wasn't unanimous, however, with that year's TUC President, Frank Chapple opining, "Those who advocate that bad laws should not be obeyed — in circumstances where such 'bad' laws are enacted by a democratically elected government — are putting at risk the entire conception of civilised society. That directly challenges democracy... the way to change bad laws is to change the government that has made them."

The irony of a trade union leader adopting such a stance clearly escaped Chapple. Had the Tolpuddle Martyrs taken such a position in 1834, he wouldn't have had a trade union to lead, or indeed a TUC of which he could be President. It was a dominant view in Labour and trade union circles, though. The demonstrable truth of social history in Britain, and internationally, that only rebellion drove progress, was not something the average trade union leader was happy to acknowledge. From women winning the vote, the right to free speech and the right even to be paid for work, the reality is that barely one single meaningful gain had ever been graciously bestowed by a benevolent ruling class or won by an adherence to the law.

While all the TUC leaders were happy, at anniversary galas and memorial dinners, to pay homage to their heroic forbears, the very people to whom they owed their privileged positions, the idea of emulating their methods was anathema.

When the 1984 Act was introduced, it expanded the scope of the earlier legislation and added to it. It included stringent requirements regarding the balloting of trade union members, the elections of officials and a complex series of hoops through which trade unions would be required to jump before a strike could even be deemed 'legal'.

The cumulative effect of both Acts was to see the TUC reverse its earlier promise to defy the law. The NUM was alone in honouring its commitment to do so. Despite sequestration, nearly a million pounds in fines and the status of, effectively, running an outlawed organisation, gaolings, phonetapping and mail interception, the NUM had shown it was possible to not only function but to sustain massive and prolonged resistance with popular support. With miners running around the country with plastic bags stuffed full of hard cash, one can only imagine the outcome if the TUC had followed suit.

Instead, the TUC went through the motions of assigning its officials to assist in negotiations and seek a settlement. By the time the New Year dawned, relations between them and the NUM couldn't have been worse. Scargill, singled out in a series of leaks to the press as someone almost mad and consistently making the most outrageous and unrealistic demands, simply refused to settle for anything less than the preservation of his members' jobs, the withdrawal of the closure plan and that the TUC keep the promises it had made in 1982 and honour the resolutions passed at its Conference in September.

As for Scargill's infamous intransigence and refusal to accept 'reality', it should be noted that he comprised but one third of the negotiating team. Also that on 11th September, the NUM, along with NACODS, had accepted a draft proposal formulated by ACAS only to see it rejected by the NCB. The following day, a second ACAS formulation was again accepted by the NUM but spurned by the Board and on the 13th a third and final ACAS settlement was again turned down by the Coal Board. ACAS then withdrew seeing no further avenues worth exploring. The only proposal that interested the Government was unconditional surrender by the NUM.

In response to protestations that the law now made secondary strikes and supportive industrial action illegal and impossible, Scargill reminded his fellow trade union leaders of their earlier promises and pointed out that the NUM was already taking illegal action and were not only still standing but still fighting.

Why significant TUC action never happened was simple to explain: Scargill, despite criticism from the hard left, some of it justified, saw his role as a trade union leader as much more than just that of fighting for the best deals for his members. Only the socialist transformation of society could guarantee complete security for miners and the working class. In his worldview, the trade unions were the vanguard of a movement that would oversee the abolition of capitalism and its replacement by a fully planned economy. The TUC, on the other hand, was an integral part of that system. Its role was to secure small improvements for its

216

members but strictly within the parameters of the market and what it could 'afford' to concede at any particular time. When push came to shove, the TUC was simply not prepared to risk the loss of its assets, perks and privileges in the crusade the NUM was waging on behalf of the working class as a whole. Indeed, sections of the TUC bureaucracy were only too happy to see the miners scuppered and, by the time January arrived, the strikers had long since passed hoping for anything of note to emerge from the TUC.

Admittedly, the NUM's attitude to the TUC, right from the start of the dispute, could best be described as suspicious. NUM General Secretary, Peter Heathfield, hadn't even written to the TUC to officially inform it that a trade dispute was taking place until several weeks into the strike. Even then he pointedly remarked that the NUM required no assistance or intervention at that time but should that change, well, don't call us: we'll call you.

It was also about control. The rank-and-file wanted control of *their* strike and were reluctant to allow the leadership to entirely dictate its course, never mind hand it over to third parties, while, for the leadership itself, the shadow of 1926 loomed large. A reprise of the betrayal and abandonment handed out to the MFGB was not going to happen this time. All of which was understandable. It rankled with the TUC General Council, though, who felt they were being treated as little more than Scargill's errand-boys. In truth, all the NUM had ever wanted from the TUC was the solidarity action to which they felt any trade union was morally entitled. That prospect was snuffed out on 7th December when the TUC officially ruled out 'illegal' action in support of the miners.

As the strike tottered into 1985, the NUM was as isolated as it had ever been from the rest of the trade union movement. Individual union branches and depots, particularly in the rail sector, had provided courageous and principled secondary action: refusing to move stocks, stopping signals and blacking transport carrying scab-coal. The NUR in Leicestershire, just one example, earned the admiration and appreciation of its tiny core of striking miners, the famous 'Dirty Thirty',[62] for its unstinting secondary action, all illegal and exposing its members to instant dismissal. It was never going to be enough but it was all the miners were going to get.

As soon as 1985 dawned, Nottinghamshire resumed the process of breaking away from the NUM. On 10th January the NEC gave notice that a Special Delegate's Conference would be convened on the 29th to discuss and vote on expelling the Area from the NUM. If at any point up to the day of the Conference, the rebels wished to meet the NEC to discuss the matter and attempt to resolve it, the NEC would be only too happy to oblige. Equally, if Nottinghamshire, at any time prior to the 29th, abandoned its rule changes and accepted the authority of the NEC, the Conference would be cancelled.

Should the breakaway go ahead, the Conference would consider:

— *Expelling the Area from the National Union of Mineworkers.*

— *Provision to be made for any Branch en bloc or individual members to retain membership of the NUM.*

— *All members to be readmitted as members of a newly constituted Nottinghamshire Area.*

— *Infrastructure of the new Area; facilities, premises, Area Council and Area Executive.*

— *The termination of contracts of the pro-breakaway Nottinghamshire Area officials.*

— *A contribution rate for members.*

— *The NEC to be authorised in taking legal action to recover funds and assets from the Nottinghamshire Area.*

— *An amendment to rules to prevent future developments of a similar nature to Nottinghamshire.*[63]

Peter Heathfield then wrote to the Nottinghamshire Area inviting its representatives to discuss the situation with a view to finding a "... solution in the best interests of the Union."[64]

Summing up the NEC's position, Scargill stated that, "The decisions Nottinghamshire have taken mean in effect the establishment of a breakaway union and I would urge very strongly indeed that they reconsider their decision. I think it is extremely sad and regrettable that people who have said that they did not want to have a breakaway union have brought in these constitutional changes which have effectively done just that."

This wasn't simply empty rhetoric either. A motion by the Northumberland Area to expel Nottinghamshire forthwith had been avoided by the introduction of a document formulated by Scargill, McGahey and Heathfield outlining several alternative options, and a proposal to suspend Nottinghamshire for six months was defeated by seventeen votes to four.

The last thing the leadership needed at this juncture in the dispute was an Area breaking away. Rightly or wrongly, mainly wrongly as far as the consistently militant Kent Area was concerned, every possible way of keeping Nottinghamshire in the fold while submitting to national authority was being explored. Although it didn't stop David Prendergast describing the NEC's decision as "blackmail". He went on to ponder that the forthcoming Conference might even be unconstitutional as many striking Areas had not held recent elections of Delegates. The working miners' friendly brief, David Negus, agreed. "If the Delegate Conference is challenged on the basis that Delegates have outrun their mandates, it is likely to be successful."

The following day the rebel Area Executive met and decided that they would not meet the NEC. Defiantly, they reaffirmed the Council's decision to delete Rule 30 and decided on a Special Area Conference to inform the Branches of the decisions taken.

Richardson and Chadburn refused to take part in any meetings where the subjects under discussion related to any sort of breakaway.

On the 11th an emergency session of the Area Executive opened to consider correspondence circulated by Richardson in his capacity as Area General Secretary. The contents contained a leaflet referring to the relevant NEC minute regarding Branches joining any future reconstituted Area *en bloc*. Richardson was not invited to the meeting, but this peculiar variant of natural justice didn't prevent the Executive from agreeing to recommend to the Council that he be suspended from his post as General Secretary. Apparently, circulating official correspondence from the Sheffield HQ was unacceptable.

The correspondence in question was in the form of a leaflet which outlined what steps NUM members would need to take to retain their membership in the event of the Area breaking away. On the reverse, a number of statements relating to Rule 51, Spencerism and a plea to "Stand with Your Union" were included.

This was deemed to be "recruiting material for the national union" and its distribution, Richardson was told, was incompatible with the behaviour of an official supposedly representing the majority of members in the Area.

The working miners soon produced their own counter-propaganda in the form of a letter, headed, *What Kind of Men Do They Think You Are?* It read:

> The leaflet handed out to some Notts. NUM members last week is based on an outright lie. Rule 51 was not proposed by Notts. Area. Len Clarke, our former President, is a man who spent his working life serving the NUM. He is a man whose integrity is beyond question. He says, "No such proposal ever came from this Area." So, the pamphlet is not based on the truth.
>
> But it's also a clumsy attempt at a confidence trick — it "invites" you to remain a member of the NUM. What a nerve! You ARE the NUM.
>
> One thing's certain — we don't think they even begin to understand you. Can they seriously believe that you will desert your democratically-elected officials to join those who attacked your homes, assaulted your mates and called you scab?
>
> WHAT KIND OF MEN DO THEY THINK YOU ARE? Your Notts. NUM Officials stand for full consultation with the membership on all the major issues in this coalfield. We stand for democracy — not dictatorship. And we leave you with this thought: Rule 51 places ultimate and supreme power over your union membership and your livelihood in the hands of the National President. This chilling sentence forms Rule 51 (d) (vii) 'The National Disciplinary Committee shall have the power to consider a complaint that a member has done any act (which includes any omission) which may be detrimental to the interests of the Union and which is not specifically provided for in this Rule.' Get out of that, brothers!

Rumours were now sweeping the County regarding the fate of those who might choose to stay with the NUM, should Nottinghamshire be expelled. Strike-breakers had stoked anxiety among some strikers by stating they'd lose their pensions and service benefits and strike-leaders found themselves bogged down addressing meetings around the coalfield to calm fears and explain the likely outcomes.

On the 12th, despite Chadburn ruling such a suspension unconstitutional, the Delegates voted by nineteen to eleven to uphold their decision. Richardson was 'allowed' to continue as a paid official but was now no longer Area General Secretary.

The 14th saw the Area Executive meeting yet again and a reprise of Chadburn's earlier ruling that Richardson's suspension was out of order. Richardson informed the meeting that, according to legal advice he'd received, his suspension was indeed illegal. A letter from Peter Heathfield was then produced. The NUM's General Secretary informed the Area that the official position of the NUM was to continue to recognise Richardson as Nottinghamshire's General Secretary.

On advice from the lawyers, now a permanent fixture at Nottinghamshire Area meetings, the suspension was widened to include all Richardson's duties as an official.

Ray Chadburn says, "That was the hardest period of the whole dispute, for me. Up 'til then I'd got Henry but on the 12th, my birthday incidentally, they had a kangaroo court."

Richardson recalls, "I didn't drive then, so I always got a taxi in and I was usually first into the office. On that day, I got there and the car park was full so I said to the caretaker, 'What's going on? Whose are all these cars?' He said there were a meeting going off. I said, 'What bloody meeting? The President isn't here and I've only just got here. How can there be a meeting?' Well, Ray turned up and I told him what was going off so in we went."

Chadburn says, "Only the Area President or General Secretary could convene a meeting of the Executive but unbeknownst to me and Henry, the Executive, all working miners, with Lynk and Prendergast, held a secret meeting, with their solicitor, a bloke called Paul Todd. Lynk had been having a lot of clandestine meetings with him. Whenever me or Henry tackled him about these meetings it was always personal business, he said, but it was just a pretext to talk about the breakaway and on this particular day, my bloody birthday, we get there and wonder what the bloody hell was going off. There were all the Delegates, the Executive Committee and a barrister, Igor Judge. I took the Chair and said, 'This is a kangaroo court.' No way were they suspending Henry. It was out of order, this meeting that was taking place."

To Chadburn's fury, he was voted out of the Chair and he and Richardson were ordered to leave the meeting while the Executive discussed Richardson's future. Once the decision had been reached, Chadburn left and went to the pub to calm down. It didn't work. "It was my birthday," he smiles. "I had four or five pints and came storming back and there was the solicitor, there was Lynk and there was Prendergast. Somebody spoke and I went for Prendergast's throat. He's flapping, 'He's attacking me! He's attacking me!' And then the solicitor, Paul Todd, said, 'Calm down, Ray. Come on outside. We're going to smash Scargill.'"

Richardson was temporarily replaced by George Liddle from Harworth pit. "Harworth," sneers Chadburn. "They used to go on strike every Friday. Every bloody Friday I'd be up there sorting out whatever it was they were striking about that week. But when you wanted them to strike they wouldn't bloody do it!"

While many Nottinghamshire loyalists were angry and saddened at Richardson's treatment, soon to be meted out to Chadburn, too, there were some who had become increasingly concerned by the behaviour of the two pro-strike officials. Clipstone strike-leader, John Lowe, was particularly frustrated. "... Ray Chadburn and Henry Richardson left me disappointed in their lack of open commitment to our cause. With Ray we never seemed to know whether he approved of what we were doing or not. Until he was actually removed by Lynk and co, he always gave me the impression he was more concerned with keeping his position; but to be perfectly fair to him, when he was put to the test by his opponents, he stuck to his principles and was sacked by them.

"Henry was always willing to accommodate our needs whenever possible and I accept that he operated under exceptional difficulties, but his low profile throughout bothered me. That he would eventually be sacked through Lynk was never seriously in doubt, and I did make the point to him: 'Say publicly what you are saying to us privately.' Unfortunately it was quite a while before Henry could find a position within what was happening in the Notts coalfield. Instead of adopting his true position at the head of the strike organisation in the County, he always seemed to be outside it, which, given his true feelings, was a great pity."[65]

The dissidents continued to wave their defiance in the face of the NEC, with Prendergast stating his and Lynk's next move would be to negotiate with the NCB on pay and conditions for Nottinghamshire miners only. Such a move couldn't possibly be tolerated by any trade union and Nottinghamshire knew it:

Lynk and Prendergast were doing all they could to provoke the Area's expulsion. "We shall not be subjected in the Notts NUM to any form of blackmail by the National Executive. We shall be the sole negotiating body for Notts miners and we expect the Board to agree with that," confirmed Prendergast.

Lynk taunted Scargill by adding, "We took a conscious decision to change the rules, fully understanding what was involved. We had the best attended Branch meetings ever held. We have given and given to the national union. The only thing we cannot do is lie down under the heels of a dictator." Moving from the political to the personal, he rubbished the NUM President stating that he "... could not negotiate his way out of the toilet. He's throwing us out to satisfy his own ego."

On the 14th, former Nottinghamshire Area President, Len Clarke, suddenly appeared to help Lynk trash Scargill. He told the *Nottingham Evening Post,* "What we have at the moment is the biggest disaster since the Titanic. Arthur Scargill has taken the most dignified workers in Britain and turned them into paupers and beggars in our streets, just to satisfy his own ego." Modestly offering his services as elder statesman if either side wanted them, he said his priority was unity but, "that does not mean unity under someone like Arthur Scargill."

For someone who had frequently boasted of his role in smashing Spencerism in the County during the 30s, the former Area chief was oddly sympathetic to the architects of the breakaway.

It was true that there were cracks appearing on the NEC with the right-wing criticising the negotiating 'troika' of Scargill, McGahey and Heathfield for the lack of progress in talks with the Board. The leadership promptly outflanked its critics by widening the negotiating team to include the entire twenty-four-man NEC. Let the Right make a better fist of things if it could.

On the 24th the NEC agreed to restart talks with the NCB, thanks to Peter Heathfield convincing the NCB's Ned Smith that this time they could be worthwhile. They weren't, though, and collapsed on 29th January. Possibly the only significant development was that the talks necessitated the postponement of the Special Delegates' Conference to consider the expulsion of Nottinghamshire. It was rescheduled for 21st February.

The strike was now forty-eight weeks old.

Chapter 14:
We Built This City

*"What lies behind us and what
lies before us are tiny matters
compared to what lies within us."*
STANLEY HASKINS

By the 1st February, the idea of a return to work without a
settlement began to gather pace. The NUM and NCB were by
now as far apart as ever and, seeing victory within touching
distance, MacGregor, under strict instructions from Downing
Street, was treading very carefully lest any slip hand an
eleventh-hour opportunity to the miners. Regarding the possibility of returning without a settlement, Scargill said, "If the
NUM did not get an agreement, the position would be considerably better than what the NCB is trying to impose on our
Union." This stance was by no means shared by all the striking
miners.

On the 4th the Board claimed another 2,318 miners had
returned to work. It was clear the Government and NCB were
waiting for fifty percent of the strikers to return to work, whereupon they could deem the dispute officially over. Even after a
year on strike, the majority were still out and, despite the back
to work numbers increasing sharply, Peter Heathfield warned
that MacGregor and Thatcher could be in for a long wait.

In a surprising *volte face,* the NUM Executive had indicated a willingness to accept the previous October's Modified Colliery Review Procedure after all, but only as a basis for reopening negotiations. MacGregor added to the pressure and insisted the NUM accept the principle of closure of uneconomic pits *first,* as a precondition to acceptance of the MCRP. NACODS were livid: what, they asked, did this now mean for *their* agreement of the MCRP when it was supposed to have meant 'due weight' and 'full consideration' would be given to any case before any closures were approved and an independent judge was to make the decisions anyway? The strike wasn't even over and already MacGregor had slipped up and revealed his real thinking and exactly how worthless the NACODS agreement was. He retracted the precondition but it was seen as confirmation of what many had long suspected: the Board and Government just did not want a settlement. A mass pit closure program would go ahead and they wanted the heads of miners, and Scargill's, in particular, on spikes. Under no circumstances could the NUM President be allowed to claim any sort of political victory.

This was not left-wing paranoia, either. Ned Smith told the *Mirror's* Industrial Editor, Geoffrey Goodman, that MacGregor had left him with the distinct impression that a deal was definitely on the table but that "something happened between that meeting and my reporting back to MacGregor and that 'something' changed the whole situation. I have no idea what it was but 'something' happened."[66]

Goodman then confirmed, "Smith remains convinced there had been a deliberate leak of his talks with Heathfield in order to sabotage any chance of their success. Nor in his view [Smith's] was it the first time this had happened."[67]

Since at least from the NACODS October settlement, David Hart had urged Margaret Thatcher to go for broke, and this was entirely in tune with the Iron Lady's desires. The truth was that unless MacGregor fumbled again and accidentally dropped an opportunity into the NUM's lap, there was no chance of any settlement even remotely acceptable to the miners emerging. From December, the strike was over and both the NCB and Government were merely going through the motions for the sake of appearances. And so the charade continued.

On the 12th, Norman Willis met MacGregor in a final effort to restart talks, and the two of them drew up a document that appeared, to the gullible, to offer fresh hope. Willis shuttled back and forth between the NUM and MacGregor, trading one set of amendments after another, none of which either side found acceptable.

Finally, on the 19th, the TUC's seven-man team met with Thatcher personally and produced a second draft proposal. The 'Magnificent Seven', as they were dubbed by NUM wags, were by this point reduced to fighting for scraps: minor amendments and concessions which might, at least, as they saw things, allow the NUM to save some face.

By now, the cracks on the NEC had widened and in addition Scargill's break from the Communist Party was almost complete. Convulsed by its own internal splits and faction fights, the CP was not long for this world, but its historic influence inside the NUM was brought to bear and they discreetly let contacts in the TUC know that their people were ready to settle. One can only wonder if that included Mick McGahey. At the suggestion of Gordon McLennan, the Party's General Secretary, Scargill's old mentor, Bert Ramelson, was wheeled out to persuade the NUM chief to take the deal on offer. Scargill is reported to have flicked through a couple of pages of the Party's suggested proposals before hurling the document to the floor and denouncing it as 'betrayal'.

The TUC proposal was put to the Special Delegates' Conference on the 21st only to be rejected by the Delegates, many of whom were to the left even of Scargill. Even the NEC's moderates felt the proposal was worse than earlier drafts. In a stinging aside, directed at Norman Willis, Northumberland's President, Denis Murphy, observed, "If you send a boy on a man's errand, you'll get big problems."

As the pressure of events mounted, Nottinghamshire was spared yet again as the agenda item to consider the Area's expulsion was shelved once more.

On the 24th, in a last, desperate effort to rally TUC support and generate action, the miners marched once more in London. Although snubbed by both Neil Kinnock and Norman Willis, tens of thousands of miners showed that, even during this final hour, the will to fight on remained. Also, once more, the police came under fire as officers attacked the demonstration and over a hundred arrests were made.

The next day the NCB announced that nearly 4,000 miners had abandoned the strike and returned to work. While the miners were by now inured to the inflated return-to-work figures and the NCB's exaggerated claims, it was by this point apparent that the 'drift back' had become at least a brisk trot. How much longer before it became a stampede?

Arthur Scargill then announced on television that if the Energy Secretary, Peter Walker, had "an ounce of integrity" he would sit down that evening and sign the NACODS Modified Colliery Review Procedure document with the NUM, "thus providing for a resumption of negotiations." Walker was having none of it. He replied, "There can now be no more talking on the main issue of the dispute. It is the common sense of the miner that must now bring it to a swift conclusion." The normally urbane Tory then descended into a quite shocking personal attack, describing Scargill as "pathetic, foolish and stupid" before referring to the latest set of proposals. "Everybody knows that that document is the only document that is going to be available on the major issues of the dispute."

Back in Nottinghamshire, Colin Clarke was unconcerned with such matters. Despite Nottinghamshire having seceded from the NUM's authority, he and the Notts Working Miners' Committee still felt justified in involving themselves in NUM affairs. They were busy looking at measures to oust Arthur Scargill from the Presidency. Having enjoyed the enthusiastic support and largesse of the Conservatives throughout the dispute, it was perhaps fitting that during its closing stages the strike-breakers finally turned to the hated Tory anti-trade union laws in a further effort to cripple their Union.

Norman Tebbit's Trade Union Act 1984, among its wide-ranging restrictions on the internal practices of trade unions, now made it mandatory for officials to stand for re-election every five years. The NUM's custom was to elect its President to serve until reaching the Union's retirement age of fifty-five, although the Conservatives insisted on misrepresenting this, describing the practice as elected 'for life' which sounded much more dramatic and undemocratic.

While the Left usually supported the principle of the utmost accountability to the membership and the right of instant recall of all full-time officials — all perfectly reasonable and democratic

— it was for quite different reasons that Tebbit had passed such legislation. It was one thing for a union's members to campaign for such measures among themselves but quite another to have them imposed by a Tory Government seeking only to restrict the effectiveness of trade unions in representing their members and opposing Government attacks.

Clarke confirmed that the Nottinghamshire Area was backing the Notts Working Miners' Committee's initiative and taking legal advice to explore ways of forcing the NUM Executive to abide by Tebbit's Act.

"We cannot see that the NUM rules would over-ride the law of the land. If not, the whole of the Executive would be affected by this method of re-election. I don't think Arthur Scargill would get back in. We hear a lot of rhetoric on television from people who are supporting the miners on so-called picket lines but a lot of these are not miners," he said.

At the same time, the Nottinghamshire NCB opened a further propaganda offensive but this time it had more subtlety, ostensibly, having little, directly, to do with the strike. Instead, bolstering the view, widespread in the County, that Nottinghamshire's productive and profitable pits would be exempt from any closure program, North Nottinghamshire Area Director, Jack Wood, painted a glowing picture of future prospects and opportunities.

He claimed hundreds of new jobs for school-leavers were being created in the coalfield. In addition, over six hundred had already been filled by school-leavers and youngsters over the age of eighteen during the preceding year, in the North Nottinghamshire coalfield, with a further two hundred to be recruited over the following few months. Apparently the Area, claimed Wood, was "... continuing to build for a long-term future as a major coal producer, with huge investment schemes now being carried out worth £116 million. Our pits are in good shape and though there will probably be a three month period of adjustment when the dispute is over, thereafter we will be on-song to achieve our objectives."

The statement went on to claim that over a hundred young people had also been recruited in the South Nottinghamshire coalfield since April 1984 with a further 250 to be taken on from April 1985 onwards.

South Nottinghamshire Area Director, Harold Taylor, shared in the glad tidings, jubilantly predicting "a great future" for Nottinghamshire's pits.

Presumably both men would have considered it churlish to mention Moorgreen pit, which had already been agreed for closure prior to the strike, and was scheduled to cease production that summer on 19th July. Similarly, the previously-agreed closure of Pye Hill, also due within the year, in no way detracted from the glorious utopia that was the Nottinghamshire coalfield.

However, it appeared that Nottinghamshire colliery managers were not fully on-message with the good-time vibe emanating from their Area Directors. Instead, they gave notice of the treatment their defiant workforces could expect on returning to their pits, with Welbeck colliery manager, Alan Isley, outlining his strategy for dealing with returning strikers. "I like to know their reasons for being off in the first place and their reasons for coming back. I mainly want to know what their attitude has been to the strike and whether they have blindly followed the leadership. That has to be management's function. We must attempt to talk to people and try and make sure they think twice before taking such action again." Taking a hardline approach to strikers and giving an insight into the kind of rough treatment they could expect, the pit boss went on to warn, "It is only fair for me to point out in Notts that management loyalties have to be with those who have been working all the time. It is no good coming to us with every little problem when they [strikers] have caused it in the first place."

Widely seen as *carte blanche* for working miners to bully, victimise and intimidate the striking minority, while management would ignore "every little problem", a macho section of the County management was clearly relishing the prospect of exacting revenge on their recalcitrant charges, something of which Ian MacGregor would no doubt have approved.

The Henry Richardson drama played on, too. The Area General Secretary had been unsuccessful in his legal bid to overturn his suspension but was still officially recognised by the NUM as its man in Nottinghamshire. While he had attended the Special Delegates' Conference, the rest of the Area had refused to go. Their Delegates claimed they had not been informed of the Conference. In reality, as per procedure, the

NEC had written to Richardson, as the Area General Secretary, to inform him of the Conference and the relevant arrangements. The Area Executive were furious that he and not Lynk, by now the 'Acting General Secretary', had been informed. Instead, the Area Executive met on the same day as the Conference but had to postpone its sacking of Richardson as he was in London.

Matters in Nottinghamshire had become farcical. The idea that the Area hadn't known of the Special Delegates' Conference was ridiculous. The manufactured pique at Richardson receiving the correspondence was equally risible. Still Lynk and company kept up the pretence, issuing one statement after another proclaiming their 'outrage' and 'indignation' at slights both real and imagined.

Lunacy was piled upon farce by a newly-formed organisation called the Law and Order Society. Comprising Conservatives, right-wing businessmen, lawyers and bankers, the Society registered itself as a limited company with seed-money of £100,000 with the express purpose of seeing Arthur Scargill jailed. Its spokesman, the MP for Leicester East, Peter Bruinvels, announced the Society's plan to see the NUM President "behind bars" as a result of a private prosecution.

Bruinvels made Norman Tebbit look like Arthur Scargill: a hardline right-winger, he volunteered to be the UK's official hangman if capital punishment was ever restored. He was also responsible for the description of the BBC as 'Bolsheviks Broadcasting Communism' which became popular with harrumphing gin-soaked Colonels and the twin-set and pearl-adorned matrons of the English Home Counties.

One imagines the terrified Scargill slept much more peacefully when the Society promptly disappeared after its public launch at the House of Commons.

At the same time, Nottinghamshire Chief Constable, Charles McLachlan, was experiencing his own difficulties with the forces of law and order. He'd started the strike as the President of the Association of Chief Police Officers and was to end it as the Head of the NRC, in recognition of impeccable service to his political mistress. He still had a rough few weeks left to ride out, however.

Leeds-based solicitor, Alan Craig, announced his intention to sue McLachlan on behalf of seventy miners wrongly arrested during the mass picket of Harworth in August. In the latest round of prosecutions, thirty miners had walked free from Shire Hall magistrates' court after the prosecution offered no evidence in support of the charges, which included unlawful assembly, intimidation and endangering public peace.

Dropping charges against eighty-three pickets from a total of ninety-one arrested was a severe embarrassment for McLachlan and his Nottinghamshire force. A spokesman for the County's Constabulary tried to make the best of a bad situation, saying, "When an officer is dealing with a public order situation, his prime concern is to restore the peace. When dealing with the prosecution of alleged offenders, other affairs have to be taken into account, such as the degree of culpability of the accused person, the cost of the prosecution, the penalties likely to be imposed, the likelihood of conviction and the experience of the courts in dealing with this type of offence.

"Our decision not to prosecute was based on the best possible legal advice and the withdrawal of serious charges is in no way a criticism of the police action at the scene."

Craig responded, "I have received instructions from more than seventy of the defendants to bring a High Court action against the Chief Constable for damages. All these people who have complained about being beaten up in the course of their arrests and being held in police cells for a number of hours, are now coming forward to make claims for compensation."

On the 27th, the NCB claimed that the magical half-way point had been passed. 93,000 miners were now back at work; over fifty percent of the workforce. NUM diehards insisted that over sixty percent were still holding out and they might well have been correct but it didn't matter: the strike was over and everyone knew it.

The recriminations, which had brewing for months, broke out as various TUC heads queued up to castigate Arthur Scargill for throwing away several chances of an honourable settlement, if not an outright victory. His foolishness, ego and stubbornness were all blamed for the strike's collapse.

In reality it was a testament to the NUM President's indomitable force of will and personal integrity that he had remained so unwilling to 'compromise'. The fundamental truth, that his critics inside both the TUC and NUM refused to

231

acknowledge, was that there was *no* compromise option available. The central question was pit closures: it was what the entire strike had been about and, for its entire duration, despite some near-errors by MacGregor, the NCB boss had resolutely refused to yield even an inch on that issue. Scargill, backed by the overwhelming majority of the membership, had equally refused to bargain away his members' livelihoods for the sake of a shameful facesaving 'partial victory', 'tactical success' or 'principled retreat.'

Even during the July talks, which had seen the NUM come achingly close to triumph, Scargill had insisted on a 'copper-bottomed guarantee' for reasons quite other than 'vanity' and 'foolishness'; quite simply the President didn't trust MacGregor and was terrified of leaving wriggle-room which would have allowed the closure program to go ahead.

The NCB and the NUM had had an agreement: the *Plan for Coal*. If the Government had decided that that needed revision then the correct procedure was to have invited the NUM to sit around the table and renegotiate, not announce the closure of five, twenty or seventy pits, with a corresponding number of job losses.

Despite the brokering of proposals containing a fudge here, a token concession there or a facesaving straw to be grasped somewhere else, Scargill had remained unmoved.

While the TUC had urged him to seize the way out, he knew such solutions were utterly worthless. MacGregor had insisted that pits should close as and when the NCB decided and in direct contravention of the mechanisms agreed in the *Plan for Coal*. For Scargill to have signed any of the various proposed agreements wouldn't have been any sort of 'compromise' at all: it would have been unqualified surrender. And worse, it would have been a betrayal of over 150,000 miners and their families who had risked everything they had in a courageous and desperate bid to keep their pits open and their jobs available for their sons and grandsons.

Defeat at the hands of a better-armed, better-equipped and more powerful enemy, while agonising, contained no shame. On the other hand, defeat at the hands of a general who'd sold his own troops for the worthless approval of those too cowardly to fight the war in the first place, would have been despicable. Scargill, whatever other faults he possessed, was never that man.

From the very beginning, miners had also been builders. They'd built entire communities and a way of life that sustained, nurtured and nourished them and their families. They'd built social clubs, community centres, bowling greens, football clubs and health centres. When a pit was shut, it wasn't just the job that died, it was the entire community that relied upon it, fed from it and was protected by it. As Brian Evangelista remarks, "Generally, miners are tremendous people; absolutely tremendous. Tremendous engineers, too. Not just mechanical and electrical engineers but the people who cut the coal; they were engineers, whatever you want to call them. And what they ended up with was a tragedy."

The strike hadn't just been about jobs, it had also been about the survival of a community whose distinctive culture and mode of living was under concerted attack.

Much has been made of Scargill's 'revolutionary' challenge to the Government. Much ink has been spilled regarding his desire to bring down Thatcher with the miners as his gullible proletarian vanguard. Again, such characterisations were to insult the hundreds of thousands of NUM members and their families and supporters all over the UK. The miners agreed with Scargill's frequent avowals that *their* jobs, *their* pits, *their* futures were not going to pay for any crisis of capitalism. The strike had been *their* strike, more than it had ever been Arthur Scargill's and the NUM President was the first to admit it.

The miners' critics condemned their hopeless naivety, their childish lack of realism. After all, how could any workforce expect to keep their jobs if they weren't profitable? No one could expect 'uneconomic' pits to stay open, surely?

As Scargill frequently pointed out, there was no such thing as an 'uneconomic' pit. There were only pits that had been badly managed, starved of investment or deliberately run down. When a pit had exhausted its reserves or was simply too dangerous to be mined, the miners had always accepted the inevitability of such closures.

Besides, what did the concept of an 'uneconomic' pit mean in any case? Even by the rigidly-defined, artificial and distorted laws of the free market, the concept was nonsense. Within the rigged parameters of the NCB's profit-and-loss columns, a pit may well show a 'loss' but what about the wider social and fiscal cost?

Close a pit and a thousand men deprived the Exchequer of income tax and national insurance revenue. A thousand men and their families then required supporting on benefits, all the while contributing nothing to the economy or their local community as shops and businesses, dependent on miners' spending power, were forced into bankruptcy and unemployment, alongside the miners themselves. Meanwhile, yet more cost was incurred as the Government imports coal while hundreds of years' worth of homegrown reserves are not mined.

The cumulative cost of the strike is almost beyond comprehension. Dave Feickert, the NUM's National Research Officer from 1983 to 1993, says, "… the economic and social costs of destroying the British coal industry have been huge — at least £28 billion. This is nearly half of the North Sea tax revenues of £60 billion collected since 1985."[68]

Possibly Scargill's biggest crime, in the eyes of the establishment, was to link the miners' fight to fundamental questions regarding the very nature of how society was organised. Why did everything need to make a 'profit' anyway? Coal was a natural resource, vital to the UK's energy needs. Only a fully-integrated energy policy, as part of a socialist planned economy could ever guarantee security and protection of his members' livelihoods. Such a vision outraged the Government and terrified both the Labour leadership and the TUC.

On 28th February, the NEC announced the convening of a Special Delegates' Conference for 3rd March. As the battle entered its final phase, the miners could only wonder what the future held for their industry, their families and their communities.

Chapter 15:
A View To a Kill

"Defeat is not the worst of failures.
Not to have fought is the true failure."
GEORGE EDWARD WOODBERRY

After months of wrangling, votes and meetings, Nottinghamshire Area NUM officially scrapped the overtime ban at the end of February. NACODS, however, had a shock in store. The pit deputies' Midlands Area announced they would not be supervising any overtime. Without them, of course, miners could not work. The Area's officers referred the matter to their NEC, due to meet the following week, but in the meantime, as far as they were concerned, the ban would be observed.

NACODS' Ray Hilton also made it clear that his Region would be making no recommendation to the Executive, either. He said, "This Area has decided to follow the instructions that were given by our National Executive back in October 1983, and that means we will not take part in the supervision of any overtime work until we are instructed to do so at national level." With an obvious dig at the Area's strike-breakers, he added that NACODS was a *bona fide* trade union and not a breakaway; therefore they'd be following their Union's rules.

Prendergast was less than thrilled and appealed to the NCB to step in and resolve the matter. "It is a problem that the Coal

Board must face up to. They should intervene in order to find some solution. It is very disappointing after the breakthrough earlier this week, but our men are ready to work at weekends if they are asked to."

Charles McLachlan, by contrast, had a much better week. At the Nottinghamshire Chamber of Commerce's 125th anniversary dinner, the guest of honour, Employment Secretary Tom King, lavished praise upon the County's working miners and the police chief whose valiant efforts had thwarted "extremists" and enabled the "brave working miners" to carry out their duty to the nation.

The Employment Secretary was on fiery form and his address was peppered with scathing condemnations of "militants" and "wreckers" who had underestimated "the good sense and bravery" of the heroic Notts men. The strike still had a few days to run but the establishment had started the celebrations early.

On Sunday 3rd March, 1985 the miners' Great Strike for Jobs officially ended. The Delegates made the decision, as they'd made all the major decisions throughout the dispute. The NEC met in the morning and split 11–11 on the question of returning to work or continuing to fight. Conference sent them back to try again. Still the leadership split 11–11 and returned without a recommendation. It was then up to the Delegates. There were four main motions to consider: one each from Scotland, South Wales, Yorkshire and Kent.

— **Kent** — *Conference demands the right to negotiate freely with the employer and agrees not to discuss any other motion or make any recommendation until an agreement is reached that reinstates those members who have been sacked during the course of the present dispute.*

— **Scotland** — *Conference proposes that there should be an organised return to work on the basis of achieving a general amnesty to protect those members who have been victimized during the period of the strike.*

— **Yorkshire** — *This Area views the situation in the coalfields with grave concern and in order to safeguard the members at the five pits and the amnesty of the men dismissed, supporting the aims of this Union, the Area Council believes that the best way to achieve these aims is: that we affirm our*

236

previous position until we are able to clarify and safeguard the above aims and that Officials, National or Area, immediately take the necessary steps to resolve the position; and that Special Council Meetings be convened on a) Saturday 2nd March 1985, in order for Delegates to return mandated on the situation; and b) Monday 4th March 1985, to hear the report of the National Delegate Conference taking place on Sunday 3rd March.

— **South Wales** — *In view of the fact that there has been a) a drift back of members to work in all Areas, and b) that it has now become clear that the Coal Board have no intentions whatsoever to have any discussions with the Union unless they sign the document presented by the TUC to the Union on Sunday 17th February, that the National Union should now organise and authorise a return to work of our members that are still on strike and that this return to work should commence on Tuesday 5th March 1985 without any signed agreement. The National Executive Committee should also be called upon to negotiate with the NCB on a national basis an amnesty for those men dismissed during this dispute.*

The Kent motion fell by 170 votes to nineteen. Scotland's fell by exactly the same margin while Yorkshire's was much closer. It too fell but by only ninety-eight to ninety-one, which just left South Wales.

Arguably, the most solid Area for the entire year (although one might imagine the Kent miners would have something to say about that), it was something of a paradox that a motion which called for unconditional surrender should have originated there. They had been warning for weeks that they'd struggle to hold their men out for much longer: it seemed that that day had finally arrived. The South Wales motion was carried by the same margin with which Yorkshire's had been lost: ninety-eight in favour, ninety-one against.

Here, again, Scargill came in for serious criticism, but this time it was harder to deflect. With the Executive tied 11–11, why hadn't the NUM President used his casting vote? For his critics it was obvious: Arthur Scargill had bottled it. South Wales President, Emlyn Williams, who, if most accounts are to be believed, had come to detest Scargill, branded him a

237

"coward". In that final desperate hour, when the miners had needed leadership most, Scargill had abdicated his duty to his members. Others saw his refusal to break the deadlock one way or the other as his way of maintaining his revolutionary purity in a self-serving manoeuvre to avoid blame for whatever decision was taken.

His supporters see things differently, with one Yorkshire Executive member stating that it would have been incorrect for one man to decide the fate of so many. He feels that with such a momentous choice to make, it had to be a collective decision to either fight on or end the strike and that he, personally, felt Scargill had chosen the correct course of action.

Dave Douglass, by no means an uncritical cheerleader for the NUM President, sees things thus: "A recommendation was problematic. This was after all a movement of *Area* strikes; *not* a national strike as such. The NEC could declare an Area strike official, but it had no authority to tell an Area to call it off.

"The National Conference was convened to co-ordinate a return or continued action. Given that the areas were roughly divided, the NEC was likewise divided. Had Arthur cast his vote to make a recommendation, which way would the recommendation go: to stop out or go back? Whichever way the NEC, with his casting vote swinging it, went, he would be damned as the one man holding all those starving miners out on strike, or else the treacherous bastard who led us up the garden path then sold us out."[69]

Only Scargill himself knew why he'd acted thus and in the thirty years since, he has remained tight-lipped.

At around 3.00pm the NUM President announced from the steps of the TUC Headquarters at Great Russell Street hat the UK's defining class-battle of the twentieth century had ended. He was greeted by tears of grief and anger and shocked cries of "traitor" from the strikers gathered outside. A chant of "We're not going back! We're not going back!" quickly struck up. But they would. They had to. There was nowhere else to go.

The following day, Monday 4th March, local leaderships made arrangements for their men to return and in a final, painful display of pride and defiance, many picket lines saw even greater numbers as thousands assembled one last time. They were bloodied, terribly so, but unbowed. The day after that, Tuesday 5th March, with heads held high, banners flying and brass bands leading thousands of them and their families and supporters through the streets of the coalfields, the strikers returned to the pits they hadn't seen for a year. Well, most of them. Kent miners, it seemed, were incapable of giving in. Their men spread out across the country mounting pickets to prevent the return. Scargill himself, leading a procession back to work in his native Yorkshire, arrived only to turn around and march thousands back they way they'd come when greeted by the perennially obdurate Kent men. Scotland stayed out, too. It would be two weeks before the entire membership was back.

In Nottinghamshire, there were no brass bands. No banners. No proud march back for the men with the support and cheers of their communities ringing in their ears. Once back at the pits, it became clear that the days of the NUM enjoying unchallenged power were over. From the first day back, managers made it clear that the new regime would be imperious, unforgiving and bent on revenge. There were a few honourable exceptions: John Daniels at Clipstone colliery and Brian Evangelista at Bestwood Workshops were seen by many former strikers as fairminded, principled and decent men who eschewed the victimisation and intimidation of most of the NCB management. For the majority, however, it was payback time. 'Facility time', time allowed during working hours for Branch Secretaries to attend to union business, was slashed or banned altogether. Militants were split up, isolated and heavily policed by management looking for the slightest excuse to dismiss those refusing to knuckle under.

Keith Stanley's experiences were typical: "At Newstead, I got isolated. I got sent down to a part of the pit where there were no men and all that were down there were the team I worked with who were all staunch NUM. They took us off the three-shift system; put us on days regular so I wouldn't see any of the men on the other shifts." Managers viewed the loyalists almost as a virus that had to be contained; one that could not be allowed to infect the otherwise pro-management strike-breakers with militancy and rebellion.

Calling a strike-breaker 'scab' was to ensure instant dismissal and men who, prior to the strike, had held prestige jobs with good opportunities for bonus earnings were relegated to menial tasks with the express intention of humiliating them and consolidating their defeat. Stanley smiles as he remembers John Benson from Thoresby pit. "He were a brilliant miner and when he went back they had him digging latrines because he'd been staunch all the way through the strike. But it were water off a duck's back. They couldn't break him. He did it like Cool Hand Luke. 'This is me digging, boss. I'm digging here, boss. I'm digging there, boss.' Brilliant."

There was an officially-sanctioned and concerted campaign of victimisation and intimidation of union activists. Ian MacGregor gloated, "People are now discovering the price of insubordination and insurrection and boy; are we going to make it stick." The NCB chief, in an interview with the *Sunday Telegraph,* on 10th March, then went on to surmise that forty pits would be added to the closure list and then shut over the following two years. This, presumably, was the 'list' NCB officials had consistently denied had ever existed.

To the glee of the working miners, NACODS once again came to their aid and that of the Board when the union U-turned on its earlier commitment not to supervise Nottinghamshire miners who wanted to work in defiance of the overtime ban. Ray Hilton announced, "We will supervise any miner who attends for work. I can't say the men were enthusiastic about it but they have agreed to do it. We will be instructing the Coal Board and the NUM that we will be supervising overtime now."

It also fell to the clearly embarrassed Hilton to get his General Secretary, Peter McNestry, off the hook. The NACODS leader had previously completely ruled out his men working with non-TUC affiliated unions, breakaways or 'scab formations'. Hilton wriggled and squirmed, eventually saying, "We have not said we will only work with unions which are affiliated to the TUC. What we are saying is that if Notts miners break away from the NUM or if they are expelled, we will continue to supervise them but we will not take any other action in support of their aims."

Generally perceived by NUM loyalists to be 'treacherous' 'gutless' and 'mealy-mouthed', Hilton's statement pretty much killed off any lingering shreds of NUM goodwill that might have existed in the County where the Deputies were concerned.

Swimming with the tide, the Area Executive resurrected Liptrott's earlier attempt to expel former strikers from the NUM by the back door, for non-payment of dues. With the

Nottinghamshire Area free from the authority of the NEC and, to all intents and purposes, a separate breakaway union, Lynk felt confident in trying the move again. On the 12th, he sent out a letter to all the Area Branch Secretaries containing six points:

1. *Persons who have been on strike shall be called upon to pay 50p for each week on strike, over and above the first eight weeks.*

2. *Branch Secretaries must submit to this office a list of members who have been on strike for more than eight weeks.*

3. *In stating the number of weeks a member has been on strike, the first eight weeks should be ignored. i.e. if a member has been on strike for fifty-two weeks, your list should indicate he is to pay 44 × 50p.*

4. *Payment of arrears must be made to the Branch Secretaries and no payment will be accepted at Area Office.*

5. *Branch Secretaries must ensure that lists are delivered to this Office by no later than the end of March, 1985, when a receipt will be given. Arrears must be paid to Branch Secretaries within four weeks of this date of acknowledgement of receipt of this list at the Area Office.*

6. *Steps must be taken by Branch Secretaries to ensure that details of the arrears of contributions are brought to the attention of the persons concerned.*

This was then posted to all the relevant members with a covering letter from the appropriate Branch Secretary, which read:-

I am instructed by the Area Executive Committee to bring to your notice that you are in arrears with your contributions in accordance with Notts. Area Rule 11e.

The Area Executive has, therefore, agreed that persons who have been on strike shall be called upon to pay 50p per week for each week on strike, over and above the first eight weeks.

You are, therefore, in arrears to the sum of £................. Until this amount has been paid, and for a further thirteen weeks from the date of payment, you are considered not to be a member of the Union as specified in Notts. Area Rule 11e.

A minor scandal around the issue boiled over when Liptrott was caught by his own Branch forging the Branch Treasurer's name on the Branch's returns. The loyalists were amazed when the Area Executive found in the Branch's favour and upheld the complaint. However, the 'disciplinary' measure visited upon the Sherwood Branch Secretary was merely an instruction not to do it again, whereupon a unanimous vote was recorded in favour of taking no further action.

Henry Richardson, on the other hand, was not in receipt of such leniency. For carrying out nationally-agreed policy, he was finally sacked as Area Agent, Area Official and Area General Secretary on 12th March.

Prendergast told the press that, "the Executive has considered a complaint in respect of Mr. Henry Richardson and that complaint has been upheld by the Executive. Mr. Richardson's terms of dismissal will be given in writing. He has been told he has been dismissed."

Richardson was enraged, claiming he had been informed of no such decision. "It's diabolical," he said. "The whole meeting was a charade, a witch-hunt; nothing but a kangaroo court. The decision had already been made before the meeting. I'll be taking legal advice. I am not prepared to accept that I am no longer Notts NUM General Secretary. I'm employed on a national level and I'm still a member of the National Executive Committee, which makes this decision farcical. They cannot tear up a contract after thirty-four years in the industry. If this happened in a pit, miners would be out on strike. Trade unionism has gone out of the window in Nottinghamshire. I have been sacked because I made a stand and followed national policy."

Just two days later, Richardson was given cause to be optimistic when he won his job back, if only temporarily. He was granted a temporary High Court injunction which prevented the Area Executive from carrying out its decision. Mr Justice Steyn ruled the Area General Secretary be restored to his post in all three capacities: Area Agent, Area Official and Area General Secretary. This wasn't something Lynk, Prendergast *et al* were prepared to swallow. Their own legal team was soon involved, seeking to overturn the injunction.

While all over the UK's coalfields the NCB was purging and victimising activists, Nottinghamshire had the added burden of having to fend off their own Area union which was doing exactly the same thing. Nottinghamshire's NUM loyalists were fighting a defensive rearguard action on two fronts.

All through 1985, the battles raged on. Henry Richardson's injunction was lifted and he was ousted for good. This time the judge, Mr. Justice Mann, ruled that, "It would be quite wrong for this Court to impose on a trade union an official in whom it has no confidence." Richardson's pro-strike administrator, Pam Elliot, also received her marching orders and joined her old boss in exile at the NUM's Sheffield HQ.

On 14th May, the NEC took its revenge. Its members voted by ten votes to nine to recommend to Conference, scheduled for July, that Lynk be sacked and Prendergast issued with an official warning.

The fight to win reinstatement for those miners sacked during the strike suffered a blow when the national member-ship voted against the introduction of a 50p per week levy to support their axed comrades. Nottinghamshire, Leicestershire and South Derbyshire, who had by now formed an informal 'Democratic Alliance', boycotted the ballot which made the final results all the more shocking, given the Left was considered to be in the majority of those who had voted.

Nationally, the final result was 50,429 in favour of the levy and 58,721 against. The turnout was low, only around fifty-nine percent. Scotland recorded nearly a four-to-one margin in favour of the levy while Yorkshire only just squeezed a majority; fifty-two percent.

Henry Richardson, in a defiant speech at the first David Jones Memorial March and Rally at Ollerton, organised by Jimmy Hood, received a rousing ovation. The first thing he was going to do when he won his job back, he told the three-thousand strong crowd, was campaign relentlessly for the rein-statement of Nottinghamshire's twenty-nine sacked and victimised miners. "They are not alone, they are not forgotten. The fight goes on," he told the rally. Ultimately, however, only eight men won back their jobs.

The next setback for the Nottinghamshire Left was the elec-tion of Lynk and Prendergast to the NEC. Unlike Richardson's sacking, this would stick first time as it was the result of a properly conducted ballot as per the rule book. Richardson and Chadburn were both replaced, with the Area President ruefully commenting, "In political terms, I suppose you could say I've lost my deposit."

There was one small victory to be savoured and that was the matter regarding strikers' subscriptions. A High Court judge ruled that the Area Executive had been wrong to try and recoup the arrears and instructed that all miners who had paid must be reimbursed. In addition, they were unequivocally *bona fide* members of the NUM. It was a rare defeat for the rebel Area which made it all the sweeter for the Left.

In July, the NUM National Conference arrived, but before the Delegates could address the Nottinghamshire problem there was the contentious matter of a completely new rule book to resolve. Rule 51 remained and a plan to reorganise the representation of Areas on the NEC was also included. Rule 11 was what raised eyebrows, though. This withdrew the President's right to a vote on any matter completely. There were two schools of thought here: one was that Scargill was sliding around Tory anti-trade union law, specifically the Trade Union Act 1984, as removing the right to vote meant officials didn't need to stand for the mandatory five-year re-election that otherwise applied. Alternatively, it was a pre-emptive strike against Nottinghamshire who had vowed to oust the President by forcing him to stand for re-election whereupon, they believed, he'd be toppled by a 'moderate' candidate.

The Left was hopelessly riven. By now, several Areas, South Wales particularly, contained very few Scargill supporters. Communist Party members were advised by their Party leadership to vote against the adoption of an entirely new rule book which was, they felt, solely designed to concentrate yet more power in Scargill's hands. In truth, the rule changes had more to do with countering Area independence so that any future struggle would not see an Area behaving as Nottinghamshire had done. For example, Rule 17B allowed the membership of an Area to be bigger than the Area itself and 17D conferred upon the Conference the right to "create, dissolve, merge, combine or amalgamate Areas." Rule 26C invested the NEC with the authority to "... call industrial action by any group of members whether in one or part of one or more than one Area." This last, particularly, went down a treat with Nottinghamshire.

Scargill had, though, paid tribute to the implacable fight waged by the women of mining communities by creating Rule

5A. The new rule, governing associate membership status, was designed to allow the Women's Support Groups entry into the NUM: a far-sighted and commendable initiative. Sadly, it was the only new rule to fall to the Conference vote.

Where some felt Scargill did let himself down was on the question of Rule 11. The right of the membership to control and elect its leaders was sacrosanct and a principle to which no self-respecting left-winger could object. Others saw opposing the rule as siding with the Right and so, badly divided, cantankerous and mutinous, the Left let the new rule book pass; which was exactly what Nottinghamshire had been waiting for (Scargill later outmanoeuvred his critics by unexpectedly standing for re-election. in 1988 he was re-elected with 53.8 percent of the vote). Their Delegation promptly upped and walked out in protest. Escorted to and from Mansfield by police outriders, the Delegation returned the next day to hear Conference vote by 81 to 13 to sack both Lynk and Prendergast. Clearly Delegates felt the NEC's recommendation of a formal reprimand for Lynk's no.2 was insufficient. Both men had clearly prepared for the move as although the decision meant the loss of their £18,000 salaries, it turned out both had already signed contracts of employment with the Nottinghamshire Area Executive.

The next day the Delegation were back to see the new rule book formally ratified by Conference and once again, they upped and left; but this time, there would be no coming back. Forty-eight hours later, on Saturday 6th July 1985, Nottinghamshire Delegates gathered at Berry Hill and voted by 228 to 20 to formally break away from the National Union of Mineworkers. Chadburn refused to endorse the move and raged furiously in hopeless opposition. The new regime promptly locked him out of the Berry Hill offices and then sacked him

In a roundtable post-strike discussion, hosted in April 1985 by the Communist Party, the Scottish NUM Vice President, George Bolton said, "We tended to assume that Nottingham was much worse than it really was." What Bolton didn't know then was just how spectacularly wrong he was. Nottinghamshire was actually far *worse* than anyone had assumed.

From July up to the Union of Democratic Mineworkers' (UDM) certification by the Trade Union Certification Officer, in December 1985, the extent of the breakaway union's collusion with the NCB was breathtaking. Not until documents were released to the National Archive, twenty years later, would the truth be revealed.

In a series of secret meetings, covert correspondence and clandestine pacts and agreements, the UDM was afforded NCB legal advice, help and support all the way through the process. Schemes were hatched to pay UDM members more than NUM members, in a bid to further weaken the NUM. Both NCB agreements and Parliamentary Acts were flouted and broken as the NCB aided the new union to break the NUM.

The NCB's Ned Smith and James Cowan were secretly letting Nottinghamshire working miners know, as early as January 1985, that recognition for their breakaway would not be a problem, in a bid to hasten the split.

Peter Walker was also involved in ensuring the NCB and UDM kept their manoeuvrings secret until the appropriate time and was at least aware of, if not directly involved in, NCB chiefs' plans to renege on constitutionally agreed industry norms. Walker had had an excellent war. Of all the key Tory players, he hadn't put a foot wrong. Whether it was keeping the tactically incompetent MacGregor on a short leash, expertly spinning the Government's line to the media, or sabotaging talks when it looked as though the NUM were nearing a break-through, the Energy Secretary had served his Prime Minister flawlessly. He rounded off a superb performance by smoothing the way for MacGregor and Cowan to act as midwives at the UDM's birth.

From at least as early as his overture to Ray Chadburn in 1981, Cowan had been angling to split the NUM. He finally realised his wish and said later that he knew the breakaway was on the cards *even before the strike*.[70]

As well he might: it's almost certain, given Cowan's actions, that he and Lynk colluded before the strike to bring about the split.

The UDM initially comprised around eighty percent of the former Nottinghamshire NUM, South Derbyshire and the newly-formed Colliery Workers and Allied Trades Association: a rump faction of mainly ex-Durham Craftsmen who had been expelled under Rule 51 for scabbing. Leicestershire was an obvious target for Lynk and his NCB overlords. It had produced just thirty-one strikers during the year-long dispute and Area

President, Jack Jones, who loathed Scargill, had happily encouraged his Leicester men to work throughout. Despite all that, Jones was pro-NUM and convinced his Area to vote against joining the UDM.

Cowan popped up again and was alleged to have tried bribing Jones into swinging Leicestershire to the UDM, saying, "You are holding up the entire operation. Leicester has got to go to the UDM. We need you for the final breakthrough in Warwickshire, including Coventry — and from there up to Lancashire. If we get that we have captured the motorway block."[71]

While the UDM never managed to make any significant breakthrough outside its Nottinghamshire-Derbyshire axis, it did the job it was designed to do with devastating effectiveness. Over the next seven years, it willingly aided the NCB in breaking the NUM's dominance in the industry as pay, terms, conditions and benefits for NUM members started to fall and pits closed with a dizzying frequency.

Once the smoke of 84/85 had cleared, it became apparent that the Great Strike for Jobs hadn't been a war after all: it had been but a battle in a long war. An unprecedented bloody and ferocious battle, certainly — an industrial Stalingrad — but a battle nevertheless. As Seumas Milne sagely noted, the post-strike world saw even greater power concentrated in the hands of fewer NUM members and, horribly wounded though they were, they were not yet down and out: the war would continue.[72]

While the leadership turned on itself and, rudderless and split, could offer little in the way of a unified coherent national response to the radically changed political climate, at pit level the miners took the war to the enemy in the form of guerrilla and unofficial actions. Go-slows, walk-outs and wildcat strikes raged across the coalfields for years afterwards, particularly in Yorkshire.

Meanwhile, Nottinghamshire faced the additional challenge of rebuilding the NUM in the County from scratch, beset on one side by the UDM and a vastly more powerful NCB on the other. "The first obstacle we had to overcome in Nottinghamshire," says Keith Stanley, "was that they recognised the new break-away union as the major union and they put every miner into that union, for administration purposes, so in the initial week

247

leading up to them coming in as the official union, my union money was going to go to them! We had to go round all our members and get them to sign saying they didn't want their money going to the UDM and that they wanted to stay with us." Management refused to operate a 'check-off' system for the NUM: weekly membership dues would no longer be deducted at source and sent on to the NUM. "We had to run around getting every miner to sign direct debit forms. Well, not every miner had a bank account so we had to operate a 'rent book' system for some of them to pay cash."

Henry Richardson shakes his head in disbelief. "If I've been a member of the NUM all my working life, and a new union comes along, surely I should have to opt *out* of the NUM to join the new union? But no: they [NCB] automatically registered every Nottinghamshire miner as UDM unless they opted *in* to the NUM. And they got all our assets, too." The Berry Hill premises, the convalescent home at Chapel Saint Leonards, and capital, totalling around £1.7 million, were all awarded to the UDM by a High Court judge. This left the NUM Area organisation penniless, with no premises and no infrastructure.

Richardson continues, "We'd got Keith and Eric running around trying to recruit back into the NUM — bloody heroes, they were. They should have had medals, the shit they had thrown at them. Victimised, put on shit jobs, weren't allowed an office even though we had as many members as the UDM at Thoresby, but they never stopped fighting for the Union — and I'm working from Jill Clifford's bungalow, with Pam. Jill were a secretary at Berry Hill; she eventually got sacked as well. Took some guts, letting us use her house and she were going into Berry Hill every day — she and her husband were out at work all day so she let us set up there, out at Ravenshead, with miners traipsing up and down the path all day, in and out of the house as we tried to rebuild. God knows what the bloody neighbours thought! It were only for a few weeks and then we set up at Mansfield, after we'd been at Sheffield, we got some premises up there."

Ray Chadburn confirms, "We slowly rebuilt. We didn't have premises, we didn't have any money but we got £10,000 from South Wales and a chunk from Durham, but we were blocked at every turn, trying to get new premises. People gloating that the NUM was smashed and Lynk said, 'They'll never get back into Mansfield.' But eventually we did get some offices. I was painting, decorating, fitting radiators and we finally returned on May Day, 1986. We loved it: it was on a May Day when they'd tried to get rid of us and it was on a May Day when we returned. We went across to the pub and had a little celebration: we were back!"

It was far from plain sailing. The UDM even campaigned to evict Chadburn and his family from their home, arguing his rented NUM property should be the property of the UDM. Chadburn eventually won that particularly lengthy and stressful legal battle and purchased the home outright.

At the point of production, Eric Eaton ran the risk of the sack every day. Even sticking NUM circulars on the notice board was grounds for dismissal. Eaton made a famous contribution at one of the post-strike NUM Conferences. Holding up a plastic bag, he asked the Delegates if they could guess what it was. "It's my office," he said, as he educated the Conference in the realities of life for NUM activists in Nottinghamshire.

Paul Whetton was eventually sacked from Bevercotes for his union activity. He, too, had pinned various pro-NUM materials to the notice board. "We took his case to a tribunal," says Richardson, "and we won. The judge said he should be rein-stated. It were blatant discrimination for trade union activity." The NCB only partially obeyed the ruling, with Whetton trans-ferred out to Manton colliery instead of going back to Bevercotes. "The first day at Manton there were a strike on so his first day there, he goes on bloody strike!" laughs Richardson. "He said, 'Brilliant pit! This'll do me!' He were a right bogger, were Paul."

Whetton's and Eric Eaton's experiences contrasted vividly with those of their UDM counterparts. NCB management had facilitated the breakaway union visiting South Wales pits on a recruitment drive. With management's assistance, UDM recruitment material was placed into the locker of every miner at the various pits they visited.

Initially, Nottinghamshire NUM membership grew steadily. "I'm sure that's why they shut Newstead," says Stanley. "We were getting really close to a majority at that pit and that terri-fied 'em. Mind you, it was the men that shut Newstead. They had a ballot in 1987 to vote on whether the pit stayed open and they voted to shut it." NUM members boycotted the ballot as, in

Stanley's words, "Ray told us, and I totally agreed with him, what right had we to vote a younger man out of a job?" Refusing to give legitimacy to the process, while understandable and principled, left a clear field for those who wanted out, and the pit closed in 1987.

Stanley worked tirelessly to rebuild his beloved NUM in the County. Elected as President of the Nottinghamshire Area, on Chadburn's retirement in 1992, he combined his full-time job at the pit with the Area Presidency after hours. Sixteen to twenty hour days were the norm and, for a period, without any union pay as the Area simply couldn't afford to employ another full-time official. Slowly, bit by bit, due to the commitment and loyalty of Stanley, Eaton and others, the NUM regained a footing in Nottinghamshire.

It was tough going as the new generation of NUM militants battled not just the UDM but bribes from the NCB. After a year on strike, part of NCB strategy was to offer enhanced redundancy terms with an even greater one-off bonus if men left before a certain date. Thereafter, the enhanced element of the package would be withdrawn. A combination of bribery and blackmail saw even previously loyal NUM stalwarts taking the cash and getting out. Demoralisation was rife and many had simply had enough. Some of the sums on offer were enormous. Upwards of £80,000 wasn't unusual — a huge sum at the time.

David Amos agrees that this was a major factor both in Nottinghamshire's decision not to strike in the first place and in the rapid rundown of the coalfields thereafter. "I think you will find that the enhanced redundancy scheme for the over-fifties, introduced circa 1981, was a significant factor in the lead-up to the start of the 1984–85 strike — many of these men had strong memories of what went off in the coal industry in the 1960s, largely under a Labour Government. Also, like my old man and some of my uncles, when you have forty years-plus in the coal industry, it was time to bail out in the 1980s to rescue a bit of what was left for retirement. As Dave Goulder put it in his song lyrics about the railways in the 1960s: 'Sixty-five his time has come, he's swopped his soot and oil, for a smart gold watch that bears his name, then at sixty-six he's covered in soil'."

Jim Aspinall, a year-long strike veteran and former miner at Hatfield, Rossington, Barnbrough and Frickley pits, sums up the bitterness, hopelessness and sadness of a post-strike period characterised by defeatism. "Let me tell you what happened in a meeting on 12th March 1989, which took place at Dearnside Comprehensive School.

"Arthur Scargill was there, along with the union men of Barnburgh pit, to boost morale as Barnburgh was under threat of closure. I was there, along with young and old, to try and find solutions to keep this pit open. Arthur began to speak, saying there were good reserves, twenty years, at Barnburgh when one of the older miners in the crowd said 'Where? On 60s face? We've had enough, Arthur, and that's that!' I just couldn't believe what I was hearing. A couple of years previously, we were all out fighting for our jobs and now the old colliers just seemed to give up; to accept enhanced redundancy packages, which I thought was selfish of them as they were not only not thinking of the younger miners but of what would follow to their own communities! Arthur just looked in disbelief. Then the same breed began to attack Arthur verbally. Us younger colliers just looked and stared. We were being betrayed by our own men! Arthur just got his briefcase and left. He walked past us and the passing glance said it all.

"I was gutted. All of the young miners were and so was Arthur. We *could* have won. Just a *chance* but no: these old 'uns wanted the money and submitted to management tactics. We wanted *jobs*! There were more people blinded by the £ sign than us. Sad, sad case. Most, as you know, blew it on cars, holidays and booze and then in streams of hypocritical martyrdom, preached to the converted, stating 'Look what they've done to our communities! It's the Tories fault'!! I'll agree the Tories were to blame but when a man goes on strike for a year, and then sees his own kind vote to close a pit, that bloody hurts!

"The union had a case, a survival plan, but greed took over. What a waste!"

Throughout the 80s and 90s a steady stream of miners left the industry as it continued to contract and pits closed. From 1985 to 1990, ten of Nottinghamshire's twenty-seven pits closed.

The immediate post-strike period also saw the NCB and the UDM working increasingly closely together to marginalise the NUM. In 1986, a meeting at Eastwood Hall saw the two organisations meet to discuss the way forward. Some

251

NCB strategists were concerned that Lynk's organisation was struggling to make headway outside its Nottinghamshire-Derbyshire base. Others were unconcerned. Those privy to the NCB's and Government's long-term plans knew that over one hundred pits would close in the period from 1985 to 1990, with the loss of nearly 120,000 jobs, and as long as the UDM dominated the lucrative Nottinghamshire and Midlands coalfields, it would be doing exactly what it was intended to do. Apart from anything else, the idea of two competing trade unions in the industry suited the Government and NCB very nicely.

Typical of the moves made by the two bodies was this: the UDM had suggested the NCB pay their members a higher rate than that paid to NUM men. This would make UDM membership a tempting proposition. The NCB were more than willing to give it a try.

Still smarting from Leicestershire slipping through the UDM's fingers, NCB chiefs selected one of its pits, Ellistown, which contained UDM sympathisers, to trial the plan.

On the 27th January, the NCB announced that any UDM members at the colliery would be paid a higher rate, backdated to 1st November 1985. The UDM and NCB then sat back and waited for the stampede as miners rushed to join the breakaway. Unfortunately for them it never happened. The NUM took the NCB to an industrial tribunal and won its case. The judge ruled it illegal to bribe one set of workers with a higher pay rate denied to a second group with the express intention of tempting the former into a specific trade union. The NCB appealed, only for the Court of Appeal to uphold the ruling. The Board had contravened section 23 of the Employment Protection (Consolidation) Act 1978.

The NUM's insistence that it would not sit down with scab unions created difficulties and generated a lot of internal tension. It left the Union in the humiliating position of relying on the crumbs of whatever deals the UDM had agreed with the NCB. Roy Lynk wasn't too happy with this state of affairs, either. At the UDM's annual Conference in 1987, he grumbled, "It's particularly galling to find after a great deal of time and effort has been spent on our part securing a negotiated settlement for our members that that very self-same settlement is bestowed on NUM members."

The splits in the NUM in the post-strike period revolved largely around two questions: firstly the response to management's increasingly draconian regime and secondly regarding the attitude to Nottinghamshire.

Some felt the NUM Left's policy of purity in the wilderness served their members badly. The Union's job was to best represent their members and secure for them the best terms and conditions. If it refused to sit down and negotiate with the Board — renamed British Coal Corporation (BCC) in 1987 — because of the UDM, what use was it to the rank-and-file? It wasn't quite that simple, however, as BCC also refused to talk to the NUM. Instead, it increasingly bypassed the leadership and its official structures and spoke directly to the workforce over the heads of the union's leaders: an American innovation, much favoured by MacGregor as part of the new 'Human Resources Management' which swept the post-strike coalfields.

Pit-level incentive schemes, dividing not just pit from pit but man from man at the same pit became the norm; coupled with a stick for the NUM while the UDM dined on carrots. BCC's strategy was intended to make the workforce identify with management; to embrace the idea that their interests were the same. The new regime suited the UDM perfectly. Except it wasn't really new at all, it was Mondism resurrected. As an internal UDM document explained, "It is UDM philosophy to negotiate with management rather than embark on collision courses. This approach does not preclude the possibility of national industrial action, but such action will always be a measure of last resort duly sanctioned by ballot. If it is not inimical to the interests of our members, we can see no sound reason for not cooperating with management if that cooperation brings benefits to the industry in which we work."

'New Realism' infected the wider labour and trade union movement. The view that class-struggle was dead became endemic. The miners' defeat had proved the futility of challenging the market and submission to capital was now the only way forward. Spencerism in Nottinghamshire and Mondism everywhere else. Scargill was having none of it and launched a blistering attack on the New Realists. In a ferocious S.O. Davies Memorial Lecture, in 1987, he ripped into what he termed the 'politics of fear' and berated those inside and outside the NUM for succumbing to its poisonous allure, particularly several Area leaderships which had moved sharply into opposition to 'Scargillism.'

At the same time, New Realism found its echo in the debates raging inside the NUM regarding the approach to Nottinghamshire. The militantly antagonistic sections refused to have any truck with the UDM while others suggested only by dialogue could men be won back to a unified national union. Ken Capstick brilliantly summed up the dilemma facing the NUM. "We had a lot of men back at work by the end of the strike. And I've got to go back to the pit and work for conciliation. I can see no other way forward. I can't draw lines. I can't have scabs, super-scabs and extra-super scabs! I can't have a sliding scale of scabbery."

Nottinghamshire's strike veterans had assumed something of the status of untouchables in the aftermath of the strike. The most loyal of the loyal, who'd refused to break and had suffered more than most, enjoyed a moral authority out of all proportion to their tiny numbers. Other Areas were reluctant to be seen betraying Nottinghamshire's stand by advocating recognition of the UDM. It was by no means as cut-and-dried as 'what Nottinghamshire said went' but it wasn't a million miles away either.

Ray Chadburn, despite criticisms from some during the strike, had resolutely kept the faith. He spoke for the entire Nottinghamshire Area — diminutive though it now was — when he said, "I am fed up with people saying we should sit down and be pals and have some sort of compromise... as far as I am concerned, there won't be any compromise. It is either us or them.

"If people think I am going to sit down with Roy Lynk, if Arthur Scargill ever sits down with Roy Lynk, it's time we wrapped up as the National Union of Mineworkers. We are not going to accept advice from people who don't actually work and live in the Nottinghamshire coalfield."

By 1990 little had changed. At that year's Conference, Scotland's Peter Neilson asked, "What happens in, say, ten or fifteen years' time if they [UDM] are still in existence? What do we do then? Do we still refuse to talk to British Coal on wages and safety? Do we sit outside the circle and allow the wages and conditions of the membership we are elected to represent to continue to fall further and further behind?"

The Nottinghamshire Delegate, in response, couldn't have been clearer: "Watch my lips and I will say it slowly: we ain't sitting down with the UDM."

Spencerism had returned to Nottinghamshire but this time there would be no reconciliation, no mergers and no reunification. Lynk's men had dealt the *coup de grace* to the British coalmining industry and now the clock was running down.

Chapter 16:
Don't You
(Forget About Me)

> *"The history of all hitherto existing society*
> *is the history of class struggles."*
> KARL MARX

1990 saw 'The Month of The Great Slander' (although it actually stretched out for several months beyond the initial allegations). The *Daily Mirror* and the *Cook Report* launched a string of allegations claiming Scargill and Heathfield had had their fingers in the NUM till. Both had used money, intended for striking miners, to pay off their respective mortgages and for home improvements. There were other allegations concerning 'Moscow Gold' and Libyan cash and their publication triggered an unprecedented hysteria as the media queued up to savage Scargill and Heathfield.

Gavin Lightman QC, who had previously been considered a friend of the NUM and Scargill in particular, condemned the NUM President in his report at the end of his enquiry, but even he had to admit neither Scargill nor Heathfield were guilty as accused. On allegations of personal corruption, both Scargill and Heathfield were vindicated. As neither had even had a mortgage at the time, it was relatively easy to do so. That no one had even bothered to check before publishing the smears was an indication of the deep fear and loathing Scargill and the NUM still invoked. The other allegations, Lightman reluctantly conceded, had arisen as a result of the NUM's complex financial manoeuvrings to retain control of their finances and avoid the dead hand of the court's sequestrators during the strike.

It was left to the *Guardian's* Seumas Milne to debunk the smears with the publication of *The Enemy Within: the Secret War Against the Miners* in 1994. Milne went even further than proving the claims were just a malicious and sloppy piece of tacky tabloid journalism. It was clear there had been a concerted campaign orchestrated by the security services, with Fleet Street, the Tories and Kinnock, either knowingly or unknowingly, in tandem. Kinnock added to the contempt in which he was held by the miners when he posed, grinning, for photographs with Terry Pattinson, Frank Thorne and Ted Oliver, the chief architects of the smears, at the British Press Awards. The trio of journalists were there to pick up an award for their story. 'Story', perhaps being the operative word: even Lightman himself described their account as "entirely untrue."

Eight years later, on 27th May 2002, the *Daily Mirror* editor at the time of the allegations, Roy Greenslade, offered a full retraction and apology to Scargill and Heathfield in *The Guardian*, for which he was then writing. The detailed penance concluded, "I can't undo what has been done, but I am pleased to offer the sincerest of apologies to Heathfield and to Scargill, who is on the verge of retirement. I regret ever publishing that story. And that is the honest truth."

Henry Richardson is sombre as he recalls the impact of the smear campaign. "It broke Peter, you know. He never got over it." Scargill, in his own way, was possibly equally damaged, his friends say. One former friend of the NUM leader says, "Arthur had always been controlling but to be perfectly fair to him that was a result of him always being in a minority and ending up nearly always being right. He always had to rely on himself. After that he trusted no one at all, apart from Nell [Myers]. He became even more paranoid and wouldn't trust anyone. Can't blame him, really, I suppose. I don't know how he didn't crack. It would have finished me off. He's an incredibly strong person but it had an impact on him, definitely. Jim [Parker, long-time personal friend of Scargill's, who doubled as driver and bodyguard, had sold his story regarding his former friend for cash to the *Daily Mirror*] betraying him like that just meant he started cutting us all out from his life. It's such a shame."

Dave Douglass is less inclined to let his former President off the hook. "No he didn't do what they accused him of; yes there was a high-level state conspiracy over the Libyan money. But Arthur is not lily-white on this. Borrowing money from the International Miners' Organisation (IMO), of which he was the President, from funds donated by miners internationally to assist, in particular, British miners, to buy a £150,000 mansion at a time when miners lived in £15,000 houses and many had lost theirs during the course of a strike he led, just six months after it was over, whether the rules allowed him to or not, was a disgrace. For an alleged communist to be so insensitive and tactless left a nasty taste in many mouths no matter how loud we shouted to defend him and close ranks against the press agenda of discrediting him in order to discredit us and the strike."*

Similar allegations would be made against a different miners' leader, nearly ten years later, but this time they would be true and result in disgrace, conviction and jail.

In 1992 Roy Lynk was challenged for the Presidency of the UDM by Neil Greatrex, former NUM Branch President at Bentinck but since the breakaway, General Secretary of the Nottingham Section of the UDM. Lynk declined to defend his office. In the words of one UDM member, "He jumped before he was pushed." Greatrex was then elected President in 1993. Allegedly representing a 'more traditional strand of trade union thinking', Greatrex's challenge was prompted by Lynk's leadership of the union, many felt, becoming little more than an adjunct of BCC. Which it had. Lynk's stewardship had seen the UDM completely transcend the accepted definition of trade unionism and become, quite simply, an extension of British Coal Corporation management, to the overwhelming detriment of its members. This shouldn't have come as a surprise to anyone. After all, the circumstances in which the union had been born meant that right from its creation it had been little

---

*The money was actually borrowed from the Miners Trade Union International (later dissolved into the IMO), drawn from the Mireds fund but replaced soon afterwards. See *The Enemy Within*, Milne, p.289.

more than a company union and a creature of the Government. Its acquiescence to any and all requirements of the NCB and later BCC had seen the shattering of the miners' historic five-day week, the introduction of 'flexible' shiftworking and a much more 'relaxed' attitude regarding health and safety and conditions at Nottinghamshire pits.

"You couldn't believe the calibre of some of them people," says Henry Richardson, referring to the UDM. "When Thatcher forced us to have a ballot on the political levy, just after the strike, there were Notts miners bragging they'd never voted Labour and always voted for the Tories, scrawling 'Vote Conservative' on the ballot papers and all sorts. These were *miners*, for God's sake! They were a disgrace.

"I always remember at one Conference, before the breakaway, we sent fraternal greetings to Nelson Mandela and Prendergast *opposed* it! 'He's nothing but a terrorist,' he said. That's what we were dealing with. That were the sort of people they were."

Despite consistently exceeding production targets and producing record profits for their BCC masters, the UDM had been a comprehensive failure in halting pit closures. Coupled with the enhanced redundancy scheme and low level of morale at the coalface, Nottinghamshire was haemorrhaging jobs and pits. By the close of 1992, fifteen of Nottinghamshire's pits had closed, leaving only twelve in production from the twenty-seven of just eight years earlier. This was in line with closures nationally. Of the 174 deep-mines operating in 1984, just fifty remained operational by 1992. New Realism had been a catastrophic failure. Not one single job or pit had been saved by cooperating with the Government and BCC.

What brought matters to a head, and saw an unfocused dissatisfaction with Lynk coalesce into an outburst of anger and sense of betrayal, was the announcement by Michael Heseltine, on 13th October 1992, that the Government and BCC intended to close a further thirty-one of the UK's remaining fifty pits, seven of them in Nottinghamshire, which would leave the coalfield with just five. Some were to shut within a week of the announcement with the remainder to be closed within six months.

The outcry was immediate and enormous. To everyone's surprise, people across all sections and classes of the UK rose as one and generated a tidal wave of fury which threatened to drown the Government; a Government which was already on very shaky ground. The Poll Tax and the Tories' traditional Achilles Heel, Europe, had seen Thatcher thrown from office by her own Party two years earlier and the new administration, headed by John Major, was sinking in a swamp of sleaze and allegations of corruption. To compound the Government's difficulties, just three weeks prior to the closure announcement, it had presided over the UK's humiliating retreat from the European Exchange Rate Mechanism. Major, as Prime Minister, and Michael Heseltine, as President of the Board of Trade, had badly misjudged the public mood.

Two enormous demonstrations, one organised by the NUM, the other by the TUC, saw over a million people marching in London within a week in protest at the new round of closures. Heseltine backed off and announced a ninety-day moratorium during which a review would take place. Harassed by a vocal Tory minority rebelling against its own Government and hundreds of thousands of people outside Parliament suddenly organising themselves into miners' support groups, it looked, for a brief, tantalising, moment, that the miners would finally take their revenge for 1984.

It never happened and the closures went through over the following months as public anger dissipated. Adding to the problems of mounting an effective campaign of resistance were several factors: the miners themselves were either lacking in confidence that such a fight could be successful or didn't even want to fight in the first place. Morale had never been so low and thousands just wanted out. Over the months following the closure announcement, BCC deployed open intimidation to force men out of the industry. They were told if redundancy was not taken now then it would no longer be available after a certain date.

A suddenly rehabilitated Arthur Scargill, now bizarrely the darling of gentrified middle-England and the subject of glowing and affectionate editorials in the Tory press, as people scrambled over each other to admit that, yes: Scargill had been right after all, had only a grim pyrrhic victory to enjoy. The received wisdom that followed in the wake of New Realism was that industrial struggle, militancy and strikes were dead. Now it was all about 'alliances', 'rainbow coalitions' and 'community-based' campaigns: cross-class popular fronts, in other words. Despite a couple of one-day strikes by the NUM and notwithstanding Scargill's usual fiery rhetoric, this time the NUM President had, by and large, played things the way his New Realist critics said he should. The result was defeat as all the condemned pits eventually closed anyway. The TUC had proved as useless as it had always been and cosy huddles with middle class housewives, vicars and liberals didn't save a single miner's job.

As one of the key organisers of the 'popular front', Dave Douglass, understandably, has a different, more nuanced, take on the miners' last stand. "It was well over one million people who marched in that week, with over half a million on each demo, as well as twelve million lost work days on the two days of action called with the miners and rail workers.

"'Days of Action' were the most we could ever hope for. It took weeks upon weeks of mass public campaigns and the women taking on the bulk of the actions before we could even convince the members to take on any sort of action against further closures. It wasn't a result of sitting on Arthur, as much as stopping him thinking we still had the same troops we had back in March '84, and declaring all out strike action. We had to build up a movement, build up an argument and show some public support; convince the men they could win this one. This was actual reality not 'new realism' or giving up strikes for vicars.

"Like the strike of '84 the tactics and direction of this movement were not Arthur's, but ours, based on the mood of the membership and their current war-weary condition. You make it sound like Arthur and the members were ready to fight but the New Realists persuaded him to do the public PR tactics instead and as a result we lost. That is not true. Most members had had the stuffing knocked out of them, they were determined they would *not* take up this fight again on their own. We had to generate a movement, we had to start a row and start getting the public on our side. These were the only weapons we now had left. It took a while to build enough steam even for joint days of action, although to be honest that was meant to include GMB and the Power Station workers, but they didn't join us.

"The mass public campaign was probably my idea and was based upon my successful speech to the Special National Conference. It was seized upon by a Union who walked into that room largely believing we were already fucked and had nowhere to go. It gave them heart and direction. Well, nobody else proposed any alternative tactics! There was nobody walking off the job this time and nobody demanding an all-out strike, ballot or no ballot."

In Nottinghamshire, things were very difficult for the remaining NUM loyalists. With many of the veterans of '84 having retired or taken redundancy, the by then tiny membership was hugely outnumbered by the UDM. There wasn't even the dubious pleasure of telling the former strike-breakers 'we told you so'. "How could we?" asks Keith Stanley. "It was still our blokes as well that were looking at losing their jobs." Stanley, Eaton and the other Nottinghamshire militants threw themselves into the campaign to keep their pits open but, in Nottinghamshire, there was little chance of success, thanks, once again, to the UDM. The breakaway union demonstrated an astonishing inability to learn from its mistakes: its members refused to back the NUM's twenty-four stoppages and crossed picket lines to work as normal. Old habits died hard, it seemed.

Roy Lynk had had a dreadful campaign. Staging a protest sit-in, the UDM boss descended 1200 feet to the bottom of Silverhill colliery and stayed there for a week. A small band of friends, still loyal to the breakaway leader applauded his 'audacious stand' while others sneered. "He's bottled it. It's just a convenient way of getting out of the way from all his angry members," said a then UDM Branch Secretary.

Lynk felt 'betrayed' and 'let down' by the Government. After doing so much to ruin both the strike and the NUM for Margaret Thatcher, the UDM President was convinced the Tories' gratitude would be eternal.

Sending back the OBE he'd received from a grateful establishment in 1990 for 'services to trade unionism', Lynk had plenty of time at the bottom of Silverhill to contemplate his own, not inconsiderable, role in bringing the UK's coal industry to the brink of extinction. Yet he felt no shame. There was no epiphany. No blinding flash of light regarding his own actions: just outrage that now he'd completed the Conservatives' dirty work, he too, along with the tens of thousands his machinations had condemned to the dole queue, was himself now surplus to requirements. Instead, he complained. "I worked hard to get Asfordby. I brought in the six-day week agreement, and I was castigated by the NUM, to make sure there were 1000 jobs created at Asfordby. I have encouraged people to work on Saturdays and Sundays to produce more coal on the grounds that if we produce coal cheap we can sell it cheap but we have cut our own throat.

"I have been betrayed by British Coal and by the Government. I get very badly treated. I have been thoroughly 100 percent betrayed. Promises made in the House towards the miners of Nottinghamshire are not being kept."[73]

Lynk and the UDM still had their fans among the Tory Party. Winston Churchill, one of the backbench rebels, said, "The Conservative Party and this Government owe those men a great debt of honour." Nottinghamshire MP, the Member for Gedling, Andrew Mitchell, chipped in with fulsome praise for the UDM. It was "modern, forward-looking constructive trade unionism" and had "saved this Country's bacon in 1984." Moreover, Lynk was "one of the heroes of the eighties" while Tory backbench rebel Elizabeth Peacock hoped the establishment would "... find a better way to reward that man for his eight years' work." Even the Iron Lady recorded in her memoirs how she and Lynk had "kept in touch" and that she had ensured other ministers "... understood my feelings about the need to protect the interests of his members." Lynk was particularly proud of his relationship with 'Margaret' as he was often heard to refer to the former Prime Minister. He had had a direct line to the Prime Minister's private office and frequently used it. As Brain Evangelista says, "The problem when you were negotiating with the UDM officials was that they always had at the back of their mind, if they totally disagreed with you, they could ring Number Ten. They had a direct line down to Margaret Thatcher and it wasn't unusual to upset certain leaders of the UDM and within the day get a phone call from Hobart House saying 'you've upset the UDM'."

None of it counted for much anymore, though. As Evangelista continues, "That changed dramatically when John Major came to power. The influence seemed to wane, there was no direct line. Obviously, it was a Margaret Thatcher baby: she encouraged the UDM, but I think Major was very cool towards it and they lost that influence, and it was a totally different ball game."

After Lynk had betrayed the NUM, he was left to choke on the bitterness of his own betrayal at the hands of the Conservatives. As one NUM member from Blidworth gloated, "Karma's a bitch, ain't it Lynky?"

Lynk was finished as any kind of trade union leader and in

1993 he left the UDM and took up a lucrative part-time post with BCC. He wasn't alone: Colin Clarke, too, was happy to accept a directorship at British Coal Corporation.[74]

Their inevitable trajectory had reached its logical conclusion. Now they weren't just helping management: they *were* management.

The extent to which Lynk had betrayed even his own UDM members, in his efforts to assist BCC and the Conservative Government, was astonishing. In correspondence in 1992 with the then Energy Minister, Tim Eggar, Lynk had advised on a series of moves to neutralise strikes, impose longer working hours on his own members, facilitate redundancies and to neuter NACODS once and for all. As part of a consortium-bid for future privatised pits, he also recommended splitting the new business into two competing halves which would render any industrial action useless.

The "stranglehold" Lynk felt NACODS exerted on the industry could and should be broken by assigning others to handle health and safety underground.

There was more: the document sensationally advised on the enforcement of longer shifts in such a manner that *his own members* would have no recourse to industrial tribunals to challenge their new contracts. Lynk concluded, "The UDM is fully aware that the role it has taken on, involving as it does radical changes for its members and possible redundancies, is self-contradictory in traditional industrial relations terms," but the UDM "... had already broken out of UK traditional trade union confines."[75]

To be fair to Lynk, he fully understood the calibre and mindset of his members. In 1994, BCC took up all his suggestions and although a ballot of UDM members returned a ninety-three percent rejection of the new terms, "Within two weeks ninety-seven percent of its members were scabbing on their own union and ballot decision and working the new package," points out Dave Douglass.[76]

The UDM's new chief, Neil Greatrex, was widely viewed as an opportunist with principles as elastic as those of Roy Lynk. He was a well-known figure in the coalfield and, as President of Bentinck Branch, had previously carved out for himself a small reputation as something of a militant. It was a wafer-thin veneer, though. Keith Stanley says, "He was no great orator, not at all, but he had plenty of mouth and he never had a problem jumping up and down and shouting louder than anyone else."

The myth that Greatrex had created for himself was that of a loyal NUM member whose Damascus-like conversion to ferocious anti-Scargillism was a result of the violence and intimidation meted out by marauding Yorkshire pickets during the early weeks of the strike. Greatrex was fond of recounting how the scales had fallen from his eyes when Yorkshire pickets overturned the car of a disabled employee attempting to cross a picket line into work.

"Bollocks!" snorts Henry Richardson. "Absolute rubbish. The car never got overturned at all. All that happened was that the lads surrounded it and rocked it back and forth a bit, as happened all the time on picket lines. No one had any idea the lad inside was disabled and it never got tipped over anyway. No way."

Greatrex, it seems, seized on the incident and made the most of it for his own reasons in much the same way that Lynk played up the rock that had crashed through the window of the Area HQ.

He was a keen and vocal advocate of the breakaway and was one of the leading figures in the formation of the UDM, rising through the ranks to topple Lynk. And so Lynk was out and Greatrex was in. The new UDM boss championed privatisation as enthusiastically as his predecessor and said the UDM's proposed bid for pits, in partnership with BACM, the union of coal industry managers, and East Midlands Electricity, would still "go ahead as long as it was supported by UDM members."[77]

Meet the new boss, same as the old boss.

Things continued to get worse for the NUM. A proposed merger of the shrinking miners' union with the TGWU ended up on the rocks. Widely perceived by some of the membership to be less a genuine merger of trade unions and trade unionists, and more of a lash-up between two sets of bureaucrats squabbling over cars, salaries and perks, an exciting and potentially game-changing development came to nothing: much to the relief of the both the Labour Party leadership and the Conservative Government. The idea of a reborn and strengthened Arthur Scargill and his militant miners suddenly becoming part of a trade union with over a million members was terrifying.

The following year, 1994, saw the passage through Parliament of the sixteenth and final Coal Industry Act. All administrative functions were transferred to the newly-created Coal Authority. The rump of a once-mighty industry was then privatised. The remaining assets in England and Wales were merged with those of private contractor Richard John Budge. The newly privatised concern was launched as UK Coal PLC, which constituted a monopoly exempt from European competition laws. British Coal was finally dissolved in 1997 and, fifty-one years after Vesting Day, what was left of the UK coal industry returned fully to private ownership.

Circumstances quite outside the NUM's control had been working against it since at least the 80s. The end of the postwar boom, the fall of the Berlin Wall and the collapse of the Soviet Union left the labour and trade union movements of the West profoundly altered.

Whatever the faults and inadequacies of 'actual existing socialism', it had represented some sort of alternative to unbridled capitalism. It had acted as a check and a brake on the worst excesses of the free market. As Milne notes, "For all its brutalities and failures, communism in the Soviet Union, Eastern Europe and elsewhere delivered rapid industrialisation, mass education, job security and huge advances in social and gender equality. It encompassed genuine idealism and commitment, captured even by critical films and books of the post-Stalin era such as Wajda's *Man of Marble* and Rybakov's *Children of the Arbat*. Its existence helped to drive up welfare standards in the West, boosted the anticolonial movement and provided a powerful counterweight to Western global domination."[78]

Following its demise, a wave of neoliberal triumphalism swept the West. Here was the ultimate proof that class struggle, militant trade unionism and socialism did not work. The New Realism of the Eurocommunists, right-wing trade unionists and social democratic parties, saw them all prostrated at the altar of high capital; capitulating willingly in the face of an orgy of capitalist gloating. This was the end of history and the market had triumphed. There was, as Thatcher famously declared, no alternative. The Cold War was a class war and the bad guys had won.

By the time Labour next won office, in 1997, Tony Blair had completed Kinnock's modernisation project, driving the Party even further to the right — aided by the enormous changes in the international political landscape — to the extent that it was barely even a right-of-centre social democratic formation anymore. It was an unashamedly neoliberal party. In 1994 Blair had symbolically marked the end of one part of Labour's history and the start of another with the abolition of Clause IV, Part 4, from the Party's constitution. Now there wasn't even a formal commitment to common ownership, not even lip service paid to socialism. Trade union influence was effectively killed with the new Prime Minister preferring to consult with the Confederation of British Industry before rolling out policies that took Thatcherism to heights even its creator could not have envisaged.

For Arthur Scargill it was the final indignity. The NUM President resigned from the Party and launched his own Socialist Labour Party, the SLP or, as his critics mockingly dubbed it, Scargill's Leaving Party. Initially, the far left greeted the Party with enthusiasm. Here was a real opportunity to forge a genuinely mass socialist opposition. Sadly, another chance to form a viable working class alternative to the three main parties was squandered. Scargill insisted there would be no federalist structure (to be fair, one could hardly blame him for *that*!) and the various far left groups would need to disband and join as individual members. No parties-within-a-party in the SLP, thank you very much. Between Scargill's inflexible and dogmatic approach and the inveterate self-serving sectarianism of the far left's component sects, the SLP's potential was squandered and it ended up as little more than the plaything of unreconstructed Stalinists and ultra-Scargill loyalists. Henry Richardson says, "That's why he and Dennis [Skinner] fell out, you know. All the while Arthur had been against breakaways so when he left Labour to form his own party, Skinner was furious."

All the while, the coal industry — privatised since 1994 — continued to shrink. There were now just a handful of deep-mine pits in the UK. The world was unrecognisable from the heady days of '84–'85 and a universe away from the NUM's 1974 toppling of a Conservative government. The miners' tumultuous and colourful story was nearing its conclusion. There was, though, one last chapter to write and, in something very close to the revenge of history, the UDM would provide it.

By 1997, "The UDM were nearly bankrupt," says Eric Eaton. "It was 'white-finger' that saved them." Or 'hand arm vibration syndrome' (HAVS) as it is technically labelled. The New Labour Government not only refused to consider reimbursing the NUM for the financial losses it had accrued during the strike, despite a motion to that very effect being passed at Conference, thus becoming official Party policy, it also signed a legal claims handling agreement for dealing with HAVS, along with other industrial diseases, with the UDM: *not* the NUM. A Labour government, *a Labour government*, as Kinnock might have stressed, preferred to deal with a non-TUC scab trade union, rather than with the Labour Party-affiliated NUM.

There were tens of thousands of outstanding and forthcoming claims and the UDM made a fortune in fees and commissions. Vendside, a UDM-registered private concern set up specially to deal with the claims, enabled the union to move from bankruptcy to a position of huge affluence and prosperity in a very short time. Its directors, who were also UDM leaders, were soon raking in combined earnings of well over £100,000 each per year.

At this stage, while nothing illegal was occurring, very shabby, grubby and greedy practice, inimical to the historically cooperative spirit of the trade union movement, was the order of the day. Blair's Government paid Vendside 'disbursements' on all the cases they handled. This meant the handling of the claims didn't cost Vendside, in reality the UDM, a penny piece in outlay: all costs and fees were paid by the Government. Despite this, a rolling percentage was still applied to every claim they handled and then deducted when the cases were won.

By 2006, even though the UDM's membership was by then measured in the hundreds, its President, Neil Greatrex, was able to draw a salary of some £115,000. This was on top of a series of 'perks' that would see the UDM chief in the dock facing fourteen counts of theft just six years later.

On 3rd April 2012, Greatrex was convicted of those fourteen counts of theft. The Judge, John Wait, stated, "Over the five year period, you stole very nearly £150,000 from the very people you were elected to protect. This was theft in breach of the highest degree of trust. It was done for greed."[79]

What the UDM boss had done was to persuade tradesmen to supply false invoices, made out to the charity responsible for the miners' convalescent home on the east coast, for home improvements. He'd had the charity pay £148,628.83 for outside paving, new windows, new doors, and a state-of-the-art kitchen, at his *two* homes and that of co-defendant, former UDM General Secretary, Mick Stevens. The offences were almost identical to the smears and allegations heaped upon the heads of Arthur Scargill and Peter Heathfield. Of course in those cases, such allegations contained not even a degree of truth and had been proven so. Here, though, were the custodians of a union they insisted had been founded on principles of 'democracy' and the utmost integrity, stealing from a charity intended to aid sick miners.

Stevens claimed he didn't know the charity had paid for the work to his property and this line of defence worked out well for him. The jury swallowed it and acquitted him of all fourteen counts. Greatrex, on the other hand, received a four-year custodial sentence. A few months later, on 13th December, 2012, he was back before the beak who ordered him to repay every penny he'd stolen or serve the full four-year term. Along with interest and costs amounting to £9,098.86, the total amount to be repaid was £210,426.37.[80]

On 10th January, the convicted thief and fraudster repaid the total amount stipulated and served only one year of his sentence.

The hysterical media campaign of slander, libel and vituperation, to which Scargill and Heathfield had been subjected, was absent in the case of Neil Greatrex. Indeed, those newspapers which even bothered to report on his crimes and conviction at all were notable for their cursory reporting of just the bare facts. *Sans* gloating editorials and extended op-ed pieces, columns proclaiming outrage, indignation and fury, it was almost as though the British media, collectively, were rather embarrassed by the whole affair...

The end for the UDM is fast approaching. In April 2013 it announced its intention to sell off the most valuable of its few remaining assets; the headquarters at Berry Hill. Its now miniscule membership is insufficient to maintain such extravagant premises. The intention is to sell the building and land to Mansfield District Council for social housing.

Representing a trade union comprising less than a thousand members, UDM spokesman Dave McGarry attempted to put a

The Ex Miner

The Journal of the Nott's NUM Ex & Retired Miners Association £2.50

June 2012

Our tools are silent but the passion still burns

Issue Number 25

GUILTY OF THEFT ON 14 COUNTS.
4 YEARS-SEND HIM DOWN !!

Photo courtesy of Page One Photography.

A retired so called Union official was convicted on the 3rd April 2012 of spending thousands of pounds of Charity money refurbishing his homes.

Neil Greatrex the ex president of the UDM was found guilty of 14 charges of theft. Judge John Wait criticised him for using his position to secure funds for himself. The Judge said "over the five year period you stole very nearly £150,000 from the very people you were elected to protect. This was theft in breach of the highest degree of trust. It was done for greed". The thefts were covered by invoices supplied from traders who were persuaded to supply false invoices in order to secure payment.

Birmingham Crown Court was told that Greatrex stole the cash over a five year period between 2000-2006 despite earning £110,000 from various sources. In total he spent £148,628.83 of the Charity's money to pay for outside paving and new windows and doors for his own

positive spin on the situation facing his fast-disappearing organisation. "Even with the closure of Daw Mill, we still have about 1,000 members at Thoresby. We think there is eight to nine years of coal left there and the workforce could then be moved to Harworth, which is currently under care and maintenance. We want to move somewhere smaller, more suited to our needs, with lower running costs."[81]

The kindest thing to say about McGarry's membership claims is that they are on the generous side. As of December 2012, the UDM officially declared 865 members. Following the closure of Daw Mill, that figure cannot be any more than 300 today.

Vendside went into administration in November 2013 and the UDM-owned concern is still the subject of an ongoing police investigation headed up by the Serious Fraud Office. Happily for Mick Stevens and current UDM President, Jeff Wood, such unfortunate developments failed to impact on the generous salary packages paid to the two officials. Including generous pension contributions, utilities allowances, car and sundry other perks, Stevens' salary from the UDM in 2012 was £123,435, with Wood scraping by on £105,842.

The NUM is scarcely in a better position. While free from the theft, greed and corruption swamping the UDM, its decline has been as dramatic. From over 220,000 members before the strike, the Union's 2012 returns to the Certification Officer showed just 1,853 stalwarts, mainly concentrated at the three remaining pits.

One can only wonder what the architects of the UDM and those who worked during the strike now think of their role in destroying an entire industry and presiding over the inevitable extinction of not one, but *four,* trade unions — NUM, UDM, NACODS, BACM — and the loss of around a quarter of a million jobs. (NACODS affiliates a total of 226 members to the TUC, while BACM, reformed as BACM-TEAM, with members outside the mining industry, reports a current membership of just over 2,000.)

Much ink has been spilled in an effort to understand Nottinghamshire's behaviour. For the purists, the county was irredeemably tainted by Spencerism and was guilty of the class equivalent of original sin. This, though, is far too simplistic and leaves unanswered several important questions. For example, what constituted a Nottinghamshire miner anyway? How did Spencerism resolve the question of nearly 30,000 miners from Scotland, the North East and Lancashire who had migrated to the Nottinghamshire coalfield during the closure program of the sixties and in steady trickles afterward? Did these miners simply become corrupted by living and working among the infamous 'Jelly Babies'? A ridiculous premise, frankly.

Ray Chadburn feels it was the transfer of labour to the Nottinghamshire coalfield that impacted on Nottinghamshire's culture, not the other way around. "It is a difficult situation when people say, 'I come from Scotland,' 'I come from Kent,' 'I come from Durham.' 'When did they fight for my job?' That is the problem that Nottinghamshire faced, whether you like it or not."[82]

Dave Douglass acknowledged the truth of Chadburn's thesis but argued that for precisely those reasons, Nottinghamshire miners should draw the opposite conclusions. At the April 1984 Special Delegates' Conference, he pointed out that, "I was moved 120-odd miles from the Durham Area into Doncaster... I, as a Geordie, had a place to come to and so had the Geordie lads who went down to Nottingham. They had Nottingham to go to. Cannot you realise that there are no more Nottinghams? There are no more Yorkshires? This is the end of the line: there is nowhere left to bloody go."

Also, if there was something innately rotten at the core of Nottinghamshire's history and traditions, how come their miners had been as loyal as any others during the disputes of '72 and '74?

For others, more subtle factors were at play. Keith Stanley remains convinced that the problem was 'green labour': younger miners, new to the industry and with no history, tradition or family ties to the principal tenets of trade unionism. He also feels the NUM itself should shoulder some of the blame. "I blame us," he states bluntly. "We should have educated these people. We should have pointed out to them that all the benefits they enjoyed had been won by miners sticking together in struggle: taking on the establishment and winning. They hadn't just been given to us by generous bosses and governments." Stanley considers it something of a tragedy that the NUM, the most politically-advanced and class-conscious of trade unions, allowed this to happen. "We should have packed 'em off to day schools and educational events and bred into 'em what it meant to be a miner and a trade unionist."

Some of the County's strikers, on the other hand, see Nottinghamshire's betrayal as purely a question of greed. "The big-hitters, the big-earners, who thought they'd be safe," states Eric Eaton. Ironically, Eaton's view is very similar to that held by none other than Neil Greatrex. Greatrex says, in an interview on the UDM website, surprisingly still visible given the shame he brought upon the Union to which he helped give birth, that, "The most divisive thing that ever happened to the mining industry was the introduction of incentive schemes. They set faceman against faceman and resulted in some men earning fortunes on rich seams while men working on a face with geological problems could see their money drop overnight. It brought a lot of division."

The hypocrisy evidenced in his statement doesn't negate the substantive point: the abolition of the National Power Loading Agreement and introduction of local incentive schemes *did* play a decisive and corrosive role in weakening the NUM's previously national unity. Their introduction showed just how surface-thin that veneer of national unity was. They also reinforced the federalist mindset and further entrenched regional loyalties to a degree where, in Nottinghamshire, certainly, loyalty to the Area was always first priority and loyalty to the national body only ever a secondary consideration and even then only when and where it didn't conflict with Area interests: something upon which Roy Lynk skilfully played as he manoeuvred Nottinghamshire away from the NUM and into the clutches of his new breakaway union.

It should be acknowledged that the working miners, like any other demographic, were not simply some single, amorphous mass. There existed no ideological hegemony. Their motivations and personal feelings were as varied, complex and as subjective as any other. While, objectively, they did betray their Union, undermine the strike and side with the Government, for every thief and crook like Greatrex, for every Tory quisling like Lynk, Clarke and Liptrott, there were others who genuinely believed that they were doing the right thing. Of course, they singularly failed to propose any viable alternative and history has proved that they, more than any other party, were responsible for the annihilation of an industry they insisted they defended. There were some, possibly from feelings of guilt, shame or even a genuine desire to help, who, although working, rendered assistance to their striking colleagues. Money, food and even intelligence from inside the working pits were given to the strikers. Admittedly not by many and not in any significant quantities but, nevertheless, such actions hinted at a layer of working miners who felt uneasy about working but simply lacked the strength to defy the Nottinghamshire majority and join the strike. One can only ponder what might have occurred if the Yorkshire pickets hadn't descended on the Nottinghamshire coalfield and, instead, the leadership had undertaken an intensive propaganda campaign of rallies, mass meetings and leafleting.

Equally, there were some astonishing gestures from the strikers, things that simply wouldn't have occurred in other coalfields, like Kent and Yorkshire, for example. The case of Bev Maycock is illustrative. Maycock was a striker from Newstead, nearing retirement age, and coming under increasing pressure from management, via stick-and-carrot, to return to work or lose the enhanced redundancy terms on offer. Nothing unusual there, and a tactic NCB management deployed for years after the strike to rid the coalfields of militants. What was unprecedented, though, was that Maycock's striking colleagues persuaded the reluctant miner to return to work and safeguard his enhanced redundancy package. He duly returned to work, with the blessing of his striking comrades, and every week thereafter until the end of the dispute donated his entire wage to the strike fund.

Post-strike Nottinghamshire was a strange world of contradictions. Working miners who had never missed a shift remained in the NUM and shunned the breakaway while committed militants joined the UDM. No one individual case encapsulates this bizarre dichotomy better than Dave McGarry and his baffling evolution from striker to UDM official. Keith Stanley recalls, "Dave McGarry, from Harworth colliery, is now one of the top officials in the UDM. He was on strike all year but when we went back to the pit and all the changes started, he joined the UDM so, he said, he could represent his men at the pit. Years and years later I ended up being a trustee on the industry-wide mineworkers' pension scheme and so did Dave McGarry. Well, I'd got a right dilemma then: how do you speak to this guy when he never scabbed? Do I speak to him or don't I? He's a UDM man but he never worked a single day during the strike." McGarry perfectly highlighted the contradictions and complexity of Nottinghamshire. Only there could such a development have occurred.

In reality, there is no one single reason for Nottinghamshire's strike-breaking. All of the above played some part and it was the cumulative effect of many varied phenomena.

Could it have been otherwise? It seems doubtful. With nearly seventy-five percent of the Area voting to carry on working, the swing required to win a majority for strike action was enormous. In addition, it should be recalled that not one single Branch in the Nottinghamshire coalfield voted for strike action. Even Blidworth had only polled forty-six percent in favour of strike action.

In addition, the overtime ban that preceded the strike was met with substantial hostility and opposition. As Ray Chadburn observes, "They kicked and they squealed about it. It was a close-run thing." As Eric Eaton and others have also observed, there were significant pockets of opinion stating, as early as the winter of 1983, that they would not take part in any national strike.

The strike-breakers, though, always insisted that had they had the national ballot they wanted, then they would have abided by the result. As they were fond of pointing out, Nottinghamshire miners had been as loyal as any other Area in the strikes of 1972 and 1974. However, a Gallup poll taken in early April 1984 showed that fifty-four percent of Nottinghamshire miners would not have joined the strike, *even if there had been a national ballot.* As Keith Stanley shrewdly observes, the strikes of the 70s had been in pursuit of pay-claims: hard cash in the pockets of miners in the immediate short-term. There had never been a strike against pit closures and, as Teversal showed, Nottinghamshire miners wouldn't even take strike action to save one of their own pits. A pit was closing? So what? We'll just get moved to another one, was the thinking. Of course one can only speculate but the very different circumstances of 1984–85 suggest that Nottinghamshire was unlikely to strike whatever the circumstances. Despite all the evidence to the contrary, the majority of Nottinghamshire miners believed they would be safe from closures. As Eric Eaton puts it, "Oh, they knew there'd be the odd pit close: one here, one there, but they thought they could just move to another one and pick up where they left off." They resolutely refused to believe Dave Douglass's assertion that there were "no more Yorkshires, no more Nottinghams."

Henry Richardson comments, "Whatever happened and however it happened, it all boils down to the fact that you never, ever cross a picket line. You just don't do it. For any decent trade unionist, that should be the most important thing. By not having a national ballot, Notts found an excuse, but even if we'd had a national ballot, they'd have just found a different excuse."

There seems to be merit in Richardson's analysis. The fiercely parochial attitude of the Nottinghamshire majority, with the historic tensions that existed between the Area and 'National', suggest Nottinghamshire might still have gone its own way, whatever the outcome of a national ballot. Indeed, there was even talk among some who went on to form the Notts Working Miners' Committee, that an Area ballot should also take place in parallel with a national one and that the Area result should take precedence. It's certainly possible that had a national ballot gone ahead, Nottinghamshire would still have opted out anyway, citing its own Area autonomy as justification.

Nottinghamshire's critics also point to it being among the first of the Areas to defy not only agreed Conference policy, but also the ballot which had rejected Gormley's Area Incentive Scheme at the end of the seventies. Nottinghamshire, it was said, picked and chose which ballot results to observe, based on which option was likely to see more money in miners' pockets.

And then there was the Lynk factor. As now seems reasonably certain, Lynk was set on a breakaway for a long time even before the strike. Certainly James Cowan, and elements in the Thatcher Government, had been angling for precisely such a development for years. Once it arrived, Lynk and Prendergast took full advantage, helped split the Area and were crucial in ensuring the coalfield kept on working during the dispute.

Lynk's actions went far beyond simply ensuring the coalfield stayed open: a conscious and deliberate wrecking strategy was undertaken which reached into the most obscure and peripheral areas.

For example, he was also involved in the curious case of Alan Mallatratt. The former NUM Head of Department for Education and Research had been employed by the Nottinghamshire Area since 1971. The Department's remit included writing conference speeches, lecturing, organising educational schools for NUM members and, crucially, scientific research. "He was a very, very intelligent man," says Henry Richardson. "A real asset to the NUM, a good socialist, too. I always had a lot of respect for him."

Mallatratt himself didn't respond to, or acknowledge, several requests put to him via a selection of intermediaries, to speak on the record but a former high-ranking NCB source tells a very interesting story.

"In 1983, Alan started research regarding the effects of acid rain, generated by coal-burn. Although he was an employee of the Nottinghamshire NUM, he worked in collaboration with some of our NCB scientists and some leading academics from Cambridge University, Nottingham University and Nottingham Trent Polytechnic. It was a joint effort.

"Anyway, acid rain and the environmental impact of burning coal were just starting to become hot potatoes, politically. Alan, with others, was researching a process whereby the production of carbon atoms could be massively, and I mean massively, reduced: we're talking over ninety percent. Basically, they found that the existing literature at the time pointed toward a process whereby some kind of adjustment to future plant and retro-adjustment of existing plant could be introduced, at a very low cost, which would virtually eliminate pyritic sulphur which, with other processes, could then produce a clean burn of coal."

Given the onslaught faced by the NUM, the negative environmental impact of burning coal was another stick frequently used to beat the industry and in the charged political climate of the mid-eighties, was something the miners could well have done without. This research then, was, potentially, politically explosive.

"You've got it," confirms the NCB source. "Precisely. Now this is where it gets interesting. Early in 1986, Alan was working for the UDM as his contract of employment was originally with the NUM Notts *Area* but that was terminated so he ended up just being transferred across to the UDM.

"So anyway, around this time, early '86, Lynk goes to see him and demands access to all his notes, research and documentation on the clean coal project. You need to understand that Alan hated Lynk. He was an old-school socialist, was Alan, and he hated ending up working for the UDM. So Lynk takes all his materials, all the back-up stuff held by his assistant, Dianne Geddes, and it never saw the light of day again.

"Now those of us at the NCB saw this for exactly what it was: the implication to us was quite clear. He'd been working to show coal was viable, that it had a future and, at least from an environmental point of view, jobs needn't have been lost. So Lynk did this because his political pay-masters, or whoever was behind it, didn't want the research to see the light of day. Anything that might have helped the NUM in opposing pit closures had to be suppressed, even if it was very valuable, positive stuff that could benefit the environment and future generations."

Life was very tough for Mallatratt under the Lynk regime, and also for Dianne Geddes. Prior to a move to the Union's Bestwood premises, Geddes was ordered to stop assisting him with research and made to carry out switchboard duties and other work she'd never been expected to do before. The NCB source continues, "I know that Alan wrote to Peter Heathfield asking for him and Dianne to be taken on by the NUM and he never heard anything else so a little later he phones Sheffield again and ends up speaking to Roger Windsor, of all people. Windsor told him, 'We're watching the situation, we're waiting for the right time but jobs will be found for you.'" One doesn't wish to stray into the realms of conspiracy theory, but Windsor's involvement in the affair is certainly interesting, given the subsequent allegations regarding the NUM's former Chief Executive.

Our source continues, "Alan never did end up back working for the NUM. They [UDM] moved him out to Bestwood and made life as hard for him as possible, all intended to force his resignation."

By this time Geddes had left the UDM to take up a place at what is now Nottingham Trent University studying for a law degree. At around the same time, Mallatratt had been accepted by Nottingham University to research for a MPhil, regarding the future of the British coal mining industry. He approached the UDM NEC for assistance with course fees. Given the mutual benefit to student, industry and trade union, one might have expected the UDM to have viewed such a request favourably. They didn't.

The end for Mallatratt came in 1989. He was approached by John Liptrott, then UDM Secretary, and told he was being made redundant. "Liptrott told him he'd get the same enhanced package as the miners and an early pension. When Alan pointed out he was as fit as a fiddle and not entitled to any pension on health grounds, Liptrott said, 'Don't worry about

278

that. We've got a pet doctor and he'll say what we tell him to say.' And that was Alan then: finished and out the door."

The NCB source says, "Lynk isn't very bright, let me tell you that, but he has a super-abundance of cunning: highly-developed instincts geared towards identifying what's best for number one. That being so, we're positive that the moves he made in this area were a direct result of advice from certain sections of the NCB or even someone in the Thatcher Government. He just wouldn't have had the intelligence to recognise the implications of this work, or the smarts to do anything about it, left to himself."

One wonders, though, if all the above is true, why others involved in the project didn't come forward and blow the whistle. Our informant responds, "You can't even start to imagine what it was like in the NCB at that time. It was like a climate of fear, like living under a totalitarian government and anyone who was suspected of being sympathetic to the miners was sidelined, isolated or sacked. Blowing whistles then would have meant blowing jobs, blowing careers, blowing pensions and blowing any chance of getting a decent job anywhere else. I signed a really tight confidentiality agreement and I could lose my pension and perhaps be prosecuted even now, nearly thirty years later, if my name came out talking to you. You just can't overstate how far the Board and Thatcher were willing to go to beat the miners. Anyone else was just collateral damage. It was vicious: a foul time, full of foul people. Frightening, really."

Nottinghamshire made one of the two decisions that wrecked the strike. Even with the TUC, NACODS, Kinnock and the Labour leadership taking the courses they did, the strike could, indeed almost certainly *would*, have been won if Nottinghamshire had backed their Union and closed the coalfield. And *vice versa*. What the NUM could not withstand was *both* Nottinghamshire working *and* the Labour leadership and TUC failing to deliver effective support and secondary action.

From the start of the dispute, there were many, particularly the heads of other trade unions, who had insisted the miners' defeat was inevitable; that the strike had been rash, foolhardy and nothing but a revolutionary vanity project for the benefit of Arthur Scargill. On all counts such thinking was wholly inaccurate. Not only was defeat not at all inevitable but the miners had come to within a hair's-breadth of winning on several occasions, not least during July and again in October. Where Scargill was concerned, while he stood in stark contrast to the other union chiefs and represented an implacable and consistent resistance to the destruction of the coal industry and his members' jobs, the strike had never been about the NUM President. While the media and the majority of the subsequent post-strike analysis has painted the dispute as a clash of the titans, a war between Scargill and Thatcher, the strike was always about the miners themselves: nearly 180,000 of them who had struck, organised from below, funded, supported and driven the opposition forward and sustained it for a full year.

With the benefit of hindsight, it's easy to point to this or that isolated tactical error made, in the heat of battle, by Scargill and attribute, as the Conservative-supporting press and the Labour leadership alike has consistently done, the miners' defeat to the megalomania of a crazed Marxist dictator, but it just wasn't true. Nottinghamshire inflicted serious damage on the strike and, ultimately, the miners' defeat lay with that, Kinnock's undermining of the miners' cause and the singular failure of the TUC affiliates to fully deliver the solidarity and secondary action all had promised to take at the 1982 Wembley Conference.

The results of the failure to oppose pit closures must be borne equally by working miners, the UDM, the TUC and Neil Kinnock and the Labour Party leadership. And a terrible legacy they left. From the many accounts of ravaged communities, one published in the Police Federation's official journal, *Police*, by a former Yorkshire police officer, Michael Downes, is particularly poignant. "The devastation of communities that were at the heart of the miners' strike actually prompted Michael Downes to become a police officer, such was his passion for policing by consent. His father and brother were miners and he was close friends with some of those involved in the dispute. He witnessed the devastation that followed the strike in his community: miners' incomes stripped bare and local shops left to rack and ruin, compounded by drug addiction and a lack of self-worth. He says the loss to communities during and after the pit closures was huge. 'Mines were not built in a community: communities were built around the mines.'"[83]

In Nottinghamshire, drugs and gang violence rushed to fill the void created by the destruction of the coal industry. The notorious Bestwood Cartel and gangs from the 'NG Triangle' all contributed to the County becoming more famous for its shootings, murders and gang crime than mining, Robin Hood and Sherwood Forest. Dubbed 'Shottingham' by many, for its escalating gun crime, Nottinghamshire was the harrowing realisation of the Thatcher project: alienation, broken communities and mass unemployment feeding violence, crime and despair. Margaret Thatcher's infamous avowal that there was "no such thing as society" became a grisly reality for many former mining communities.

Thirty years later, families and communities remain split, with the passions aroused by the strike unabated. Such passion could lead to tragedy, the case of Keith 'Froggy' Frogson, in particular, casting a long shadow over Nottinghamshire's former pit villages. Frogson was a year-long striker and a committed NUM militant. Up to his death in 2004 at the age of sixty-two, the former striker was a well-known figure in his local community of Annesley Woodhouse. He remained proud and unrepentant regarding his role in the strike, still sporting 'Coal Not Dole' badges and taunting former scabs.

In July of 2004 he was attacked and murdered at his home by former working miner Robert Boyer. He was stabbed multiple times in the face and neck and although Boyer's family and his defence team insisted the strike had played no part in the crime — pointing to the accused's mental illness and delusional condition — Frogson's old strike-colleagues remained unconvinced.

Frogson was one of the twenty-nine Nottinghamshire miners sacked during the strike, and at the time of his death was facing the loss of his job at the Kodak film plant near his home. His funeral saw a thousand mourners pay their respects, including Arthur Scargill. Boyer was later convicted of manslaughter on the grounds of diminished responsibility.

The long postwar upswing had long since ended by the time the strike arrived. The balance of class forces had shifted in favour of the Tories and while none of that made defeat inevitable, it meant that the consciousness of many miners, particularly in Nottinghamshire, was entirely different to that which had existed in 1974. Circumstances were completely changed from a decade earlier. One might almost believe Karl Marx knew what was coming to Nottinghamshire when, in

1852, he wrote, "Men make their own history, but they do not make it just as they please; they do not make it under circumstances chosen by themselves, but under circumstances directly encountered, given and transmitted from the past."

Chapter 17:
Wake's Wake

"Go to sleep now and rest. Our job is done.
You kept your promise and I kept mine..."

MAGGIE OSBORNE

Any account of the miners' strike in Nottinghamshire, aspiring to the status of definitive, would, ideally, feature extensive first-hand recounting of the views and opinions of those members of the Notts Working Miners' Committee and the UDM whose roles were so crucial. That *Look Back in Anger* falls short in this respect is not the fault of the author. David Amos enjoys the singular honour of being the only leading working miner and UDM official who was prepared to speak to me.

I contacted Neil Greatrex via the Prison Service and requested an interview. He declined to respond.

I visited David Prendergast at his home on Wighay Road in Hucknall. He lives in a plush cottage-style property, set in leafy grounds, with spacious additional buildings. A vintage red sports car gleamed smartly in the open garage.

He cut a peculiar-looking figure. In his late sixties now, the former UDM official wore red corduroy trousers, a blue blazer, checked shirt and a garish, clashing tie. The impression was that of an eccentric academic from a gone-to-seed provincial university, still trapped in the 1980s. I introduced myself, explained my presence and requested an interview. He was instantly wary, shortly becoming overtly angry.

"Why don't you ask Scargill, in his Barbican flat, why he daren't walk around Barnsley anymore?" he retorted.

I said, "Everyone knows Scargill's views. They're the same now as they were twenty-nine years ago. No one knows your views, though. That's why I'm keen to get you on the record."

"I don't talk about the strike anymore."

"Why not? Are you ashamed?"

"It was about democracy and that's all I'm saying."

"Well, if that's the case, how do you justify trying to sabotage NACODS' democratic ballot in October 1984? How do you…" He interrupted, by now angry and upset, "I've told you I'm not interested: now please leave before I call the police." And that was that.

I'd been told that Roy Lynk would not speak to anyone about the strike now but I had to at least try and get his side of the story. So I drove out to see him.

He'd clearly done well out of the Nottinghamshire miners — living in a big detached house on Huthwaite Road in Sutton-in-Ashfield. There was a large silver Mercedes on the drive with a vanity plate that reads LI INK J. Except the grass was uncut, there were weeds scattered around and the house paint was chipped and peeling. Most of the curtains were drawn. Worse, there were binbags dotted here and there and a plastic bucket next to the front door, filled with empty litre bottles of vodka and whisky. The place reeked of neglect and despair.

I never got to see Lynk, now in his eighties. Passing my card to the woman who answered the door, and explaining my reasons for wanting to interview him, she said she'd "see" and closed the door. She returned a few minutes later with the remark, "'Print what you like,' he says: he aint bovvered." I expected to feel pleased to see how the once-mighty had fallen. But in the end Lynk was just someone else used by the Government and thrown away when he was of no further use. At least he'd been well-compensated for his treachery before he was betrayed in turn. Lynk fitted perfectly the scathing remark, popular after the strike, usually directed at Scargill by working miners: that of starting the strike with a small house and a big union but ending it with a big house and a small union. I felt an odd mixture of pity and contempt.

* * *

On 3rd March 2013 documents from Thatcher's Cabinet Office, dating from 1984, were released to the National Archive under the thirty year rule.

In the main, the revelations contained few surprises, confirming most of what many involved in the strike had long-known or at least strongly suspected. There *was* a secret closure program, long and stridently proclaimed by Arthur Scargill, during and since the strike, and strenuously denied by both Thatcher and MacGregor. The documents revealed that the scale of the planned closures exceeded even Scargill's predictions.

Thatcher herself *had* intervened *directly* in the matter of policing picket lines, demanding, as one document shows, evidence that the police were "adopting the more vigorous interpretation of their duties which was being sought."

Although there was no proof that soldiers had been dressed in police uniforms and had infiltrated picket lines — a strong suspicion ranging to an outright certainty among thousands of striking miners — the documents *did* reveal detailed plans to use the army to break the strike, declare a state of emergency and make whatever legal changes were required to facilitate the process.

Possibly of most significance was the disclosure that the Government *had* come very close to defeat, particularly in July, at the time of the dockers' strike, and again in October during the threatened NACODS' strike, as asserted earlier in this book. This was something else also much repeated by Arthur Scargill but, as with so many of the former NUM President's statements, it had been dismissed and rubbished by his critics and 'friends' alike.

The dockers paid the price for not seeing their strike through, when the National Docks Labour Scheme was abolished in 1989 by a triumphant Thatcher administration. The Victorian insecurity of casual labour and men queuing for work on a day-by-day basis then returned to Britain's docks.

Other discoveries included discussions on every possible aspect of the dispute, with Thatcher involved in astonishingly precise levels of micro-management: to calculating coal stocks and numbers of lorries, the Prime Minister was personally involved in every conceivable area of the dispute. The conclusion was inescapable: Arthur Scargill, the most maligned and vilified trade union leader in British history, had been right all along and his nemesis, Margaret Thatcher, had consistently lied and misled both Parliament and the public before, during and after the strike.

Mike Simons, writer and contributor to one of the most hard-hitting photographic accounts of the strike, *Blood, Sweat and Tears*, and the Executive Producer of the 2014 documentary about the strike, *Still The Enemy Within*, says, "For me the important thing is the Cabinet papers show the Tories were fighting a class war as a civil war. There are too many who claim to be on the left telling us today that class politics are old fashioned. They are *not*. The rich fight the class war every day and they are very conscious of what they are doing.

"The other important thing is to be proved right. Nothing I've read yet in the cabinet papers is a surprise, but we were called fantasists and propagandists at the time. Now there is no argument that the Tories were cynical liars thirty years ago. That makes it easier to say don't trust anything they say today — about strikers, about immigration, about schools or the NHS.

"People don't trust the Tories about generalities. The stuff out today helps us say don't trust them about specifics either and that is useful when our side has its back against the wall in a particular struggle.

"One thing I've learned doing the film [*Still The Enemy Within*] with young people is that they haven't learned what we learned and they can't conceive of such things until they hear a set of people involved or see long-lost archived accounts or see stuff like these cabinet minutes. It is very important to see things with the eyes of someone making a discovery for the first time. Old hat to us — although nice to be proved right — devastating to someone who had a few illusions or hasn't experienced what we experienced."

It seems that the release of material vindicating Scargill was not welcomed in some quarters. Since his retirement as NUM President in 2002, and assumption of the Union's Honorary Presidency, he has been involved in a series of disputes with current NUM General Secretary, Chris Kitchen. Kitchen is himself currently under attack from current and ex-NUM members for the questionable nature of his 'election.' The Trade

Union Certification Officer was forced to intervene and install the current General Secretary in his post. Much of the current bad blood between Kitchen and Scargill has revolved around this question.

In return, Kitchen has attacked the former NUM President for his insistence that the NUM's Barbican flat is something to which he is entitled. One may question Scargill's judgement in pressing the matter, given the financial burden on a trade union with less than two thousand members, or even whether such arrangements should have existed in the first place (as had been the case for all of Scargill's predecessors), but it is reasonably clear that this was no more than Scargill's contractual due.

None of this has stopped Kitchen linking the Barbican flat to discredited allegations in an attempt to trash Scargill. Kitchen appeared on the BBC1 program, *Inside Out*, in January 2014, to rail against his former comrade and cooperated with presenter Dan Johnson in resurrecting the smears of the early '90s. Despite Johnson claiming the program was not a hatchet-job it obviously was. Seumas Milne Tweeted "Ludicrously slanted BBC Yorkshire hatchet-job on ex-miners' leader Scargill last night: rehash of 1990 smear campaign with same 'witnesses'."

Milne and Ken Capstick had been initially invited to appear on the program only for the invitations to be withdrawn. Instead, Roger Windsor was wheeled out to repeat the old allegations previously disposed of by Milne in *The Enemy Within*.

The program contained, in contrast to Johnson's protestations, no "fresh allegations" at all and, given its proximity to the release of the thirty-year Cabinet papers, there was only one conclusion it was possible to draw — nothing which proved Scargill had been correct and had told the truth about the pit closure program could be allowed to stand unchallenged.

In 2014 the impact of Thatcher's assault on the miners and their industry, coupled with the accompanying privatisation of the electricity supply, couldn't be more dramatic. Fuel poverty has hit the country hard. A poll for the Press Association revealed that one in ten pensioners are forced to stay in bed to keep warm and for hundreds of thousands more, not just pensioners, exorbitant fuel costs mean a choice between eating or heating. Meanwhile there are nearly a thousand years of coal reserves trapped beneath the nation's feet.

Maurice 'Mog' Wake and Iris Wake. Summer 1984.

* * *

My mother-in-law, Iris Wake died on 19th September 2009 and
her husband, Maurice 'Mog' Wake, followed on 27th July 2012.
He was seventy-seven. Naturally, as has been their custom ever
since the end of the strike, the dwindling band of Linby strike-
veterans planned to bring the strike banner to the funeral as a
mark of respect for their fallen comrade. Nothing is ever quite

that simple in Nottinghamshire, though. There were members of Mog's family who had worked for the entire course of the dispute. Might they be offended? Might they see the gesture as an insult? On the one side, my wife, Susan, was chief among those who cared not one jot: the strike might have occupied just

The author (left) and Jimmy McDowall (right) at Maurice Wake's funeral, August 2012, with the Linby commemorative strike banner.

one year of Mog's life but he had been immensely proud of his role in it and it was as much a part of his life as his love for his family and his passion for fishing and music.

Susan says, "Everyone had the right to remember my dad the way *they* wanted — and to say goodbye in their own way — and those men loved my dad. They'd all been through so much together. They had as much right as anyone else to pay tribute to him in the way *they* wanted." Others, while sympathetic to this view, understandably didn't want the funeral turning into a rerun of the dispute. A funeral was no place to settle old scores. Had Iris been alive, the debate would have lasted about ten seconds. Eventually the decision was made to grant permission for the banner to be displayed, just as Iris and Maurice would have insisted. This was Mog's day; it was all about him and if anyone felt offended, well...

In the end the day went off with no rancour. Quite the reverse: the mourners were deeply touched by the old strikers' gesture and those who might have felt otherwise sensibly maintained a respectful silence. As we arrived at Bramcote Crematorium, there they were: Eric Eaton, Jimmy McDowall, Les Dennis, Kevin Parkin, Ian Morrison and the rest, maybe a dozen men, solemnly forming an honour guard with the Linby strike banner. On it inscribed the names of all 102 Linby men and one woman — Dot Hickling — who had remained 'Loyal To the Last'. By unspoken agreement, the retired miners acted as pallbearers, and so Mog's old comrades carried him to his final resting place.

At the wake, held at Bestwood Miners' Welfare, Mog's former colleagues occupied one side of the room, swapping tales, anecdotes and jokes, while those who had worked occupied the other, with Councillor Denis Beeston cutting a solitary and forlorn figure, on his own in the public bar. Such is the legacy of the strike in Nottinghamshire.

Later, when that moment that takes place at all wakes arrived — sadness momentarily giving way to laughter, as everyone shares their memories and funny stories regarding the departed — I slipped outside for a smoke. It was a beautiful late summer's afternoon. Sat on the back steps, the bowling green's lush emerald shimmering in the heat-haze, I was joined by Les Dennis. We sat quietly as, from the 'big room', we could hear the muted strains of Bestwood Welfare Black Diamonds tuning up as their rehearsal got underway. Bestwood Village might have seen its pit close the year I was born, in 1967, but the colliery band was still going strong.

An unmistakable melody snaked through the building towards us and then seemed to hang, almost suspended, on the humid summer air. I stared at Les and he stared at me. Silently, he pointed to his tanned forearm — with the NUM tattoo above it — where the hairs had all stood up on end. "You couldn't make it up," he said, softly, as, of all things, *Gresford — The Miners' Hymn* played on. Lost in our respective thoughts, we turned and looked away across the green.

Nottinghamshire Collieries
1984-2013

Year of Closure	Colliery
1985	Pye Hill No. 1 Pye Hill No. 2 Moorgreen
1986	Hucknall Babbington
1987	Newstead
1988	Linby Mansfield
1989	Sutton Blidworth
1991	Gedling Cresswell
1992	Cotgrave Sherwood Silverhill
1993	Rufford Bolsover Bevercotes
1994	Ollerton
1997	Bilsthorpe
1998	Bentinck
1999	Calverton
2000	Annersley
2003	Clipstone
2005	Harworth*
2008	Welbeck

*mothballed

Afterword
Paul Mason

I cannot remember the first time I smelled coal: it was all around me. I grew up in a landscape where slag heaps were forbidden playgrounds, where men had unexplained blue scars on their arms and foreheads.

At rugby matches during the 1970s, there would be a moment during the game when the shift came up out of a nearby colliery, and the shunt of the winding gear would echo across the terraces. Men in the crowd would exchange glances when this happened – like sighs of relief – but their meaning was never clear.

In their daily lives miners would come up with equally inexplicable acts of solidarity. My grandfather's "job" in the community around Butt's Bridge, Leigh, was to pull people out of the canal who'd fallen in. This was what he was known for, on top of his other job, which was 800 yards deep at Astley Green Colliery.

We now know that coal is one of the great destroyers of the earth's climate. But it was one of the great creators of human solidarity.

What we call today "social capital" was found everywhere, and for free, in the mining communities of Britain.

The coal industry was not destroyed for reasons of climate science, or even economics. It was destroyed to rip the heart out of the British labour movement – which was achieved.

During 1984-85 I was in Leicester. When the Kent miners arrived to picket out the Leicestershire coalfield the pervasiveness of the social capital mining had built up was clear. After picketing from around 5.30am until 8am, once the last cage had gone down at Desford Colliery, the local management opened the canteen for a second shift and fed the Kent men breakfast. For free.

Thirty years on I got to sit in the National Archive at Kew and leaf through the Cabinet minutes of that time. The Home Secretary, Leon Brittan, was urged to put a rocket under the local police: to demand more arrests, tougher policing, faster processing of the arrested by the courts. Within days the Kent miners were being stopped, arbitrarily, under no legal power other than force, in their cars at the Dartford tunnel.

It's a myth that the miners could not have won. By June 1984 they were winning. John Redwood, Thatcher's policy chief, wrote to the cabinet that the National Coal Board was "crumbling" and urged the government to resume its "war of attrition". When the dockers come out, the minutes show Mrs Thatcher's handwriting in the margins – calculating the number of RoRo ferries, the number of lorries, and tonnes per journey they would need if they took – as they considered – emergency powers and sent the troops in.

The myth of the miners strike as a working class Balaclava – a pointless charge at loaded guns – dies hard. It's joined all the other myths about working class history that result, in the end, from not studying it.

As a journalist and social historian my rule is to go to the sources: the diaries of strikers, the casualty lists from massacres, the almost meaningless demands of prisoners scrawled 150 years ago. Sadly, with the miners' strike these sources are too few.

The survivors lives were blighted – not just by the imposition of mass redundancy and the destruction of social cohesion in their stranded villages – but by the stark contrast between those twelve months of freedom and what came next.

The human instinct is both to romanticise and forget. When I went to the funeral of Malcolm Pinnegar, the leader of the 30 Leicestershire miners who defied their region and went on strike, he'd written – in a message to mourners – "some of you may know that for a year I was a miner went on strike". The chapel was full of men with blue scars, crying. But he had a point: it was one year out of forty as a trade union activist – 67 as a brother, husband and Dad. Lives moved on, other stories happened. That's why so much of labour history remains trapped in the oral culture – and disappears.

This book adds not just to the record but the detail of the strike. Above all the story of how the Notts and Leicestershire coalfields were lost, and lost the strike, will be of interest both to social historians and those who lived through the events themselves.

But in the detail of what happened one thing stands out: what we lost when we lost the miners – whose culture and humanity lay at the heart of the wider culture of the British working class. It took 200 years to build and less than a decade to destroy.

Paul Mason is the author of *Why It's Still Kicking Off Everywhere: the New Global Revolutions, Meltdown: The End of the Age of Greed* and *Live Working, Die Fighting*

Endnotes

1 Justice For Mineworkers, http://www.users.ic24.net/~terrynorm/ Justice/index.htm

2 *Weekly Worker* 523, Thursday, March 25, 2004

3 *Scargill and the Miners*, p.147, Michael Crick (Penguin Special)

4 *Nine Days That Shook Mansfield*, p.6, Barry Johnson (The Ragged Historians)

5 *The General Strike*, pp. 157–160, P. Renshaw (Methuen)

6 *Marching To the Fault Line*, p.1, Beckett and Hencke (Constable)

7 *Great Contemporaries*, Churchill

8 *Nottingham Evening Post*, May 1, 1926

9 *Labour Research*, July 1926, Vol. 15, No. 7

10 The General Strike in Nottingham, *Marxism Today*, June 1972, p.172, Peter Wyncoll

11 Alarmingly, this appears to have been even worse in recent years. The BBC reported that in the period from 1999 to 2007, for every one hundred deaths before the age of sixty-five in the richest ten percent of areas, there were two hundred and twelve in the poorest ten percent. This compared with one hundred and ninety one deaths in the poorest areas from 1921 to 1930 and one hundred and eighty five deaths from 1931 to 1939 http://www.bbc.co.uk/news/health-10730095

12 http://www.unionhistory.info/timeline/1939_1945.php

13 http://www.labournet.net/ukunion/0305/wartime1.html

14 Ibid

15 http://www.bbc.co.uk/news/special/politics97/background/ pastelec/ge45.shtml

16 http://www.num.org.uk/History-NumHistory-nationalisation.html

17 *The Enemy Within; the secret war against the miners*, Seumas Milne (Verso)

18 http://www.guardian.co.uk/politics/2002/nov/01/uk.military

19 http://www.minersadvice.co.uk/reviews_%20civil_war.htm

20 Much has subsequently been made regarding the Cortonwood

announcement by other commentators. Beckett and Hencke, in their 2009 retrospective, *Marching To the Fault Line*, breathlessly 'reveal' that Hayes had 'misunderstood' his brief and had not followed procedure and that therefore the whole strike was predicated on a huge mistake, something which Adeney and Lloyd had already addressed twenty-three years earlier in their book, *The Miners' Strike: Loss Without Limit* (Law Book Co). In his review of Beckett and Hencke's book, Dave Douglass deploys excellent analysis on this question.
http://www.minersadvice.co.uk/reviews_%20marching_to_the_fault_line.htm

21 *Ghost Dancers*, pp. 34–35, D Douglass (Christie Books)

22 *The 1984/85 Miners' Strike in Nottinghamshire: Spirit Alone Won Battles: The Diary of John Lowe*, p.26, Jonathan Symcox (Wharncliffe Books)

23 Dean Hancock and Russell Shankland

24 For a detailed and fascinating account of this historic Conference, the reader is advised to consult Dave Douglass's *Ghost Dancers*, pp. 52–59.

25 *The Link-Up of Friendship*, Butcher and Seymour, p.13 (self-published)

26 http://www.morningstaronline.co.uk/news/layout/set/print/content/view/full/81057

27 *The Link-Up of Friendship*, Butcher and Seymour, pp. 26–27

28 Liz Hollis was active in many campaigns in Nottinghamshire. Those who knew her still mourn her: she committed suicide while still a young woman.

29 *Hearts and Minds*, J Witham (Canary Press)

30 *The Guardian*, 7th March 2009

31 Ibid

32 Ibid

33 Ibid

34 *The Enemy Within: The Secret War Against The Miners*, Milne, p.371

35 http://www.redpepper.org.uk/From-Orgreave-to-the-City/

36 *Ink In The Blood*, Williams, pp. 170–172 (Woodfield Publishing)

37 Ibid

38 *Mansfield Chad*, 5th July 1984

39 *Nottingham Trader*, 11th July 1984

40 *Hucknall Dispatch*, 18th November 2009

41 *Nottingham Evening Post*, 19th July 1984

42 Ibid

43 Ibid

44 *The Guardian*, 11th August 1984

45 *A Turn of The Screw*, Walker, p.66 (Canary Press)

46 *The Guardian*, 11th August 1984

47 *A Civil War Without Guns*, Smith, p.64

48 *The Guardian*, 17th October 1984

49 Ibid

50 *Observer*, 21st October 1984

51 Ibid

[52] *The Guardian*, 17th October 1984

[53] *Observer*, 21st October 1984

[54] *The Guardian*, 17th October 1984

[55] Ibid

[56] *Observer*, 21st October 1984

[57] *Marching To the Fault Line*, Beckett and Hencke, p.162, see also *The Enemy Within: the secret war against the miners*, Milne, p.130

[58] *The Times*, 12th December 1984

[59] *Nottingham Evening Post*, 17th December 1984

[60] *Scargill*, Paul Routledge, pp. 174–175 (HarperCollins)

[61] *The Miners' Strike: Loss without Limit*, Adeney and Lloyd, p.268

[62] There were actually 31 striking Leicestershire miners, but one individual remained uninvolved in the activities of the 30 and his role was not discovered until after the strike.

[63] *Nottingham Miners Do Strike!* Stanley, p.95 (Nottinghamshire NUM)

[64] Ibid

[65] *The Diary of John Lowe*, p.145, Symcox

[66] *The Miners' Strike*, Goodman, p.173 (Pluto Press)

[67] Ibid

[68] *The Guardian*, 11th February 2004

[69] http://www.minersadvice.co.uk/reviews_%20marching_to_the_fault_line.htm

[70] *Loss Without Limit*, Adeney and Lloyd, p. 274

[71] *The NUM and British Politics Volume 2*, Taylor, p. 289 (Ashgate)

[72] *The Enemy Within: The Secret War Against The Miners*, Milne, p.13

[73] *The NUM and British Politics Volume 2*, Taylor, p.309

[74] *The Enemy Within: the secret war against the miners*, Milne, p.367

[75] *The Independent*, 14th December 1992

[76] *Ghost Dancers*, Douglass, p.58

[77] Ibid

[78] *The Guardian*, 16th February, 2006

[79] *The Ex Miner*, issue 25, June 2012

[80] Ibid

[81] http://www.bbc.co.uk/news/uk-england-nottinghamshire-22293605

[82] *The NUM and British Politics Volume 2,* Taylor, p.189

[83] *Police*, March 2009, p.6

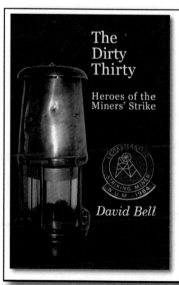